Cocktail Conversations
by the
CONTROVERSIAL COUNSELOR

Diane

Thank you for supporting my endeavor as I strive to reach the top seller list. Its always special to have hometown love and especially from someone that is very fond of my mother so I know your heart is in the right place. Please share my endeavor with others. If you have any questions throughout reading get back to me.

Your new friend

David

Controversial Counselor

Cocktail Conversations
by the
CONTROVERSIAL
COUNSELOR

DAVID GLOVER

Copyright © 2014 by David Glover.

Library of Congress Control Number: 2014919096
ISBN: Hardcover   978-1-5035-1008-1
           Softcover   978-1-5035-1009-8
           eBook   978-1-5035-1010-4

All rights reserved. No part of this book may be reproduced or transmitted in any form or by any means, electronic or mechanical, including photocopying, recording, or by any information storage and retrieval system, without permission in writing from the copyright owner.

Any people depicted in stock imagery provided by Thinkstock are models, and such images are being used for illustrative purposes only.
Certain stock imagery © Thinkstock.

This book was printed in the United States of America.

Rev. date: 12/03/2014

To order additional copies of this book, contact:
Xlibris
1-888-795-4274
www.Xlibris.com
Orders@Xlibris.com
677474

CONTENTS

Chapter 1: Relationships 21

    1. Chasing Skirts 21
    2. Endless Love..24
    3. Is White Always Right 25
    4. Marchless Madness..28
    5. Nothing in Common 31
    6. Overtime or Bedtime 34
    7. Sometimes People Never Learn....................................36
    8. Take It or Leave It 38

Chapter 2: Family 41

    9. A Blow for a Blow at the Barber 41
    10. A Joke Is Only a Joke When Both Parties Find it Funny......44
    11. Blood Is Thicker than Water..47
    12. Chat Line 50
    13. Family Means Everything..53
    14. Home is not a Home..55
    15. Hurt People Like to Hurt People 58
    16. Wedding Notification thru Facebook 60

Chapter 3: Child Drama 64

    17. Fancy Pants 64
    18. Fight or Flight 70
    19. Free Willie 77

20. Hidden Pain 80
21. Ice Cream Social..84
22. Search and Seizure...90
23. The Creep Show 92
24. Triple Whammy 94

Chapter 4: Health Issues 98

25. Can I Hold Your Whip 98
26. Don't Open One Door without Closing Another 101
27. Following Your Dream or Following Your Heart........105
28. Getting My Drink On...107
29. Got It Going On..109
30. Something Just Ain't Right 114
31. Trying to Reinvent Myself...118

Chapter 5: Education 122

32. All Work in No Play..122
33. Crack the Code 125
34. Grooming at It's Finest..128
35. Parental Ignorance...135
36. Respect and Protect...139
37. Summer Loving Happen So Fast 141
38. Sweet Appetizer..145
39. When Enough is Enough 148

Chapter 6: Work Issues 155

40. Disappearing Acts 155
41. Empty Bed 159
42. It's All About Me..162
43. It's Getting Hot Up in Here 166
44. Pimping Pastor..169

45. Show Me the Money 173
46. Time for Myself 181
47. Three Way Split 183

Chapter 7: Friendship Issues 189

48. Don't Hate Participate 189
49. Homie Lover Friend 191
50. Johnnie Blaze 193
51. Last of the American Virgins 196
52. Marriage Over Friendship 199
53. Reunited and It Doesn't Feel So Good 205
54. Snitches Get Stiches 208
55. So Fine You Blow My Mind 212

Chapter 8: Loyalty 219

56. Baby Boy on the Run 219
57. Daddy's Little Girl Angry World 222
58. Go with What You Feel 225
59. I Need That Earned Income Credit 228
60. No Brazil No Dancing 233
61. No Child No Future 236
62. Where Is My Daddy? 242

Chapter 9: Mistrust 250

63. A Missed Opportunity 250
64. Closet Lovers 254
65. Confirm My Schedule 257
66. Games People Play 267
67. I Can Make It Better 272
68. Income Tax Sniper 276
69. Snake in the Garden 278

Chapter 10: Dating Game 285

70. Don't Settle 285
71. Free Spirit Doing Me..287
72. I Don't Do Dutch 292
73. Let's Try It Again After Going Dutch 307
74. Life or Death...310
75. May Day 312
76. No Texting Rule 323
77. Nothing to Offer 326

FOREWORD

I AM HONORED TO have participated in the "Cocktail Conversations" with the Controversial Counselor. I have had the pleasure to participate as an observer and contributor, and sometimes I have been the devil's advocate that was needed to get the conversation going. David Glover has introduced conversations to a social media setting that has allowed many to have the courage to speak their mind in a way they may not have been able to in other arenas. Now he is sharing them in print for others to share and expand the conversations.

David addresses topics that are real and very valid within his community and may be close to our hometown of Niagara Falls, New York. The participants were not just allowed to respond, but also to expand and explain the emotions behind their responses. Certain topics brought up a number of emotions. I am sure the questions asked of consenting adults are the same ones our adolescents are faced with everyday. I challenge David to expand to a series of topics that can be used to help our youth become transparent, and let their parents, mentors, teachers, and other leaders guide them along the way.

Having grown up with David, I know he has always had a sense of community and helping others. He was also encouraging others to look at alternatives to decisions and make the best of situations. This is the purpose of Cocktail Conversations. Maybe you are "Chasing Skirts" or "Have Nothing to Offer" and someone may say something that will help you in your situation. Perhaps that health issue you have been struggling with or your loved one has seems hopeless, you will find an answer in someone else's testimony. There are many of those in the responses. You will also find cries for help in different scenarios. David has been given the charge to expand to blogs and radio, so it is possible you may be able to help someone.

There is no issue that is taboo parenting, relationships, health and education and all of these the hottest topics out there no matter your race, creed or social-economic status.

I am truly humbled I was asked to submit this foreword. I had a scenario make the final cut, and although it was very harsh, it was also rewarding and enlightening to get strangers' input. The raw responses were very eye-opening to a situation that I was too intimately involved in to make a sound decision. Nonetheless, David has accepted the challenge to reach the masses to make changes in decisions and how we react to situations that can affect our futures. In a way, he has become an intermediary between the angel and the devil on our shoulders.

I am looking forward to the success of Cocktail Conversations with the Controversial Counselor and the dialogue it produces.

Venom Patton

COCKTAIL CHRONICLE PARTICIPANTS

FIRST OF ALL, I don't have the typical authors, news reporters, or entertainers speaking on behalf of my book; but what I do have is a group of individuals that are rich in heart who bought into my beliefs and vision, for that I owe each one of them much gratitude. Thank you all; I appreciate your support throughout this journey.

In my perusing on Facebook one night, I see a post from my very good friend David Glover, about a scenario of real-life situations. Finding it very appealing, I read the scenario and commented. After a few minutes and nine comments later, I found real dialogue with people I never met before; I was intrigued. I found myself anxious to see what others had to say and what advice was given. I applaud David in his abilities to open up a forum for all people of all backgrounds. No matter what age, race, sexuality, or religion, this has been a great medium for people to talk, share, and listen. The scenarios he presents are from real-life situations that people are facing, a social forum where the human race can come together. (Kathryn Perdicho)

Interesting and intriguing. (Abeer Shinnawi)

Entertaining and interesting, helps with research for my book. (Lisa Nunn)

To see what others think and how they react to real-life situations. (Herbert Lewis)

I find the scenarios interesting and I like to see how other people answer. (Sandra Gusdez)

I participate because I find the scenarios interesting along with the different point of views. (Cheri Bradberry Hudson)

I like a good healthy debate. (Gerri Glover)

I read your scenarios because it's not only provides a stimulating intellectual dialogue but it also allows me to see another perspective, which I may never have thought about when dealing with my own real-life scenarios. (Lori Hamilton Minor)

One thing that I really appreciate is the fact that people share what is going on in their lives. So many times I've gotten tons and tons of support from the Facebook world and most of them don't even know how much they really helped me so, more importantly I think our comments and feedback actually help people rock on. (Chanell Owens Johnson)

There are several reasons that I follow up with *Cocktail Conversations* that are posted but the main one I would have to say is that it forces you to see different viewpoints to the same situations; everyone sees it *differently* and it proves that how a person views things is limited to life experiences. If they are able to see other person's views, then it gives them another perspective that they may not have realized. This is something that is lacking in the world today. If people actually sat down and discussed their different views instead of just staying around the same people that shared their views then the world would be a better place. (Tomeka Allgood)

David Glover is an affable comedic counselor, whom has spent countless hours helping young people grow into the confident young adults of our society. He has been a great role model for many people and has the ease of transferring the strength and courage within him, onto the lives of others. His heart is to bring the drive and positive attributes of others out of themselves, so that they can have positive attitudes toward themselves and toward the lives of other people they touch. (Marloe Jordan, former colleague at Bryant & Stratton College)

Today's society is filled with motherless girls and fatherless boys. Losing my mother at the age of twelve to cancer put me in that category. Although my father tried to raise me the best he could, there were some qualities he was lacking. One of them is not being interested in higher education. Under these circumstances, I found myself with no education or guidance. When I came to Bryant & Stratton College, I felt deprived. Upon meeting Mr. David Glover, he immediately took me under his wing. He not only advised me in regards to my education, he motivated and showed me that he believed in me. His recommendations along with my efforts of making the dean's list, made me eligible for many privileges, including but not limited to school activities, work study program, and the Graduate of the Year Award. I also received full-time employment with Bryant & Stratton upon graduation. It was then that I professionally witnessed his great work ethic. Over ten years later, I have appreciation, gratitude, and a deep respect for Mr. David Glover. His example is one every person needs. Mr. David Glover, advisor, role model, and friend. Thank you Rachel Allen (former student and colleague at Bryant & Stratton College).

David was very influential person in my life. He motivated me at Bryant & Stratton College, believed in me when there were times I didn't believe in myself. He was an excellent academic college advisor. I went on to finish my bachelors and I'm currently working on my masters and a huge part of that is due to David. Thanks, David, for believing in me when I did not. (Ronell Hardy former college student at Bryant & Stratton College)

When I was in high school, I always knew that I could go to Mr. Glover for help with anything. Sometimes, I needed help with deciding what classes to take or with my college application; other times I needed advice on how to deal with a problem with a family member or classmate. Looking back, I can comfortably say that having Mr. Glover as a guidance counselor is one of the biggest reasons I am in medical school and realizing my dream today." "I always felt and feel supported by him." (Ayobami Ajayi, former valedictorian at New Town High, current medical student at UPenn)

You were a nice comforting school counselor that helped out all your students. It wasn't just college applications and SAT's that you helped us with; you were also a genuine person to talk to when it came to everyday life struggles. You're still the best counselor New Town has seen. (Diamond Flowers former New Town High School and current Howard University Student)

Mr. Glover has helped me as a counselor by helping me improve and be successful. When I have hard times in school, Mr. Glover always pushes me to do even better. He also made me understand different things, if I have problems in class or with teachers. I also thank Mr. Glover for being very helpful and there for me to be successful. (Brianna Thomas former 8th grade student Golden Ring Middle School)

I think I realized early on there were two sides to David. The one I saw on weekends, ready to party at college or some event in town. And the other holding down at most times two or more jobs getting his finances in order and taking care of his family. While other specific upbringings were different, it was the same ole story. Single-family homes, raised by our mother's and mentored by those we came across in the neighborhood.

I saw him pushing to the limit at all times, saying "Don't become a roody pooh Johnny come lately," meaning a man goes out and works hard to get what he wants, and doesn't use setbacks as a reason not to try. He pushed me toward my college education, a job at that very campus that I loved and opened my mind to crush the stereotypes that I am less than because of my color or economic standing. He gave me the ability to see past the mess, hear the message, and formulate an end game (goal) so I didn't get stuck in a dead end job. His sports mind pushed me to never quit, pick up and dust off when I fall and to always be ready to catch my blessings.

He is my friend, my brother, and I will always remember the jewels of life we shared. As brothers, white or black, we must motivate, elevate, and encourage each other to break barriers and to reach excellence; but always remembering, we are but works in progress. Peace and love (Brian S. Archie Sr., friend, coworker, student at Bryant & Stratton College).

My name is Jerome Brundidge from Niagara Falls, New York. I can recall when I was thirteen years old, my first year playing organized football for Cataract PAL Eagles being bullied by a group of veterans on the team. My dad would give me money to stop at the store on my way home from practice (back then we rode our bikes). To fit in, I would give the guys my money. I was too afraid to mention this to my coach and my family. This behavior affected my play on the field. One Sunday on our way to a road, game David witness those guys receiving money from me and made them give it back and told me that I had nothing to fear, he had my back. From that day forward, my confidence went up and my play improved and I took over the starting role at cornerback. Thirty years later, David is still helping those who can't help themselves. There has been many times in my personal, professional, and coaching life I had to reflect on that time when someone stood up for me and I returned the favor. Today I would like to take the time out to thank David for changing my life thirty years ago.

I grew up as the middle child with two sisters. My mother, my only present parent, was a very hard working woman. As a child, I wondered about my father and wanted him around. But, more than that, I always wanted a brother. After living in an apartment complex that was multi-cultural, my hard working mother bought a house on North Avenue, an African-American neighborhood. That's when my life changed as a child. On North Avenue, I met "my brothers"—the Glovers, David, Carlos, and Dedrick. I was with Carlos and Dedrick every day. We did everything together. David noticed how tall I was and said, "Man, you need to be playing some sports." We went to work after this. He did not let up on me. We practiced and played basketball, football, and boxed. Through the time we spent practicing and playing, I started finding confidence in myself. I actually became good. So good that my "big brother" David and I were always on the same team. We won a lot in whatever we played. But what was happening was so much bigger than winning and losing games. When I reflect on this time in my life, I now understand how important David was at that time. He took me on as a brother first of all. So now, I'm in a brotherhood. Second, he helped me realize the talent I had inside and hard work does pay off. This developed the confidence to know that whatever you "study" or "practice" you will definitely be great in. Today I am in the medical field and historically carried several leadership positions. (Lemoyne Bennett, friend)

COCKTAIL CHRONICLE CONVERSATIONS

Controversial Counselor David Glover

I WAS INSPIRED to write this book for several reasons but it came together one Sunday on February 9 when my brother stop by and I was reading one of my scenarios from Facebook that I post almost on a daily basis, and he made the comment "where do you get those scenarios from" and I responded that you can't make this stuff up, many of the scenarios came from my personal or life situations that I might have observed. He stated "Why don't you write a book?" I responded that I am not a writer, which led him to say actually you are a writer and has always been a great storyteller.

Well the ability to tell stories was part of my painful past that I experienced, there are a couple major experiences that caused storytelling to be a part of who I am; my father was someone who was very mentally abusive to me because of the jealousy of the relationship I had with my mother and because at certain times I was not progressing as fast as the other kids, so I would be called all kinds punks and pussy's on a regular basis, his presence made me very nervous and took away much of my self-confidence. For the longest, I would shake or have tremors when I had to perform a task that made me feel uncomfortable. Another dark experience from the past was when I was molested by a male in the community who lured me and this other boy into his basement and he attempted anal sex on both of us and would even attempt to have us perform it on one another. I never mentioned the molestation experience to anyone until I reached the age of twenty-one; I had the uncanny ability to block it out and try to survive the pain on my own. This is when the art of storytelling came into play; every weekend I would tell my younger brothers, Carlos and Dedrick, a story about these two dirty boys that had no parents, nowhere to live, struggling to eat on a day to day basis, and they wore the same clothes every day. When telling the story, I made my brothers think that the boys were them; but in actuality, they were me combined in to two, symbolizing the pain I felt, loneliness as if no one was there for me, I was living life on my own with no help at all. This story helps me express my pain but at the same time I had an audience that was engaged with my abilities.

Storytelling was always something in my heart, but one of the final things that tied all this together was my profession as a counselor along with teaching critical thinking at Bryant & Stratton College. I enjoyed teaching that course because it gave me a forum to have my student's problem solve and give their diverse perspectives on many day to day topics. Once I left Bryant & Stratton to become a fulltime counselor, I always missed teaching that course so I started a Critical Thinkers Social Group at one of my former high schools and many of the top students stated that this was the best group the school had to offer because they learned about life situations and how to solve them.

Last year in May, the vision came for me to use Facebook as an outlet to continue the critical thinking component, so I begin writing scenarios involving relationships, education, child drama, family, loyalty, work issues, mistrust, the dating game, and any other life situations. The more I put the scenarios out there for the public viewing, the more participation I received. I realized I had a great brand when people began sending me personal messages stating that they had a scenario or situation that they wanted some feedback on. They appreciated my forum because it was an opportunity to get feedback from a diverse group of people who were coming from different walks of life, financially, educationally, and culturally. These perspectives happen to be very therapeutic and I look forward to sharing these short chronicles and I hope they can be a starting point of conversations to many and I truly understand many of us go through struggles on a day to day basis but only get opinions of people in our inner circles, *Cocktail Conversations* will open your horizons to how to deal with certain situations and how not to, but the bottom line you will learn from these courageous conversations.

My ultimate goal with my scenarios or short stories is for people to imagine new perspectives, inviting a transformative and empathetic experience. These scenarios allow individuals to actively engage in the story as well as observe, listen, and participate with minimal guidance. My readers will be able to create lasting personal connections, promote innovative problem solving, and foster a shared understanding regarding future decision making. The readers can activate their knowledge and their perceptions to form solutions to the scenarios. Together the participant and readers can seek the best practices and invent new solutions. The scenarios have multiple layers of meaning and readers will need to read closely to identify the underlying knowledge in the story. The scenario will teach the readers to respect other's real-life issues, value the inner-connections that are created by relating to someone else's issues, and identify strategies to overcome adversity.

Hopefully the end result will be for individuals to identify facts, issues, problems, dilemmas or opportunities, for growth in each scenario. Account for different perspectives, and value the individuals who stepped out on faith to present their scenarios. Individuals provided feedback based on practical/empirical/theoretical knowledge that might be relevant to issues in the scenarios and raise questions about additional knowledge that might help inform decisions. Individuals will provide actions or suggestions based on what they know, experiences they have been through, and come up with positive courses of actions that they may take if they are faced with challenges presented in these particular scenarios.

After each scenario, I always have a presenting question or questions for the participant or readers to predict the likely results based on the upside and downside, intended and unintended of proposed actions. I can easily see *Cocktail Conversations* used in a collegiate environment, at friendly social gatherings, as icebreaker conversations, happy-hour functions, and any other venues that great intellectual conversations need to be sparked up at for discussion purposes.

CHAPTER 1

Relationships

Scenario 1 Chasing Skirts

GREG COMES HOME from the end of sixty-hour-work week and just wants to have a beer and relax. His homeboy Dwayne calls him up and says "Let's hit the strip club, homie, so you can spend some of that OT money." Greg decided to meet Dwayne out at Becky's Backside. When Greg came home, Tab, his fiancée, was dressed in a negligee and attempts to seduce him and he says "Not tonight, baby. I am too tired for sex." She storms out the room and for the next week she denies him sex. What should he do? And why do most women play these games?

CA: OMG, LOL, do women actually behave like this? LOL, sounds like a child throwing a tantrum.

PC: Greg should have got it when it was hot,

C2 (Controversial Counselor) You already know the games they play, maybe not specifically but I am sure you know some women that does it, unless it's a black women thing.

TF: He deprived her so he has to pay for that.

VS: SMH why is it a game played when the man is denied? She wanted it but he was too "tired" so what should she have done? Whatever it is should be the outcome for the next two weeks. People get in relationships and get selfish. They probably had sex every day until they made it official, so now what? It should always be 60/40 it's not a game it's a lesson,

TC: Only 2 weeks? If my man turns me down because he is too tired after being away from me 60 hrs that week working and going out with his friends, he won't get any until his balls turn blue and fall off. If I get sexy and waited up for him, he better take one for the team whether he is tired or not.

C2: Why couldn't she get broken off something the following night, now that is understanding?

DJ: He wasn't too tired to hang with his friends. He told her not tonight. She told him not tonight for a few weeks. Okay that will teach his ass to man up?

NM: If he was too tired for intercourse he could taken a few minutes to please her in other ways.

DP: A man or a woman in a relationship should not deny each other, unless there are circumstances that warrants it. I do not believe in holding out for weeks or even days. You are only hurting yourself. Sex is not a weapon to be used to teach someone a lesson; we must learn to communicate with each other better to do better.

LN: How is attempting to seduce your man into sex, a game? He's been busy hardworking 60 hours, who says they've had sex during that time. If your man likes watching female strip, why not give him a show. Many men wish they could get their women to be a freak sometimes. Turning your partner down for sex is never good on either part. If he can be too tired, then so can she, until she feels desired. Maybe Greg is a trick and is too tired because he already paid the stripper for private services. HMMM

COJ: His tail better stay home next time, he will learn eventually,

CM: The Vagina is not a belt or a disciplinary weapon. Children are to be disciplined, not adults. Do not start using sex as a way to control your mate. That very thing you use could very well be the thing he ultimately use as an excuse you when he exits out of your life.

TA: What should Greg do? I'm lost; I think he already did it. He went to the strip club then denied his woman afterwards. Translation he did not put her first. He was able to get everything but she was left hanging. That is not cool withholding sex for 2 weeks isn't a game. That is a sign she is done with him. There is never a good reason for either a women or a man to withhold sex, period, she needs to move on and leave him with the boys. Not because he didn't break her off but because he didn't put her first.

MJ: They both are wrong, if Greg was that tired he should have told Dwayne he was too tired and could have gone another time. Tab is wrong for throwing a temper tantrum and withholding sex for 2 weeks. Our goodies are not for controlling. There has to be a compromise. Puppet Master is not the title I want nor do I want to play with any puppets.

Issues: Greg worked sixty hours this week and originally stated he was tired but ended up hanging out at the strip club with Dwayne; after returning home, he denied his woman sex, she became upset and now threatens to withhold sex from Greg.

Perspectives: Many of the perspectives felt like Tab was right for her actions because Greg did not put Tab needs first, so this was viewed as punishment. There were some other perspectives that centered on women should never use withholding sex as a way to get back at a man.

Knowledge: Based on the knowledge, Greg's plan was to relax that evening after working sixty hours but he decided to go to the strip club. In my opinion, when someone works that much it should not be an issue if that person wants to take some time for themselves.

Action: If it was me in this position, I may have done the same thing if I was tired but rest assure my plans would be to make it right the next day.

Consequences: Based on this scenario and Tab holding back on sex, I can easily envision Greg hitting the strip club again and possibly finding someone to service him.

Scenario 2 Endless Love

Kate Met Wayne many years ago and they hit it off from the beginning; they had love and respect for each other. Wayne had a job offer out of state and took it knowing Kate had love for him. She encouraged him to go achieve his professional goals all through the ten or so years they have kept in contact and still have love for each other. They both had a child but those relationships did not work out. Over the holiday, they saw each other in after all these years; it's like they never missed a beat. He has become very successful and still doing great things in his life and she has a great job and is doing well for herself; they are now older and are each other's number one fans. She wanted to be in a relationship with him years ago but put her feelings aside, he has always been the apple of her eye and she would love to rekindle their love, he has never spoken of a significant other so she assumes he is single. How do you think Kate should approach this situation?

HM: She should find out what's with him and his status . . . single, dating, etc. After she knows then she can decide if she is going to pursue him or not.

COJ: Do nothing, they don't live in the same place, or maybe they should see how far apart they live and see if a long distance relationship can work. Side note: I don't believe in long distance relationships but that's just me.

C2: In this day and age with the lack of decent men, women have open up possibilities they would never do before, hence online dating or all the million chat lines.

CA: Lol, there are many good men out there; it all depends on where you look... its simple choices.

TA: Nothing if a man wants you he will pursue you. The question is what's up with Wayne.

C2: Wayne does well with the ladies and I will leave it at that.

KP: I think Kate needs to have a convo with Wayne and see if he is interested in a relationship with her or if he is content just being a ladies man. Long distant relationships are hard and will always build a gap in a relationship. If either of them is willing to relocate and they want the same thing. Then maybe they should just go for it. Real men are hard to find… But a serious discussion is a must.

YW: Just ask

Issue: Two former lovers Wayne and Kate have dated in the past and the feelings were still there for each other at least on Kate's end. Wayne relocated for a career opportunity and recently over the holidays, they reconnected and realized that the connection has not lost a beat.

Perspective: Most perspective was based on Kate asking Wayne about his status to see what he wants out of this relationship. Another perspective is long-distance relationships are difficult to maintain and they don't work.

Action: Kate needs to have a conversation and see if Wayne's heart is with her, maybe she is jumping the gun and he enjoys her conversation and they have great sex but he has no interest in her coming to join him.

Consequences: Kate may be in love with the concept of being with Wayne but he prefers her to stay put and when he comes to visit, they hang out and do what they do. Also they do have children to consider in this matter as well.

Scenario 3 Is White Always Right

Dion always liked his black sisters and never felt comfortable talking to white girls until he laid his eyes on Beth. Beth had recently started at Dion's job at Dept of Motor Vehicles, and boy, was she stacked every time she walked by Dion; he had thoughts of "boy the things I would do to her." As time went on, Beth would always come to Dion's area to talk smack as if she knew she had a hold on him. One evening all the colleagues decided to go to a happy hour and Dion was invited;

typically, Dion would decline because he was antisocial. Beth told the coworkers she could convince him to come and she did just that; while out, Dion and Beth remained close, drinking and laughing throughout the evening. Everyone was shocked to see Dion so content. At the end of the night once everyone cleared the parking lot, Dion and Beth went at it like nothing else matter to them. They acted as if they were not making out in a parking lot. When they returned back to work, Dion seemed more social; he started dressing differently, and Beth had a lot of influence on him. She made comments such as you are really white trapped inside a black man's body, and if you are to get any place in life, you need to upgrade your standards and cut those ghetto black chicks out, they don't deserve you. Dion took her advice to focus strictly on Beth. There was one problem with this situation—Beth was engaged to be married to a white man. What do you think of the new and improved Dion? So what do you think became of Dion and Beth?

AM: Wow if he had any respect for himself and his mother he would have put Lil Miss Racist White gold digging adulterous whore in her place. After what she said to him there should have been no further communication except to let her know about her inappropriate comments. SMH come on now does she not know if they have kids that they would be black? SMH ignorance is frustrating.

AE: I agree her comments were definitely inappropriate. What I found upsetting was the fact that Dion was so blind to Beth's comments he had one thing on his mind.

AM: The sex seems to be all she is good for anyways; she's already cheating on her fiancé. I mean what does he expect her to do with him. She probably is just dealing with Dion because of some Mandingo fantasy she already had. Someone needs to tell her fiancée to save her from a scandalous life of insatiable whoredom.

C2: What do you think about the comment that the black women don't deserve him and do you think some black men feel like that?

MJ: I'm totally disgusted by this; it reminds me of someone I use to work with. Beth is the one who doesn't deserve him. Its ghetto girls like her that needs to be cut. Home wreckers ugh I'm livid right now.

HL: Any improvement that Dion had is a blessing to him, but it has come with a price as some successes do. The unfortunate portion is his involvement with someone who is scheduled to be married. Beth and his relationship may end but who knows. If he was to continue on with her. I'd advise him to do so cautiously.

AM: It would be foolish for him to continue a relationship with her. She may have caused him to improve things about himself but that would happen if anyone he was interested in reciprocated his feelings. He should really want to do things for himself.

HL: From personal experience that your comment about a black man having self hatred/lack of love for himself is not the reason we date interracially. The answer to why we do is in the scenario, but as so many do, they choose to ignore it. The only conditioning that people suffer from is the one that comes from others in the form of judging before they walk in other shoes.

KP: I see where there is a major struggle and perceptions that have brought out issues that black and white society has misconstrued; Beth obviously has not been educated or has lived her live around enough ethnic people. Her perception may because her lack of knowledge and upbringing. Shame on her for being a cheater, she had loyalty to herself and I hope her fiancé finds out and dumps her ass. As for Dion maybe he needed that boost of confidence he was missing… gave him the swag he needed. Some comments have been about a white man in a black body. I have also heard this from white and black girls to some male friends. I have also heard a black man in a white man's body. This is crazy! We need to stop putting labels on each other and just be us!!!! Sad thing is our own races are the ones that are creating these stupid statements. Act black…. What's that? Act white…. What's that?

TA: First, nothing became of Dion and Beth because his pockets are not deep enough for her. Beth is playing him like a game of monopoly and the only racial color she sees is green. Secondly, Dion is not new and improved he is lost. Any adult who needs to be validated in order to be able to participate in life by someone as shallow as Beth is an early target for manipulation.

Issue: A black guy dating a white woman who is already spoken for and scheduled to get married, also she makes demeaning comments about his race.

Perspective: Many perspectives dealt with the disgust of this man tolerating her behavior toward him, along with her being disloyal to her fiancée. People felt he is getting manipulated and used. Another perspective is this woman was good for him because she was building him up and taking him to heights he has never been before.

Knowledge: Dion's dealing with Beth had a lot to do with his sexual attraction to her, and besides that he was always curious to be with a white woman.

Action: If Dion knew he was not in it for the long haul, and then maybe he was okay with his relationship with Beth, because he was having the best of both worlds, sexing her up with no real commitment. I would only hope that he would put Beth in her place regarding his race and stand up proud to be a black man.

Consequences: Sooner or later, her fiancée may find out and end it all with her, which may cause Beth to come running to Dion for emotional support. The question Dion would have to ask himself is that does he want to be connected to Beth trifling ass emotionally as well as physically.

Scenario 4 Marchless Madness

Giovanna met Floyd at the CIAA tournament last year and things became hot and heavy mainly a lot of steamy getting self-acquainted conversations happened over the past year. Giovanna planned to visit Floyd and had everything mapped out on how she would take him to this euphoric state and make him her man despite the distance between them, secretly she wanted a change and would entertain relocating from Virginia to North Carolina. The time has arrived for her to go down to North Carolina and she made a trip to Frederick's to seal the deal. When she arrived, Floyd left a key under his rug mat for Giovanna; she prepared some finger foods and made some grand marnier chocolate covered strawberries so the table was set or it sounds like she was trying to get set on the table. Well when Floyd arrived and Giovanna was lying across the couch, she left nothing for his imagination; he looked at her and said I know you don't expect anything to go down tonight? Giovanna was so pissed she got dressed and left within thirty minutes and headed back to Virginia at 10:00 p.m., a five-hour ride. How would you handle this situation?

DP: Um… Giovanna poor thing. I mean she should have considered that maybe she was more than a booty call. I mean if her goal was for a lasting relationship why give the milk first before the cow. I'm curious to know the conversations prior to her visit that made it seem like sex was such a priority. Her leaving so hastily let Floyd know he wasn't anything but a fling to her. Definitely a lack of communication from both. Also, if he knew she was coming why wasn't he available to greet her. He should have had dinner ready. If she drove 5 hours… so many things wrong with this picture. Bottom line bad communication.

LMH: First and foremost I would never put myself out there for any man!! You have to respect yourself before you can expect anyone else to respect you. She assumed and labled herself as being easy and deep down inside men want a lady not someone that's going to give it up so easy unless it was meant to be a booty call. What she should have done after he made that statement was apologize, get dressed and sit down with him and have a conversation. Maybe somewhere in her past that's all men were interested in. What some women don't realize is that a lot of men want a woman that can have an intellectual conversation. Don't get me wrong sex is good in a relationship but it shouldn't be the focal point and the only thing the relationship is built on.

C2: Typically after the chase and the dates the sex comes into play, in my opinion women already know if they are planning to sleep with a man, so I guess cut through the crap and get it in.

KP: Floyd should have told Giovanna he was flattered. Told her to cover up so they could have a heart to heart about the expectations they both have and after the discussion, proceed accordingly.

TA: This one is little tricky but first things first . . . Giovanna was wrong to overreact. She doesn't know this man well enough to be ready to "put it on him" so to speak. Therefore giving him an opportunity to explain the "why" is necessary. Her kneejerk reaction was childish. This entire situation was created by Giovanna and the story she created in her head about how the weekend would go. Women have the tendency to do that more than men, in my opinion. Technically all Floyd did was walk in the door. She was the one who went over and beyond the call of duty to prove herself worthy to a man who hasn't earned the opportunity from her yet. I think it's irrelevant why he didn't go for it. I think she has issues thinking that sex was her way to make him hers. Women need to realize that if a man doesn't have an emotional connection to you than its nothing special to him. So to be honest it wouldn't be me 'cause I'm not doing anything like that for a man who isn't mine. Plus, who knows why men do half the stuff they do. I stopped trying to figure that out years ago . . . lol.

HL: Sex is great, but not to be done with everyone that crosses your path and offers. Sounds like he wasn't into her for that or at the point in time.

Issue: Giovanna drove down to North Carolina, which was a five-hour ride to see Floyd; she set the mood with the lingerie and appetizers preparing to get broken off something by Floyd after he got off work.

Perspective: Several individuals felt that Giovanna put herself out there for Floyd hoping for something long term, but was not sure if that was something he truly wanted. Also some felt that Floyd could have been more sensitive considering Giovanna drove five hours to see him and was going to give him the work.

Knowledge: Giovanna and Floyd had been dating for over a year and Giovanna was hoping that this weekend would be a deal breaker because she was actually looking to relocate for a change.

Action: Giovanna could have laid out her expectations once she was rejected by Floyd and just maybe after a long conversation it could have led to some intimacy. I don't think throwing a tantrum and storming off was the best idea, communicate and leave in the morning if things don't go your way.

Consequences: Based on her reaction to Floyd's rejection and deciding to pick up and leave, it's safe to say she will not be getting an invite anytime soon by Floyd; stick a fork in it, she is done.

Scenario 5 Nothing in Common

Tiffany and Jarvis have been in a serious relationship for almost two years and have been discussing marriage. Tiffany has been married before so she understands the ups and downs of being married; she is very cautious of getting married again. Over the past two years, Tiffany has been through a lot and has made big changes in her life; she stop drinking heavily, got a promotion on her job, and has earned the ability to work from home; she went through financial difficulties, relocated, lost her father and grandmother; through it all, Jarvis was there for her. Tiffany feels there are some things that will become major issues in her relationship and she is wondering if she is being too cautious, or if these are serious issues that should keep her from marrying Jarvis. First of all, they have different interest; Tiffany enjoys going on wine tours tasting and he refuses because of his personal beliefs. Tiffany wants to take a trip to New York City to see the Wendy Williams Show and go shopping; he refuses, Jarvis does not like Tiffany's friends because he feels there pulling her back into a negative lifestyle and he feels they should make friends together with other married couples. They have different parenting techniques although they will not be having any more children together; Tiffany's youngest is sixteen years old. Tiffany wants to relocate and he refuses and would like to stay where he currently lives. Despite these obstacles, where do Tiffany and Jarvis go from here.

TS: Different interest shouldn't be an issue but unwillingness to compromise should be.

EG: Marriage counseling preferably a Christian centered with a bible base theology to affectively address worldly issues in a Kingdom minded arrangement.

HL: They should sit down and see what it is they want as well as what they can come together on. Put all the cards on the table, honestly and truthfully.

KP: The cards are already stacked against them . . . seems as if their commonalities are very few. Too many obstacles are in the way to overcome. They seem to have to find a reason to stay together . . . . their list of cons are more lengthy than the pros… What is the foundation of their relationship based on? All of the mentioned obstacles are major issues that they both should be concerned about now and discuss what they both need and want.

DM: If both parties are willing I think they should definitely give counseling a try. However, they have to both be willing to go open minded and truly listen to what it is the Counselor has to say as I know a couple who once went to counseling, one of the parties did not agree with what this person had to say therefore it was really a waste of time of the others person time. As adults I do not get how we do not understand that nothing in life worth having comes without hard work, loyalty and dedication, if it comes to easy it is probably because it is not real. Someone is playing a role to get what they want out of it (can you say opportunist) No two people will ever come together and be in total complete agreement with one another. I think that Jarvis is being a little petty by not being willing to do some things that he claims to care about wants to do. Now, if these are the friends that use to drink with it is probably in her best interest to listen to Jarvis, the person who has been there for her through these trying times. As in that case he is correct you can't make changes in your life and still be friends with the same people that you use to run with in party, as they eventually pull you back down. I think that their issues can be worked if they both truly willing. If one of there hearts isn't truly in it, the other should tell him or her so and just let it go.

C2: Well I am not sure if the counselor can make someone feel passionate about things that you are not interested in, I guess those things you have to grow to like, certainly many of us are set in our ways and the first thing we try to say is that person is trying to change me, well damn it sometimes change is good.

C2: I am wondering if Jarvis is a bit controlling, it seems like he is not willing to compromise. Also, with everything that Tiffany has been through she may need more time to adjust to all the changes in her life. Not to mention she has been married before and may have had a bad experience so maybe they should take things slow and see how things turn out.

KJP: There are the main things that I believe need to be strong and understood before taking the plunge. All else can be worked out...LOL (Money, Religion and Children)

Issue: Tiffany and Jarvis have been dating for two years, but Tiffany is questioning their relationship because she is realizing they have nothing in common; everything she wants to do, he doesn't want to do and he thinks it has no meaning behind it.

Perspectives: Many of the perspectives is based on compromising in a relationship for the good of the couple. Other perspectives are centered around Tiffany and Jarvis receiving counseling to work toward their issues especially if they plan on having a future together. Finally, the last perspectives were they need to go their separate ways because counseling will not make Jarvis appreciate the things Tiffany likes in life.

Knowledge: Tiffany is very reluctant to move forward in this relationship because Jarvis is thinking about marriage, but she realizes they have nothing in common so what connection can they possibly build for the future.

Action: Tiffany needs to find out what Jarvis's interest are and see if they have in common ground, I would also find out why he shoots down all of her ideas and see if he is willing to compromise some of his values for her happiness.

Consequences: Tiffany can remain with Jarvis but unless he changes his mindset and open up to a new possibility with Tiffany, she will end up miserable and unhappy. Tiffany can walk away when the getting is good and break it off because he appears to be dominant and too controlling. "Tiffany know this is you, it's his way or the highway," so pick your poison carefully.

Scenario 6 Overtime or Bedtime

If you are dating or in a relationship with a guy who is a dedicated sports fans and during the pivotal part of game 7 championship game, which was headed for overtime, you decide to make a sexual advancement toward him; but during this time, he happen to be still be glancing at the TV and preoccupied, do you have the right to get upset?

EG: Controversial Counselor, I am about to catch heat for my response but here we go, emotions have no timing and should be taken advantage of when called upon. The sporting events are designed to distract any way, separating us from more serious contact humans.

YB: Being the tomboy that I am, I would be watching the game with him. But if she knows he's into the game like that, she should wait until the game is over.

PN: No, I will say he could say baby as soon as the game is over he will make me happy with a kiss.

HL: Nothing comes between me and the Super Bowl. I make that known from the first time I plan to be exclusive with any woman.

KM: Nothing comes between me and my woman!!!!!!!!!

OW: Would not be mad but feel some kind of way, you men want it when you want it and sometimes we do too. If you wait till later I may not be in the mood, your loss.

C2: When women want it during these times is it about attention or you trying to control a situation?

HL: Thinking like OW is what gives men the impression that being in the mood equate to not being in the mood because of a headache. I'll let you all have that one and take it where you want to. I call it BS though. If a woman only want to have sex when the mood suits her, then she may as well hire someone to answer her beck and call. That is one of the most outlandish things I ever heard.

OW: Man C2 when the mood hit you damn it you not thinking bout nothing else. What you doing, working, cleaning, feeding the kids, or watching the game, my itch needs to be scratched and if you don't do it I will get some batteries (get it) now you decide. LMAO

TA: Does she have the right to be upset? Yes but then again so does he! That is the equivalent to him trying to get with her during the last 5 minutes of Scandal!!! Lol

JC: Hell Noooo!!!! She suppose to save that for halftime and/or to celebrate the victory afterwards. LOL

CA: Whatever happened to delayed gratification…. Geesh have some patience lol, WTF

Issues: How women are so damn attention seeking, wanting sex during times where men may be watching a game and simply don't want to be bothered at the time. Should men cave in or have them wait?

Perspective: There were many different perspectives, some women who think like men felt it was not that serious wait to the damn game goes off. Other women felt like if you come on to your man, he needs to be prepared to walk away from the game and have sex to fulfill her needs at the time.

Knowledge: This particular guy was out at a bar watching a game, and as his woman was talking, his focus was on the TV and she was distracting him; she became upset and said he was being rude and he does the same thing at home when she comes on to him.

Action: Both parties can come to an agreement that when they are having "me time" for the others to respect those boundaries, certainly guys can't use the sports card every night because they will create an imbalance, but never should women use their vagina as a control method; if you have seen one, you have them all.

Consequences: It works both ways if needs are not being met, someone may be inclined to seek it elsewhere, it will all boil down to communication, should sex be centered around obligation or timely passion?

Scenario 7 Sometimes People Never Learn

Tina has continued to let Tony use her car after being warned by coworkers and her parents to stop letting this man use your car. Despite that feedback, evidently he was laying the wood really good because she continues to let him drive her car around. This particular day, Tina had an appointment to get her car inspection done because it was due to expire. She had been calling Tony all morning and texting him but no answer, she became frantic and called a cab to ride around to see if she could locate her car. She called the police to report her car stolen, but they said there was nothing they can do because she gave him the keys, so technically it's not stolen. Finally at 4:00 p.m., he showed up walked in the house and overheard Tina talking about him on the phone, and his first words were "I know you are not putting those bitches in my business?" What Tina didn't know that behind him was Tony's girlfriend who followed him to Tina's house to make sure he got all of his shit out of the house. That was very bold of Tony, but his girlfriend wanted to make sure and that he would not be leaving any of his belongings at Tina's house. Have you ever been in a situation like this, and if so, please let us know; there continues to be people out here that are stuck on stupid and just sometimes never learn.

MJ: Oh wow!!! I would take it as a blessing in disguise. Let him leave and make sure all his stuff is gone!!!. Take her keys and change the locks on the door. She will be hurt for a while but time heals all wounds. She wouldn't get rid of him so God removed him for her.

C2: Sometimes when you meet men like Tone Capone, it becomes a conquest for women to see if they can become the woman to tame that wild dog. Agree or disagree?

LH: The good me agrees with MJ's answer. The spiteful me says she was a dumbass and what did she expect? Fool me once shame on you, fool me twice shame on me.

MJ: C2 you hit the nail right on the head with that statement. Many females do think they can make the man tame but they can't.

TA: Firstly, no I haven't been in that situation. Secondly, yes you are right and wrong C2, there are females who think they can tame a man but I wouldn't say they were women. In my experience, a good and grown woman will not tolerate Tony's behavior. Usually females who find themselves in this situation are not mature (which has nothing to do with age) I consider myself to be a good and grown woman and Tony wouldn't know what to do with someone like me cause I am a woman with requirements. Females who don't are the ones that end up with Tony's so to speak.

C2: TA, so are you saying these females are little girls? Some times laying the wood could be the equalizer that break good women like yourself down.

TA: Being immature and a little girl are two different things. A little girl is age related while immaturity is behavior. Good doesn't equate mature either. Laying good wood isn't a factor with me. It's important but before you get to that point with me I will know if you're even qualified and poor "Tony wouldn't have even made it to the point of knowing my address or phone number for that matter. A grown woman has enough life experiences to know that laying good wood doesn't equate to a good man either.

Issues: Tina had been advised to stop letting Tony use her car by her parents and coworkers because he is taking advantage of the situation. Tina had an appointment to get her car inspected and she could not get a hold of Tony; when he finally surfaced, he returned the car but brought along his girlfriend to make sure he got all his belongings.

Perspectives: Several people felt that it was a blessing that Tony was out of Tina's life, she did not have the power but God intervene to remove Tony. My perspective was many women think they are the ones who can tame a man and possibly be the one that will change the guy's behavior. Another interesting perspective was Tina being immature and Tony not being able to handle a real woman so he takes advantage of weak women such as Tina.

Knowledge: What I know from this scenario is that Tina was going through a divorce and was dealing with pain and got involved in this relationship to compensate for her loneliness and now she is settling.

Action: Tina needs to realize her self-worth and understand that Tony has nothing to bring to the table and he will continue to use and abuse her as he joy rides in her car but sleeps with her when it's convenient. Is getting some wood laid to you worth your self-dignity?

Consequences: Tina runs the risk at being cut off by parents and coworkers behind her stupidity because ain't no one got time for her crap. She was never over her husband and how she wants to be able to say she has someone for the sake of saying it, as my grandfather use to say, a man can't be a man without transportation. Tina needs to tell Tony to hit the highway with his carless ass.

Scenario 8 Take It or Leave It

Louis and Victoria have been together for ten years, Louis never mentioned he had a child eight years prior when they were just messing around. Papers came in the mail for support and the paternity test. The results came back he is the father 99.99 percent. When questions in the past about the pictures of the little girl, Louis lied and said it was his cousin's baby. Now he wants to spend time with a child and expects Victoria to be a stepmom and role model. Victoria refuses because of the numerous lies Louis told about the now-proven daughter and the issue is constantly causing arguments between the two of them. Is Louis wrong for expecting Victoria to warm up to the idea? Is Victoria wrong for refusing? The caveat to it all is that Louis daughter's mother is always trying to find a way to start trouble in his relationship. How do Louis and Victoria overcome this hot and sticky situation?

NG: How can Louis expect Victoria to step up and be a step mom and mentor to a child that he lied about and denied for 8 yrs.

C2: What choice does she have if she wants to remain with Louis

NG: You just said "what choice does she have if she wants to remain with Louis", I say if Louis wants to keep Victoria in his life, and be a father to this child he needs to stop all the lies. Start to have a relationship with his daughter and give Victoria and the Child time to warm up to one another.

COJ: Louis should have never lied on his kid. The balls of him to say it was his cousin's baby!!! Men who lie on their kids are wimps. Dump his tacky ass and move on to the next.

PF: Leave it, If Louis can lie about something so serious what more has he lied about? The trust is gone and nothing good comes out of a relationship without must.

TA: Are they married? If they are not, she needs to do whatever is best for her. She doesn't owe him anything. I don't understand how in the world a man always wants a girlfriend to play the "wife" role. He is asking her to commit to him when he hasn't committed to her. I'm sorry but if I were her, I would be out just on the lies and the audacity to think I am obligated to help raise his child and be a good example. He needs to get his life and she needs to upgrade. The day women realize that we can always do better than being with someone that does not treat us with respect.

HL: The child is a non issue. I don't tolerate deceit. I read tea leaves well and I'd always have to question what is true. Not a good way to live. I'd have to advocate leaving.

Issue: Lewis and Victoria have been together for ten years and throughout their relationship, Louis was hiding the fact that he had an eight-year-old daughter. Once Victoria found out, Louis wanted Victoria to come to terms and accept his child.

Perspectives: Many have responded that due to the years of lying, they don't think the relationship can turn for the positive and Victoria should leave him. If Victoria plans to stay, what options does she really have but take the situation and roll with the hand that she was dealt with currently. Another perspective is that it boils down to the couple's status; are they married or not, if not, bye-bye.

Knowledge: What many don't know is that Victoria ended up staying with Louis, but it's not a day that doesn't go by that she has not struggle with her decision of staying.

Actions: If I were Victoria, my thought process would be where I go from here; I can leave and start over, but do I really know what I am going to get from the next man; the grass may not be greener on the other side of the fence.

Consequences: Victoria can have resentment toward the child and mistreat her when Louis is not present. Reoccurring arguments between Victoria and Louis due to a lack of trust, or all ends well and they work together to overcome this major conflict.

CHAPTER 2

Family

Scenario 9 A Blow for a Blow at the Barber

RAY IS AT the barbershop and share with the guys that his wife stepped out on him with another guy; she did not sleep with the guy but just gave him head, but Ray decided to forgive her and they remained together. Meanwhile the next week when Ray comes in for his appointment, the guys are sitting around after the shop closes and Keon ask Ray how does it feel to kiss his wife after knowing she went down on another man? Ray walks out to calm himself down. What do you think is going to happen once Ray goes home and sees his wife?

NJ: If he decided to forgive her when it happened than nothing should happen when he gets home. He chose to share that information with his friends, so he's going to have to deal with the immature comments and not take it out on his wife. If you truly forgive someone you move on from their mistakes and don't use it against them later.

C2: Hey NJ only in a perfect world if forgiveness worked like that, I am sure that he shared that info at the barbershop to try to get someone to validate his decision.

NJ: That's how forgiveness should work. Unless those men are his close friends he should have kept his mouth shut about his home life. There are some things you don't talk to acquaintances.

C2: Secrets keep you sick, he had to let it out and the truth of the matter is you are taking a major risk anytime you share with people. My mindset is out of 10 people only 2 or 3 may your best interest at heart.

NJ: I'm not saying keep it a secret but share with people you really know. Everyone has at least one person in their life that they can tell anything to and not be judged. At least one I know I do.

CA: Ray and his wife need a lessons and boundaries! WTF

TF: If he decided to forgive her that should be the end. I know since his friends through it in his face, Ray is pissed again. When he gets home to the wife its going to be a family battle.

DB: First of all this doesn't make sense because this isn't typical men behavior because most men can't take seeing your beautiful lips and eyes, which you can't hide, so she slopped the knob and instant forgiveness. I will tell you what the bible says what will happen.

KH: Ray is going to think about the relationship that his wife had with the other guy. But truly this is probably a feeling that he already thought about and will be able to get pass it. Because if he already agreed to forgive and continue on its not going to bother him. It's just that trouble making Keon trying to start stuff.

PC: Well for Ray to forgive his wife knowing what she had did, he also knowingly understands that not everyone is going to understand his decision to do so. When he returns to the shop, he should check Keon on the level of disrespect that he is showing regarding a situation that does not have anything to do with him, unless Ray's wife gave Keon some head.

HL: If Ray is content with his decision to stay he will brush it off his shoulders and continue to try and build trust between them. After all it is 2014 most women who get married are not virgins at the alter. If men always walked around with that attitude toward it there probably would never be a first kiss. You don't think about what a woman did with her ex before you. So for the sake of salvaging the marriage he should just leave it alone and move on or get a divorce if he can't make himself get over it.

EG: C2 I am back that's why it's so important to have scripture on your heart for situations just like this. A great place to have the Bible right next to the bed, lol. Scripture says you have to study to show yourself approved. Always willing to share truth.

KM: Rules of the jungle: (1) It's in a man's nature to have more than one woman to spread his seed to dominate the world with his genes. I'm not saying it's right. It is what it is. (2) It's not in a woman's nature to have more than one man usually. As for the brother Keon who was ribbing about the wife oral activity, if your wife wasn't a virgin when you met her, she did the same thing to another man or woman as well. I'm just saying, it's not what I do.

FJ: I believe there were problems from the beginning for her to step out on her husband, or he knew his wife was promiscuous when he met her. If he can't take the heat (ribbing), he should have never told anyone. He's going to go home and argue or cry because he would've beat her already if he were going to do so. Either leave the relationship or forgive and move on. Knowing that it could happen again, weather she slept with him or whatever she cheated.

MJ: As I was reading this I was thinking what PC said. I wouldn't have had a conversation about my business in a barbershop in the first place though.

CA: I believe married people may want to think about getting divorced prior to stepping out of their marriage on the level that happen between Ray and his wife.

Issue: Ray shared at the barbershop that his wife stepped out on him by giving another man oral sex, but he has forgiven her. Meanwhile, Ray received some teasing from one of the barbers and it instantly pissed him off. How do you think Ray will handle his anger in regards to his wife?

Perspective: One of the perspectives were that if Ray had made the decision to take his wife back, then he needs to let his anger go. Another perspective was Ray needed to talk about it and the barbershop as an outlet, but he was putting his business out there at his own risk. Third perspective was that Ray needs to leave his wife; there is no way a man can rebound from the reality that his wife was with another man. Fourth perspective was more than likely his wife was not a virgin when he met her so Ray knows she has been with other men at one point in her life. The final perspective was if Ray was going to put his hands on his wife, it probably would have already happen and violence is not going to change the fact that it was done.

Knowledge: What many don't know about this scenario is Keon lives to get under someone's skin and put things out there to be a jackass, it's the simple case of KYP (Know Your Personnel) when you are sharing information with others because you never know what someone is going to do with that information.

Action: Ray could have shared this info in a more private setting or could look into counseling. Personally, I think it will be an uphill battle to work through this but it can happen. I wish him all the luck in the world because marriage and parenting may be two of the hardest roles to maintain stress free.

Consequences: Ray and his wife may experience turmoil throughout their relationship and Ray must be prepared for constant triggers of infidelity that may send him over the edge. I hope sucking the chrome off the 57 Chevy was well worth the pain she may experience.

Scenario 10 A Joke Is Only a Joke When Both Parties Find it Funny

Steven and Kimberly have been married for twenty years, have three sons, and are living a good life. Steven is a chemical engineer and Kimberly is a stay-home mom. On New Year's Eve, they attended a party and Steven got pretty saucy. That night when they went home, Steven was passed out and did not hear his phone vibrating and Kimberly decided to open his text message and what a surprise did she get, several pictures of nude guys. When confronted, Steven stated it was a joke from his coworkers. Now should this matter be addressed?

AM: If she didn't sign a pre-up. Those texts were all proofs she needed. It's a touchy situation because of the kids. I don't think divorce should be the first step, I think more investigating needs to be done.

MJ: Is he gay? Before she married him there had to be signs. That's messed up

HL: There is no evidence he has done a thing. All the conclusions being formed are very short sided. There is nothing that says he was a part of the pictures so anything along the lines of divorce are speculation of what he has done.

EG: My man I am going to disagree with you on the trust issue, it should be an open book, according to the word of God. C2 Christian status actively involved in the church or Easter visitors?

HL: I don't have an issue with relationships being open in terms of info. I just don't think she would have checked his phone if he was awake. To me, that is the bigger problem. Correct me if I am wrong, but if she doesn't look at his phone, then anything else is a mute point right.

DJ: I would have to investigate but if his ass is gay ain't no working it out. He can take his happy ass somewhere else.

C2: That might create a hardship for Kimberly's non working ass

TA: Don't jump to conclusions, I have 20 years of marriage on the line and I'm not going to walk away from it for a text message on my husband's phone. Technically I don't think it's even a valid reason to get a divorce. Especially since he has the right to have an expectation of privacy (legally). If this is someone that I have known for 20 yrs of my life and this is the first time anything happen like this, please. I'm not doing anything, I will make a mental note and keep one eye open but for now, nothing to worry about. That is the problem in today's world. We jump to conclusions without all of the facts. I'm the type that will build my case before presenting evidence. I wouldn't even have told him I saw the message either.

RT: She got what she was looking for, if it was a joke or not if she never poked her nose in (she decided) it's a non issue. But since it's out there, now he has some explaining to do. Whatever happened to boundaries in relationships? Its one thing if they have an agreement, she must have suspected something in the first place.

DJ: That's why I said I'd investigate further and if it's true may God forgive me because it's over. Can't be with a man who wants a man (FOH), no one should snoop but if you're married it should be open book.

Issue: Kimberly and Steven have been married for twenty years and on New Year's Eve went out, Steven got really saucy and when they returned home he passed out; his phone kept buzzing, Kimberly decided to open his text and found nude pictures in his phone. When confronted, Steven stated it was a joke from his coworkers.

Perspectives: (1) Is he gay? (2) No evidence was found other than the pictures that would cause for his wife to consider divorce. (3) Kimberly was out of line for going in his phone in the first place. (4) Marriage is an open book and all parts of the relationship should be shared with spouse. (5) Too many years together to even consider a divorce based on a text message.

Knowledge: Steven coworkers did not send the message, they happen to be sent by those actual guys; Kenny has not done anything physical but he enjoys looking at the male anatomy. Steven is ashamed of his attraction especially how disappointing it will be for his sons to find out.

Actions: I feel that Steven needs to be honest and let his wife know what the deal is; my gut feeling is there are thoughts, feelings, actions, and behaviors, sooner or later he will act on this situation and that is where things get sticky and tight. Give his wife the opportunity to leave on her own instead of putting her through this embarrassing pain.

Consequences: The consequences of this scenario is more than likely Steven will continue doing what he is doing until everything comes out in the light; he will forever live in shame and embarrassment, involving his wife, children, and career. If only this was a joke, unfortunately men are leaving their families to take on this alternative lifestyle on a regular basis. Women, know your man before the joke is on you.

Scenario 11 Blood Is Thicker than Water

Graduation time was meant to be good times, but in this case, someone had to deal with pain and betrayal. Brianna was graduating from high school, but due to the shortage of tickets given out by her high school, four tickets, she had a major decision to make. One ticket went to her mother Helen, two other tickets went to her grandparents, that means she had only one ticket left. Certainly, that ticket should go to her stepdad Eric who has been a part of her life since she was three years old and has been the only Dad she knows. Her biological dad was informed by his sister that his precious daughter who he had nothing to do with throughout her life would be graduating from high school, so Leon contacted her two days before graduation and stated he wanted to start over and very much would like to attend the ceremony. Brianna was confused but always wanted that love and acceptance from Leon, so she told her mother that she wanted her dad to attend the graduation. Helen informed Eric of the news and he was devastated and upset. Helen pretty much told him that this day was all about Brianna and he needs to build a bridge and get over it. What should Brianna do? Do you think Helen handled this situation correctly? Where does Eric go from here after being betrayed?

TF: Hopefully this will not break up their marriage. Brianna knows Eric deserves that damn ticket. I understood her wanting a relationship with her father, she can go to dinner with him after the ceremony, or invite him to her celebration. Helen knows Eric deserves that ticket too. Eric will not get over it.

KP: Helen should have explained to Briana how devastating this will be to Eric even though he was not a bio father that he was father that her bio father should have been. Helen needs to have a convo with Leon and let him know that he can rebuild his relationship with Brianna after her graduation. Leon has no right to share a day that he had no part in Brianna's success. Eric needs to voice his opinion.

TA: Helen is wrong and should support her husband period. The biological hasn't earned the right to attend graduation. He hasn't contributed to anything in the daughter's life since she was 3. Eric needs to tell both Brianna and Helen that he doesn't agree with the decision but it is her to make. However, going forward they need to make sure they let the biological know that since he is ready to step up and be a part of her life now that anything Brianna needs (college tuition, car, wedding paid for, etc) he needs to handle it cause he is done.

C2: I am sure the dynamics will be forever ruined between Eric and Helen, next thing we know Leon will staying over night because that is what Bri wants him to do.

EG: C2, at some point parents will have to set boundaries. Dialogue is key and continue to be the main point in the majority of the scenarios presented. It is to easy to throw time away and much harder to work at the relationships. Team Mayweather Hard Work and Dedication.

HL: Helen needs to re-evaluate her sensitivity toward Eric, her comments show a lack of appreciation for his contribution toward her progression to this day. Eric may need to search his soul to understand that if he has done his job as a father, then his day would have arrived sooner or later and that he has raised a young woman to make decisions for her best interest. While the sting of being passed over will be great, as with time it will heal. His daughter's desire to have her biological father in her life can't and shouldn't be under estimated and he better not let her down.

TS: I disagree that the dynamics between Eric and Helen "will be forever ruined" this was just about her special graduation day and the relationship between Brianna and her father not from Helen and some ex from forever ago.

AM: Eric wasn't portrayed. Brianna wanted to get to know her biological father. There is nothing wrong with that, when Eric decided to be active in Brianna's life he should have understood that since she is not his he may need to share her love and attention with her biological father. I get that he hurts but he should focus on the fact that the young lady he helped raise is moving in the right direction, Graduation is a special moment but how many of those has he had and will be continue to have with her in the future? He needs to kinda step back and look at the bigger picture. His wife was right.

Issue: Brianna is graduating from high school and has limited tickets for the ceremony. After giving one to her mother, grandparents, she has one remaining; she wants to give the final one to her dad after he popped out of the woodwork leaving her stepdad Eric without one, which has Eric without one and has him feeling some kind of way.

Perspectives: Stepdad deserves the final ticket and Dad needs to do dinner with Brianna. Mother should have had a conversation with Brianna regarding how giving the ticket to her dad would make Eric feel. The dynamics will be ruined between Eric and Helen. The opportunity for Brianna to spend time with her biological dad should not be undervalued. This day was about Brianna's happiness and not Eric's; if she wanted her dad there than old well, Eric needs to get over it.

Knowledge: Brianna's dad had been locked up for years and his ultimate goal was to get close to Helen; he wanted what he thought was his and the quickest way to get to Helen's heart was through Brianna.

Action: Helen should have put the hammer down and said, "I will not do that to my husband who has been there all of Brianna's life; he deserves better to share this day with you and my recommendation is your dad take you out to eat; this day is about family and Eric was a key part of the equation to get you to walk across the stage."

Consequences: Eric will detach himself from Brianna and Helen; anything that has to do with Brianna, he will not participate or make an excuse on why he can't be a part of it. Helen and Brianna needs to find out what her dad's motives are before hurting Eric. Blood may be thicker than water but in this case, water is pure and dad's blood may be contaminated. Always make sure you pick your poison carefully.

Scenario 12 Chat Line

Charles worked three to eleven at General Motors and it was typical for him to come in the house, stop in the bedroom, and kiss his wife Ellen on the forehead while she was sleeping. He would head to the kitchen, warm up his dinner, grab a cold Corona, and head down to his man cave in the basement. He would get caught up with the world of sports on ESPN or maybe just check out a late night game, depending on what night it was during the week. Charles was also a frequent visitor of the Tango Chat line, where he had a membership; he love to browse the line and connect with different women all over. This particular night, he decided to connect live with this particular woman. During the conversation, they shared sexual pleasantries, which led him to moan and groan. His wife Ellen happen to wake up this particular night and walk to top of the stairs and overheard Charles in a state of total bliss. Should Ellen confront him or should she take her ass back to bed? Do you consider this being unfaithful?

PC: She should respond the same way he would respond as if it were her down in the cave having online sex. Now if the wife is not giving up the booty, then she has no right to say anything.

KP: The first time will lead to another than another. I had a friend who was very lonely in her relationship with her husband and she started to "Chat". Pleasing herself was the beginning then it started turning into an emotional connection. She became attached to a man across country, and her marriage fell by the waist side, her husband had caught her emotional emails and pictures to this other man and confronted her. Luckily they worked it out and she stopped going on chat lines. Charles may just want to get his bliss but chatting with someone I think he crossed the line. Ellen should confront him and see if there is a disconnect in their sex life, the earlier the better. If Charles needs a sexual stimulation then he should watch a movie where there is no contact with a real live person. Ellen needs to step up her game so Charles will not have a need to chat with anyone but her, spice it up girl!!!.

DP: Ellen should maybe go downstairs and not confront but comfort. He seemed to love his wife but perhaps did not want to disturb her sleep. Ellen should let him know those interruptions are good ones.

EG: Lol, there we go putting monkey wrenches in a seemingly good relationship, Charles need to have a dialog with his wife about his likes and dislikes, this should have happened before marriage. Ellen should confront because she is part of the problem. Open up dialog, confront issues, forgive/pray, have sex and fall asleep.

C2: EG my brother unfortunately we live in a drama filled world.

EG: Lol, C2 that's why I am a particular individual according to scripture-1 Peter 2:9. I am living my life on purpose, flawed yes but determined to walk according to his direction. I have done it according to the world for to long so I desire to see results.

RC: I would confront him about it because he could've been moaning and groaning with me and I'm right upstairs!!!!.

C2: Its just not that simple he still loves his wife but not physically attracted to her no longer.

KP: Not attracted, let her know tactfully and see what they can do about it. Explore the possibilities. So many things that can help just have to be willing to open up to each other.

C2: Sometimes a marriage ends up being a business management nothing more and nothing less.

KP: True C2, but if both are willing to have a loving and sexual marriage then they will exhaust and possibilities. If not then go your separate ways! No matter what sex is a big part of the relationship and if you are not a willing participant then why put yourself through a sexless one. (There are some that have mitigating circumstances and should be handled carefully.

NM: We would have to have a conversation about this. A confrontation is possible considering he is living with someone. Yes this is being unfaithful

KP: Not at all C2, but men are visual creatures and if they see something they like their endorphins kick in much faster than woman when they are visually aroused, but some men are dogs.

C2: I am concerned because he has a membership which leads me to believe that Slick has been doing this for years, just maybe he likes variety.

KP: Variety is fine if he finds it with his wife, she should be concerned with his behavior, unless she is ok with it, and maybe she turns a blind eye to it because it is a marriage of financial convenience.

Issue: Charles works three to eleven at General Motors, and when he gets home at night, he comes home and kiss his wife on the forehead, warms up his dinner and heads to the man cave, to watch sports and talk on the chat line. One night, Ellen, his wife, got up and heard Charles moaning and groaning. What in the world should Ellen do?

Perspectives: Go downstairs and confront Charles and ask him is there a reason he needs to do that over the phone. Maybe Charles is no longer physically attracted to Ellen. If sex is a part of their marriage, then something has to be worked out for Ellen to take care of Charles's needs. Maybe Charles simply likes a variety of ways to get off and Ellen needs to accept it.

Knowledge: Charles is an undercover freak and this is what he likes to do; hence, why do you think he has his membership to Tango Chat line, he may feel like he makes good money and he will do what he wants to do.

Actions: In all reality, Ellen may not do anything but go back to bed like she does every night and get in where she fits in, sad but this may be the case. Charles is the breadwinner so Ellen eats her humble pie and waits her turn.

Consequences: Eventually Charles will meet someone local on the chat line and instead of the phone one-to-one conversation, he will be meeting with someone after work while telling Ellen he will be working overtime, so instead of coming in after 11:00 p.m., he will be rolling in after 7:00 a.m. in the morning.

Scenarios 13 Family Means Everything

Geary shared to Maria about his newborn baby, recently four years ago, Geary stepped out on Maria and got someone else pregnant, but later found out the child was not his. His ultimate goal is for Maria to accept his newborn and they get back together. Maria does not want to go down that road so she told him congrats and that she wished him the best; Geary has been blowing up Maria's phone and sending crazy text saying he wants a family with Maria and family is everything. Maria was alarmed so she contacted Geary's mother to say he finally has that child that he has been waiting on and she has her three-year-old daughter Angel and she is happy so there is no need for her to deal with Geary. When Maria first had Angel, Geary shrugged the situation off and as if he does not want anything to do with Angel. Maria finally sent Geary a text and said that it was never meant to be and was happy for him and his daughter and wish them all the best and please stop texting her. Geary called back in tears very angry and said I am glad the damn church is working for you and you are a fricking hypocrite because he has always been there for Maria and Angel. Maria tried to be nice as she could but Geary was not having it. What should Maria do about Geary?

MJ: Call the Cops

AM: He's just hurt he'll get over it. I wouldn't get the cops involved unless he starts making threats.

DP: Geary messed up and is hurt because Maria is done with him. He feels the rejection are caused by outside factors and not previous actions discussed by Maria. He wants to blame anyone but himself for the failure. Block his number and eventually he will get over it. Unless there is something in the past that should alarm Maria this too shall pass.

TS: So did he impregnate the other chick while he was with Maria? If so she is justified in her actions. He is just hurt and is responding as such. She needs to just ignore him now and things should settle. Definitely involve police if he becomes threatening though

EG: If the world hates you, ye know that it hated me before it hated you. (John15:18 KJV). Maria has found direction in her life, the last thing she needs is to remain in the world she just escaped. Encourage this young man to have a relationship with his child, pray for him, remain polite but always remain stern in your commitment to Christ.

TA: What is up with all this crying, whining and begging? He doesn't get a vote on how she wants to move forward in her life. She gets to decide what and who she wants to be with and it isn't him right now. That is the risk that both men and women take when they step out and dishonor their relationship. There are consequences for every action whether they are intended or unintended. I'm always amazed at people that think someone owes them something. She isn't his wife. She doesn't owe him another chance or anything else.

CA: Damn Geary, keep it in your pants, nasty ass lol

DP: Maria should continue to move on. Geary is not responsible

JE: Ummm let me get this straight, they both had children with other people after they met each other? Seems like a no brainer to me. Neither one seems truly interested in starting a family together so they should just move on. Nor does either seem like they have a solid gasp on the concept of effective family planning for that matter.

KP: Maria should tell Geary to take a hike, he started out the relationship hiding a potential child so what else has he been hiding? And what else will he hide from her in the future, a relationship not worth having.

Issue: Geary had stepped out on Maria during their relationship and thought he got another women pregnant but it came back that the child was not his, but recently he called Maria and said he finally has a child and he wants to be a family with Maria and her children but Maria does not want anything to do with Geary.

Perspective: Geary is hurt and angry because of his past and can't handle the fact that Maria is in a better place with her life. This is the risk that happens when you decide to step out in relationship. Geary need to keep his Johnson in his pants. Geary and Maria need some effective child planning courses. Geary started out hiding things in the relationship and will continue to do so.

Knowledge: Maria is better off without Geary; when they were together, he half-assed handled his business and never accepted Maria's daughter when he found out about her. Both parties keep it moving.

Action: Maria can choose to remain as a friend to Geary and accept the situation for what it's worth and understand that if she takes him back there will be a lot of bitterness and resentment to work out.

Consequences: Geary and Maria may not end up speaking again behind their issues. They made a run at a relationship years ago and now two children have been brought into the equation, which will complicate matters worse; family means everything, but some bonds need to be broken for the betterment of certain individuals.

Scenario 14 Home is not a Home

Robert leaves his wife of fifteen years along with their eleven-year-old daughter and nine-year-old son, to be with his mistress. Robert's wife was solely dependent on him financially and this has left a severe hardship on his family to the point of almost homelessness. Robert has refused to pay child support, finally after one year he was court ordered to pay child support.

LB: Bull Shit but real for so many women

C2: Talk about it, how do you think the father actions will impact his family

TF: Robert is an ass because he is responsible for taking care of his children! His new woman is an ass also. Who would deal with a male that does not take care of his children???? A stupid ass that's who, I will date a man with 1000000 children, he better be taking care of all of them.

DP: Acceptance is why this happens. Mothers accepting the son's behavior when they come home with their mistress, sister and brothers downing the wife and saying she wasn't good enough instead of condemning the actions of the brother. Fathers lack of proper role modeling and providing in prior generations. It is a cycle *we* as a community should not tolerate this behavior by being the mistresses and promoting family.

LFJ: I can relate! The father can have his life however give respect where it's due. Give the mother her child support. Its hard raising kids however I didn't depend all on his money, but damn we as women don't make the children by yourself and another thing, I would've left him with the kids to be with my side piece I would've been called a whore, unfit mother and so on but males can do it and think that their balls can hang free. Yeah let those m fers hang free for a second and then I'm going to hit you where it hurts in the correct way which the males scream that the woman is bitter. Hell yeah that may be the case but pay your share and life is good. Please don't get me started with the topic. LOL

EG: Robert was dropped, his name is Mephibosheth. (2 Samuel 4:4 KJV) and it was not his fault. He does not realize he is the family's protector and should be working for reconciliation instead of separation. He witnessed a lack of intimacy from his parents, have no leadership ability and lacks fruit so the title of Godly man is out of the question.

C2: Robert has failed his family and it breaks my heart to know he would leave them for broke to chase this other new adventure and like TF said what kind of woman would let this take place.

LFJ: Must say that the females that get those males swear they have a prize, in fact they do for the moment because they provide for attention so in a long run Karma is a bleep that you don't want to mess around with at all.

LB: Men who equate their relationship to the female are an ass. If we females had the same response no relationship means I don't need to be a mother to the children, this place would be even more messed up, and i.e. being a parent is a life time not just during the relationship.

LR: We all go through this very same issue give or take. If the mother was being supported by DSS his butt would have been under the jail, have no driver's license and being pulled into court with every raise and bonus. It all goes back to responsibility and respect for you, your kids and God. When those things are overlooked then it becomes cyclic. Unfortunately the society that we live in tolerates this from our men so it becomes common place.

Issue: Robert left his wife along with his two children to be with his mistress, his departure left his family with a serious hardship that almost left them homeless.

Perspective: Robert is an ass for not taking care of his children and refusing to pay child support. This behavior is a cycle that is allowed by mothers who let their sons behave this way. A situation like this is double standard; men are allowed to behave like this, but when women do it, they are called all kinds of whores. Robert needs to have reconciliation instead of separation; he is lacking leadership in the home. What kind of female will allow a man to not take care of his children and she knows about it.

Knowledge: Robert has went on to become a successful physician, but to this day, his relationship is scarred because of the way he treated his wife and children and that is something that he has to live with for the rest of his life.

Actions: Robert should have let his wife know he was unhappy and sat down and discussed a plan on how he was going to financially support his family; never leave your children in a position of potential homelessness or wondering where their next meal will come from, too many times men are gallivanting around town flossing their goods while their kids are looking for something good to eat.

Consequences: Pain, hurt, and mistrust comes out of situations like this, and in most causes, everything fathers touch ends up ruined. They say God does not like ugly and in some cases home is not a home, and when that is the case, talk to your spouse about it, attempt to make repairs before you evict yourself from the situation.

Scenario 15 Hurt People Like to Hurt People

Dexter and Glenda have been married for fifteen years; they have two children, Darnell, nine years old, and Carlton, seven years old. Glenda works the three-to-eleven shift, and most of the time she works, her mother keeps the children. The other times Dexter keeps them, but only if Glenda knew that while under her husband's care, Dexter is a serious heroin addict; he invites his drug buddies over and they shoot up dope. Also Dexter is very abusive to Darnell calling him punk ass, pussy ass, and bitch ass on a regular basis, especially if he is not competing on the level with the other children his age. This often made Darnell very sad so he would go hide in his grandmother's bathroom for hours at a time. Eventually Darnell's grandmother will realize he was in the bathroom and would hear Dexter yelling "Come outside pussy, stop being afraid." Grandma would threaten to hurt Dexter if he didn't leave her baby alone. This verbal abusive behavior continued every time Dexter was high or drunk. Poor Darnell, he was living a life of pain and hell; every day, young people are being abused at home and are faced to deal with these issues, who is going to help Darnell during these valuable years of development.

DCJ: He's the punk letting a bitch ass drug kick his ass

HL: Hopefully an uncle or someone from the community. If not, then his mother needs to somehow become aware and get him out of this abusive situation. Why the grandmother hasn't spoken up is beyond me.

Glenda being unaware of his drug habit tells me that she isn't paying attention to what is going on. If she was, she might be able to pick up clues about their son being abused,

MJ: The grandmother needs to speak up on and take action. This sickens me and hurts my heart to the core!!! Herbert is 100% correct and the mother needs to be told. When she finds out, if she doesn't kick him out or leave with her babies herself, then she is guilty by associations.

C2: I wonder if Dexter was apart of the vicious cycle

MJ: Like you said hurt people hurt other people it's quite possible

C2: So many of our men abandon their sons and leave them in this world to fend for themselves, where they seek manhood lessons from the streets

LN: I'm upset with Glenda; clearly she is not communicating with her children. If she was, she would be aware. Grandma must speak up for that child, she probably a victim of an abuser and is afraid to address what she's witnessing, poor kid. Karma is real. Dexter may overdose, and then all will be right with the universe. Was that too harsh.

MJ: No LN you're on, you definitely reap what you sow

DP: Confused why grandma is silent and Glenda is not talking to her children. Heroin is a very violent addiction. I'm wondering is she being passive about it.

C2: Some grandmothers are ole skool and they let their children work through their issues without getting overly involved.

KP: There is no question that Glenda needs to get these kids and get out!! There are so many programs and avenues she can utilize to help her and her children. For her to let things go on this long is beyond me... Can not tell me she didn't know her husband was doing drugs or hurting the children... For Darnell and Carlton to have a fighting chance in society and to break the cycle that Dexter has been exposed to she needs to leave and don't look back.

HL: True C2, but she has stated that she would hurt him if he doesn't leave her baby alone, just makes me wonder.

C2: Maybe that statement was the Band-Aid approach to stop the bleeding for the time being HL.

HL: Very well could be, either way, it is destructive.

Issue: Dexter was suffering from a drug addiction and the vicious cycle that caused him to be verbally abusive toward his son, mainly during times when Glenda was at work. Darnell's grandmother witnessed the after effects of Darnell being abused, she would address it with Dexter but Glenda remained clueless.

Perspective: Darnell needs support from relative, community members, to get him out of the situation. Glenda needs to pay more attention to her son's needs. Grandmother needs to be more proactive and speak up about the matter. I am upset with Glenda for not communicating with her children. Glenda needs to get out of the situation; there is a lot of community support that can help her.

Knowledge: Glenda did eventually leave Dexter after years of physical abuse she suffered from Dexter herself; once she left Dexter, he walked out of his children's life and never had much to do with them other than occasional here and there.

Actions: Grandmother could have let Glenda know to speak with Dexter about his behavior and suggested that she considers leaving before more damage is done. But sometimes grandparents may step back and let their children go through experiences on their own.

Consequences: Some of the consequences from Dexter's actions are Darnell growing up with anger and resentment, lacking self-confidence, and severed relationships due to all the pain caused by Dexter.

Scenario 16 Wedding Notification thru Facebook

Seventeen-year-old girl Kendra finds out through FB that her father Tim is getting married without her knowing about it; Kendra currently lives in Los Angeles and Dad lives in Cleveland. Kendra is very upset because she asked her dad about being in a relationship and her dad denied it; Kendra feels that her dad is wrong and his fiancée was stupid because her dad didn't have the decency to mention his wife to be to her. Do you think Kendra is wrong for how she felt? What are your views regarding her dad? How do you think the fiancée should feel?

BM: The fiancée and daughter should both feel like were left out of the most important things in his life... denial, betrayal, and dishonesty has his two favorite girls as his two worst enemies.

N: I feel she is right in her feelings but the sad truth is regardless of how you are connected to someone be they a father, boyfriend, friend and etc. You can't force someone to be in your life. You can't make people like or love you. It may hurt but the quicker you can see that fact the sooner you can start your moving on and self healing.

CA: Wow that is Rude! Her father is an asshole and a liar.

C2: What about the fiancée?

CA: Did the fiancée know she had a daughter?

CA: So why didn't this man tell his daughter about his significant other?

CA: is the daughter invited to the wedding?

C2: She refuses to go because of the way she found out

CA: Strong willed!!! I like this young woman

CA: Her father is disrespectful and apathetic to the emotional needs of his daughter

TF: I agree CA; the father has been disrespectful to his daughter. He has also shown both his daughter and fiancée that he's selfish. Basically he showed that both of their feelings didn't matter.

C2: The crazy thing about this situation, Tim doesn't have any other children so why wouldn't he share this special occasion with his one and only beautiful daughter.

PC: Well Kendra should feel upset because her dad lied to her. Outside of that she is old enough to understand that her dad has his own life to live and he is entitled to live it how he sees fit. Kendra is out of place for addressing the fiancée although Kendra is angry with her dad.

C2: Come on now she is 17 an emotional teenager and the child of Tim, that has to be tearing her up inside, she may feel like she was not good enough for her dad to share this occasion with her, I can see if she was 25, her dad is dead ass wrong

PC: Not really they live on two different coast, her dad should have said yes I'm getting married, instead he lied and by denying it his daughter has the right to be upset just because she is an emotional 17 year old doesn't mean she can order the burning of the fields, storming of the castle and beheading of the Queen

C2: And I think that's the initial point of him telling the truth, there is cause and effect to everything, when you are dealing with children problem it typically stems from an adult making a wrong decision.

CA: Sir PC you apparently have some respect issues going on here, regarding women and children. Your lack of empathy is quite repulsive.

Issue: Kendra found out through Facebook that her father Timothy was getting married after she asked him and he denied being in a relationship? She also felt her father's fiancée was stupid because how could she let this go on.

Perspective: Fiancée and daughter should both feel left out on this very important day. You can't force someone to be in your life and do what they are supposed to do. Father is disrespectful and apathetic to the feelings of his daughter. Kendra is okay to be upset but she has to understand that her father can live his life how he wants. Father should have treated his daughter with some value considering she is his only child.

Knowledge: Needless to say how Kendra was treated she decided not to attend the wedding because she did not feel like she was wanted.

Action: Kendra's reaction was age appropriate and I think her dad went about this whole thing completely wrong and I am not sure why he could not be honest.

Consequences: Kendra will have resentment toward her dad and will definitely lack respect for her stepmom because she did not have the decency to promote for the presence of Kendra being at the wedding. Am I wrong for thinking that Kendra should have been in the wedding?

CHAPTER 3

Child Drama

Scenario 17 Fancy Pants

NADINE ALWAYS KNEW something was wrong with her eighteen-year-old son Tristan and that was never more apparent when her fiancé Walter, the father of her youngest son Andre, came home early from work to find Tristan parading around in some fire-engine red stilettos with a Chrissy Snow blond wig on. This sight floored Walter initially, but then he instantly became filled with rage and disappointment when speaking with Nadine. She was just as upset and confused. Tristan was relieved that the cat was out of the bag and this was the stamp of approval to be free and express himself. Something he has been hiding the last two years. There were several problems wrong with Tristan's behavior, Walter was very ole skool and totally despised Tristan, also Andre begin emulating Tristan, which was the biggest issue because no way would Walter allow Andre to go down his path. Tristan's flamboyant behavior has caused a strain on Nadine and Walter's relationship. Walter feels to protect his son is in the best interest that him and Andre get their own place. How can Nadine continue to raise Tristan but maintain a healthy relationship with Walter and Andre?

LN: Nadine has to Love her son no matter what, especially during this time, so she should talk to Tristan about getting his own place, and until he does, his flaming behavior must be displayed outside of their home and away from his younger brother. Andre needs to discuss with his son, the behavior his brother is displaying is not appropriate for a young man, and it may be time to discuss sexually, since it's been displayed to him. Andre can only protect him so much

JLO: Sounds like Walter is nothing more than an "ole skool" homophobic! He and Nadine should sit down with Tristan and ask him to keep his dress up time more private as it's something his little brother doesn't need to see to warrant explanation at a young age. Walter shouldn't be as ignorant as to worry that Andre will "catch" anything . . . . sexuality is something predisposed at birth . . . . not learned.

C2: it predisposed at birth or is it a fad?

JLO: You may consider it a fad if he's leaving the house dressed like this . . . . .?

LN: Dressing like a Drag Queen is not predisposed behavior, it's a choice.

JLO: Right . . . but the reason he's dressing like a drag queen was from predisposed behavior.

C2: I do not understand where at birth it will determine that a boy will be rocking heels

HL: Nadine's job of raising her son is complete. Now, from this day forward, she needs to be supportive of him in whatever he does. She may be best without a person (Walter) in her life if he isn't going to be supportive of both of them. Her son is her son and that will never change. Walter's concern about his son emulating what he has seen should be all the more reason for him to teach his son now as opposed to waiting until an "appropriate" age. If parents refused to educate their children first, something or someone else will. I'm seeing some of the respondent may need to research the Gay Gene Theory.

LN: Dressing like a Woman is one thing, but Blonde wigs and Red heels, What tha?

SBC: I am familiar with the assertion that people are predisposed to be gay or heterosexual; however, I feel as though that really has nothing to do with the topic at hand. Regardless of whether Tristan was predisposed or not, his behavior is having an impact on his younger brother and, in my opinion, the adults in the situation should speak with Tristan about his behavior around his little brother.

KP: As for his brother . . . . Education is the key . . . Kids are more accepting then adults . . . they only know what they are taught

SBC: No, I don't think it's quite that simple. It's a delicate situation because there are many different dynamics at work. Tristan is gay and there is no changing that and most certainly you do not want to make him feel as though you no longer love and accept him; however, as a parent, you must balance your love and compassion for Tristan with love and compassion for the younger child while attempting to raise him in the way that is mutually agreeable to the two parents. Child rearing, as I'm sure you're aware of, is one of the hardest tasks a person will ever take on. I myself have a son who I believe may be gay and while this is a whole new world for me, I am attempting to deal with it in the most effective way possible because I never want him to doubt my love; however, I personally would not be gay because it goes against my religious beliefs. That being said, the task of balancing my religious views without pushing my son away has been a daunting task. But all that in mind, he is my son and for all I care he could be a murderer and while I would hate his actions I would still love him.

HL: Information is key to any situation a person may find themselves in IMO. Tristan may not be gay, but in need of gender transformation. That might explain the cross dressing. That is one of many signs. Coupled with the fact that he was hiding it for 2 years, also is a reason to look into while he is young enough. The younger child is a separate issue for this reason only. It has been shown that children don't not have formed sexual beliefs as do adults. That child, if instructed properly, will be more accepting of Tristan than most adults.

AM: Tristan is grown. He is even relieved that the cat is out the bag. It is important to discuss appropriate behavior in the house and when around Andre. As for Walter, you can't force a man to stay if he doesn't want to. All she can do is propose that they stick together and try to stay strong as a family. This is Tristan's lifestyle choice; it doesn't make him any less family. If he decided to go to the army instead of college even if was against his family's wishes, it's still his decision and he is still family. Walter should not have married Nadine if he wasn't willing to consider her other son as family and treat him as such. Gay people need love, family, support, *and* guidance as much as anyone else.

C2: its okay to live your life by the choices you make, but understand the rules and norms in the household follow them and respect them or you can be jeopardizing your stay and it doesn't matter who you are in my eyes.

TM: I have peopled whom I love in my life that is gay. I love them very much, and they know not to expect me to march in a parade or engage me in any conversation about their lifestyle. Why should I feel bad or ridiculed for it? For those who have a faith, know that any sin whether you are an adulterer, thief, murderer, homosexual goes against the will of God. Hence the statement "Love the sinner, hate the sin." Will one day society be accepting of murder? But I know some will say being homosexual does not hurt anyone, indirectly it does because children are impressionable at a young age. You now have the young man in David story emulating the behavior of the older brother. Walter's concern is totally understandable. We also need to question ourselves about what is normal and abnormal behavior. We are living in an "anything goes" society. This is why moral values and the consideration for others are quickly being depleted. The young man in David story is 18. Has he even considered how his flamboyant behavior may affect his younger brother? Or the way how it would affect his parents?

HL: Education trumps ignorance. If they haven't indeed informed him that if actions jeopardized his living at home, then they should do so. The best way to stop a runaway freight train is to not let it start.

DP: I am late on this. I may have missed some comments. However, here is my two cents "Gay Gene Theory" and all of that. I am very familiar but I will say as a woman it is very offensive to me to see men emulate me as a woman because they feel they were "born that way" or predisposed to the behavior. Let me disclose that I am not a mother but I would probably have a harder time then my husband accepting my son in that manner. So in tho scenario I would have to side with Walter. Now there are a few other observations I would like to point out. Nadine has two sons but two different men and I am going to make the assumption (David left it out) that she did not marry Tristan's dad and is not married to Walter. So neither Walter nor Nadine has set an example for Tristan or his brother on a strong family unit. Walter is shacking up with Nadine. Social factors are contribute to the "this behavior" that Tristan is displaying, he did not just wake up and put on high heels and a wig. So there are so many other issues to point. Walter is now walking out and turning away from Tristan so quickly was there ever a bond between them . . . . ok I think I am done now.

TS: We are missing some information here . . . and therefore it is hard to comment. People are definitely ignorant of what it means to be either transgendered or gay . . . which are actually different things. But regardless, the little one won't "catch" either . . . There are worse things than a boy wearing heels . . . people should be more worried abt their young boys being exposed to video games and media that display excessive violence, drugs and explicit sex . . . of any type or variety

HL: TM: Is that why so many young boys end up being teen fathers and not helping the mothers in taking care of their children?

TM: The way how "societal laws are set up it makes people believe the abnormal to be normal. As a person of faith, there are many things we do on a daily basis that is wrong, and go against the will of God. No one is perfect. But at the same token I know that adultery, homosexuality, murderer, thief, etc is a sin. As stated in the Holy Bible. And yet all are still loved. As I stated above I have love ones who live that lifestyle, do I love them any less before I found out? No. We have wonderful times together, but they know neither to engage me with conversation about their lifestyle nor to look to me for support. No I do not believe in the "Gay gene theory". I believe in choice making as well as making decisions based upon overwhelming urges, and feelings people allow to consume them, even myself. It doesn't make it right and I am aware of it and I choose to change it because of the ultimate price I have to pay if I continue. "Everything is permissible, but not beneficial.

Issue: Walter got off a work early to walk in the house to see his stepson Tristan dressed up in a blond wig with red stilettos. Walter was infuriated to see Tristan parading around the house in this matter. While Walter was concerned for his five-year-old son, Tristan was relieved that his sexuality was out in the opening. Nadine was totally confused on what to do.

Perspective: Nadine has to love her son regardless, but he needs to know that this behavior can't be displayed in the household. Walter sounds like a homophobic and he needs to sit with Tristan along with Nadine to let him know he can't display this behavior in front of Andre. Nadine may be better off without Walter if he can't support her during this challenging time; if he wants to leave, let him go; her son will be her son and that will never change. Nadine needs to have a balance on the way she shows love and compassion for Tristan as well as her younger son Andre. The religious perspective of homosexuality being a sin, not that individuals should be loved less, but you can't force your lifestyle on people who disagree with it.

Knowledge: Walter and Nadine had issues throughout their relationship; Tristan coming out party was the tip of the iceberg and because Walter's ole-skool nature, this behavior would never be acceptable in his eyes, so any other perspective is beating a dead horse.

Action: If I were in Walter's place, I would probably respond like, "It's one thing to being gay, but all the flamboyant activity is unacceptable and would never be tolerated by a real man."

Consequences: There are many factors to consider in this scenario, many feelings needs to be taken in consideration: Tristan, Andre, Nadine, and Walter. Typically, you lean on the side of the child, but being he is eighteen years old, he may need to take his circus act elsewhere; it comes down to decision and choices, and unfortunately, not everyone can end up happy. Fancy Pants need to tickle his fancy elsewhere, meaning it's time to leave the nest.

Scenario 18 Fight or Flight

Darvin was a dedicated dad and always stuck to his commitment of getting his four-year-old daughter Alisa. At times, Darvin and Alisa's mother, Camille, had a rocky relationship because of mistakes they both made in the past, but never was he prepared for what Camille has in store for him. It was Darvin's weekend to pick up Alisa. When he went by Camille's house, the place looked vacant, so off to Alisa's grandmother's house; and when she answered the door, she seemed to be cold with her statement "they're not here" and shut the door. Darvin was confused; it's not like Camille to not to contact him regarding Alisa. Darvin left several messages on Camille's phone but no answer. A week went by but he still has not heard from Camille or Alisa. Darvin was a wreck at work and spent his spare time crying at home. Darvin's mother and his sister called Alisa's grandmother and asked her "what the hell is going on." Darvin has been too good to the baby for him to be treated like this; finally Alisa's grandmother admits that Camille and Alisa have left the state and relocated to St. Louis. When Darvin's mother called to tell him the deal, Darvin burst out in tears; he was devastated, he just felt like dying. What will he do without his daughter, and what could possibly be the justification for Camille to leave.

TS: The obvious answer is to get the courts involved. If they have joint custody didn't the mom technically kidnap her?

LN: Camille is very selfish, her daughter and Darvin must be considered when decision-making on matters like relocating, Its obvious by Camille's behavior, he should go legal asap, get custody order or enforce current one. Be cordial; maintain his composure, no flying off the handle on Camille, his constant role in his daughter's life, should work in his favor.

C2: Some men do not like to leave their fate in the hands of the wicked court system, but you are correct that is kidnapping.

DM: Devils advocate: If they were NOT married nor did he pay child support then technically it is not kidnapping as he does not have any parental rights!! Sadly, this is what happens when people do not communicate . . . I need more facts as there are two sides to every story. Just because he was picking his child up and spending some money on her does not necessarily mean he was a good DAD!! How do we know that she did not take her daughter away from a bunch of drama that she just could not take anymore and wanted better for her and her child . . . Drama from her family or her baby daddy and his family!!

C2: Well Darvin paid support did that, check, he was the most stable person in his daughters life check, just maybe Camille was running because the reality could have been she didn't make the cut to be with Darvin and could not handle it

DM: I hear what you are saying David but, this still sounds to one sided for me!! Everything that glitters is not gold; you previously stated that they both made mistakes in the past. I learned the hard way as I had totally believed EVERYTHING a person told me and was a number one fan however; as time went along I begin to see there was another side that should have been heard before I jump on the ban wagon!!

C2: Its one sided because that is what you perceive it to be, they both made mistakes because Darvin strayed away at times in their relationship and she could never maintain any of her personal goals as far as school and work.

DM: Before I reply with what I want to say by strayed away do you meant cheat??

C2: He had other relationships but does that have anything to do with breaking the bond between father and daughter.

KP: Where does Alisa's well being come into play . . . Screw the parents and what dirt has been done to each other . . . She has formed a bond with both of her parents . . . It's not about them anymore . . . That stopped when they had a child . . . They both need to stop being selfish and put their shit aside and work together for their child . . . . ..if Camille is not going to be an adult and talk to Darvin and work something out. Then Darvin needs to go through the proper procedures with the court system . . . He can not handle it in his own . . . It may just hurt him more then help.

EG: David in response to the man up commit made in my earlier post and your response, the decision should have been made after marriage, home, savings stability of some sort, a plan for life. In your field of employment you tell your students all the time you have to have a plan. Life is the same.

KP: EG . . . Where is Camille's responsibility in this? In this day and age . . . Love then marriage then baby carriage is just a nursery rhyme

DM: Yes, it does . . . I am a product of that and it does affect the child! He was a cheater and she had personal issues within . . . Sounds like they did not communicate well at all. What did he cheat because he felt neglected because she was trying to deal with her personal life goals (maybe wanting a better life for the three of them)? Sorry everyone has issues that they must deal with within them; NEVER DOES STRAYING AWAY BECOME ACCEPTABLE!! I would have a hard time dealing with a Man that Cheated on me . . . REALLY he not only cheated on the women but, on his DAUGTHER as well . . . He just might be a womanizer and NO WAY would I want him to be having my daughter. Selfish people like this do things and don't realize what there kids may see and hear . . . This is one of the problems with people today . . . They grow up around parents who cheated on each other, demeaned each other, did not Love one another, did not communicate with one another and so on . . . These kids grow up with these same issues and then they wonder what is wrong with there kids . . . I would take my daughter away as well if he is a womanizer as I would not want my daughter to grow up thinking that it is ok for a man to do . . . .

C2: So removing the daughter out of his life is the correct thing to do because it did not work out between Camille and Darvin that sound asinine.

DM: David it is a MUCH BIGGER picture then it just did not work out between the two of them; he cheated on Camille; unless you have been in that kind of situation you can NEVER understand how it affects a Child . . . Sometimes the best thing a Parent can do is to realize that as much as they love their child they need to get some help to fix themselves and then re enter into that child's life. Parents need to stop being so selfish and realize that everything that goes on in your life, is going to have some type of positive or negative effect on their kids. Who is to say that when he gets his daughter he may not be having her in Michelle's face this week, Tina's face next week and on the phone with Kim right after Tina walked away? You are speaking from your heart and as a dad; I do not think that you are looking at the whole picture . . . REALLY, would you not say that people have issues within as a result of the environment in which they grew up in. If he is a womanizer, his daughter will grow up either letting men cheat on her or she being a cheater (meaning cheating on her man or with someone else's man). Hummm sound strange that she would run off and not tell him anything another man or not; just sounds like there is still more to this story . . .

C2: In this day and age with the state of absent dads in their childrens lives there are not too many reasons I can think that would constitute Camille's actions and we can take this statement to the bank.

DM: I hear what your saying however, I still beg to differ; as I believe an absent dad is much better than a present Dad who cheats, lies or steals from the mother or who may physically/mentally abuse her as that is no good for a child. Let me just say this though, I believe that if a man is made to pay child support . . . the courts should take the first few checks to pay for a law guardian who would come out to spend time with both parents with the child and use that to decide who REALLY is the better parent to have the child reside with them . . . as there are some women out here that look for good men with good jobs to Get A Good Support Check . . . . To some women it was never even about having a family. As far as the grandmother goes...a mother is going to always protect her child . . . she more than likely didn't want her daughter to get back with Darvin after he cheated on her daughter . . . . and happy that she finally left him for good!!!

C2: I don't think you have the best interest of the child, the issue in hand is did Camille have the right to leave town without informing

Darvin? If so since she left does that mean all of his financial duties have been relieved because who wants to spend money on something that is not tangible.

CA: Ok, this scenario infuriates me!!! How fucking selfish. I would NEVER, I repeat NEVER do that to my son's Dad or my son for that matter. Get a damn good attorney. Shit, I think I'll go to law school just to represent people like this! WHAT the FUCK is wrong with people! I feel like slapping the shit out of someone right now!!!!!!!!! GRRRRRRRRR!!!!!!!!!

HL: No justification and he should contact the local authorities as well as those in St. Louis to report the kidnapping DM: I'm going to say something and I HOPE TO HELL IT RESINATES WITH thick skulled women . . . . . . a child is not to be referred to as 'MY CHILD', it should be OUR CHILD!! That shit irks me!!! His infidelity has NOTHING TO DO with his ability to be a father. That mess is something that scorned women use as a crutch to get a pass for acting in a selfish manner and are rarely called on it

NG: What Camille did was messed up, their relationship was rocky, and they both messed up. Now it's up to Darvin to go to court and have the judge make her move back. And Camille's mother has no business being upset with Darvin because her daughter was no angel either, and anyway this isn't about Camille and Darvin's relationship this is about a man who has and always was a father to his child and now he is being denied that.

KP: There are always 3 sides to a story hers, his, and the truth . . . .these so called adults need to put their energy and focus on this child. No matter what happened between them she will start having resentment toward her parents for not considering her as their priority and putting themselves above her well being . . .

DM: Yes, KP you are correct and being a child that was in that kind of situation; I have to say that I LOVE MY MOTHER DEARLY but, for years I resented her for NOT leaving him and letting us Grow up in that Dysfunctional Situation. CA: I don't condone lying or cheating, but if we are going to hold past deeds against others, then virtually no one will ever have solstice from any transgression they have ever made.

HL: It is as an I've heard from a woman . . . 'A man should only be punished ONCE for his wrong deeds'. After that, it comes out as bitter behavior no matter how it's looked at because I don't believe any reasonable, rationale person who deprives a child of a parent. When Camille took their child and fled, she not only negated his ability to be a father, she only potentially began to build a foundation for her daughter to misbehave and act out because of the intentional rift that has been caused by the lack of a male presence in their lives. More often then not, the man receives the lion's share of the blame for what he did to cause a situation and what he didn't do to fight for his right to be a father. How easy for women to have the ability to fall back and their inability to deal with their emotions. Men are taught daily that we have to learn to control our emotions and not respond with the physicality that we could and use better judgment. The greatest double standard I've EVER heard of. If that were a man taking their child and running off, I'm sure there would be few women who would stand for that! Most would ask who do he think he is and so and so. Call the police . . . I can hear it now!! I mean how silly is the notion of a person having to fight for their right to be a parent! Yet and still, we see how the courts favor women and consider them to be the 'better' parent for a child and is given custody and in some cases, sole custody. When it happens that a man is given that same custody, all hell breaks lose and the end of it is never heard. And just for ANYONE who believes I speak from the perspective of a scorned man, I DO NOT!! I have no children, but I see the damage everyday!! Senseless people need to be stopped no matter their gender. It all has destructive repercussions that are unseen and never fully understood until it is too late!

DP: Just catching up . . . Bottom line - Shame on Darvin and Camille for not having a formal custody arrangement in place. Unless you are married then there should be a formal agreement, even it is just a sworn affidavit with a witness. We always want to look at the courts as adversarial however; it is in these situations that they prevent the shenanigans. Moving out of state without involving the other parent is irresponsible. The damage that will be down to the children can be unimaginable. I see comments referencing the relationship between the parents ending bitter but the bottom line is the children loves both of her parents and being separating suddenly for one of them can be devastating.

Issue: Darvin went to pick up his daughter for his usual weekend visit but when he arrived there no one was there, and in fact, the house looked vacant. So Darvin went by his daughter's grandparent's house and ask was she there and she said no and shut the door. After that, Darvin felt something was wrong and he was right; finally Alisa's grandmother confirmed they have moved out of town.

Perspective: Camille is selfish and never considered her daughter or Darvin in this decision to relocate. Just because he was picking up his child up and spending some money on his daughter does not mean he was a good dad. Marriage would have provided stability in this relationship, stop having children out of wedlock. There is no justification to run off with a child and removing the father out of their lives, totally unacceptable.

Knowledge: Their relationship was doomed with their child before it begin, Camille had a poor work ethic, never could accomplish or complete goals. She was a runner when things got tough, she runs instead of trying to solve problems. She makes irrational thoughts without thinking things through and then suffers the consequences down the road.

Action: Personally I would have tried to work the issue out instead of putting it in the hands of a random eighty-five-year-old judge, who knows shit about either individuals past. My heart aches for Darvin because all too many times women use children as a leverage of power.

Consequences: The child may pick up some of Camille's behavior due to her lack of stability, or may have resentment toward her mother because she removed her from a stable figure in her life (Dad). Also I am sure Darvin may have some ill-effects with trust and also may become emotionally detached from any future children.

Scenario 19 Free Willie

Your twelve-year-old son is one of the top seventh grade basketball players in the city; Coach Willie has taking him under his wings as a positive role model. You found out that coach has been arrested and served time for drug possession on numerous occasions. Do you continue to allow your son to continue this relationship with Coach Willie?

C2: I don't know if he is doing it or not I guess it's the chance you have to take.

C2: Personally I need that info listed on the application when you sigh up to be a coach

JP: Where I grew up if I stayed away from everyone who had a sketchy past, I would have stayed in a bubble.

KJP: How is he able to be a coach with numerous convictions?

C2: It happens everyday in our little league and recreation basketball leagues

KJP: Multiple convictions is problematic for me . . . yea everyone deserves another chance to get right . . . .but my baby could have been the one he sold to . . . so kick rocks and no I'm not trusting a multi offender . . . bye!

C2: In my opinion the best coaches come from structured disciplines such as educators and military background for example, although the prison system is structured doesn't constitute Willie to be a Coach just my opinion

EG: No because I need the coach to be a better example for my child. I abhor the assembly of evildoers and refuse to sit with the wicked. I am teaching my family values and morals; the last thing I want to introduce to my family is chaos. This conversation would take place with the coach and I. Dialog is so important!

MJ: No I would not. That's not setting good standards for this young man.

C2: I would like to see all Rec coaches have criminal record background checks, our kids are to precious to be put in the hands of fake playground legends and wannabee coaches

K: Absolutely not . . . My son would eventually learn of these dealings and mimic his coach's actions as he grows into a young man . . . Coach may also be grooming him into his shady ways . . . . Take no chances!!

TA: Based solely on my gut feeling, no I wouldn't. However, our society is full of some judgmental folks that fail to realize that not everyone that has a record is the same person they were when they committed the crime or maybe wasn't even guilty of the crime in the first place. Going off what things look like vs. what they are is the root of most assumptions and you know what they say about assumptions. Please focus on the truth and then make decisions based on that information. Also, please note that most of the time the people who you think are shady (because of what you heard) are the ones that will be the most honest with you. It's the people that come across as squeaky clean that scare the hell out of me . . . lol!

EG: TA, Amen but like you said solely on my gut feelings, no. I feel we can't have it both ways, you are standing for a principle in your life and I don't think your being judgmental, you are using the discerning power granted you by your Father in Heaven. We are all born into sin but must not remain there but elevate our lives so we might be used as vessels in the earth.

TA: EG, the reason I said solely my gut is because I wanted to answer David's question. My gut or as I call it "women's intuition" has never been wrong. So when I say "my" gut, I literally mean "mine". I can't speak to others. There is no rule that you can't have it both ways. Again, I can't speak for other people but for me, I don't always have a gut feeling about everything. Therefore, IF I get a gut feeling I go with it. However, in general I don't judge anyone without cause. Even in this particular scenario, I'm not judging Willie. He has the right to do what he wants where he wants. I am just making a parental decision to not have my child be potentially at risk. That is what a parent's job is. I have that right. Its not being judgmental it is making a decision as a parent as to what I feel is best for my child.

EG: Once again TA, you are operating out a biblical principal, your gut is the Holy Spirit and it is never wrong and we are not to judge unless we be judged but decrement is very important part of our lives . . .

TA: EG you are confusing me. What are you talking about? I was providing a view point based on the scenario and my experiences. Just for the record, biblical principles should be something that is understood. Where I come from what is understood shouldn't have to be explained. I am a child of God and know who my Father is. Anything I say should be considered to be from biblical principle because it always comes from a place of love and/or forgiveness.

EG: Amen TA sorry for the confusion expression comes in many forms

Issue: Seventh grader who happens to be one of the best basketball players in the city and you find out that he is being coached by Willie who happens to have a sketchy past. Should you end the relationship between your son and Willie?

Perspectives: Required background check on all rec league coaches, no one with felony charges should be coaching children. If we stayed away from everyone with sketchy past, we all live in a bubble. Need the coach to be a better example for my child. I don't want to pass judgment because people do make mistakes but I would go with my gut feelings and that has never failed me wrong. Multiple convictions would be a problem so I would say bye-bye Willie.

Knowledge: Every day, throughout the country, we have adults in coaching positions that should not be; many of these men were legitimate players either in high school or in college. If they did not make it, some chose the fast life in the streets but always had passion for sports; but coaching youth, I question if you decide to do the fast life.

Action: I would not have a problem with Willie showing my son a couple of moves, but as far as coaching, I rather have a high-character guy in that position. Like the great saying goes, "Character is doing the right thing when nobody is watching." Willie has some areas he needs to clean up.

Consequences: Young people are very impressionable and if that young man looks up to Willie, he may put him on a pedestal like God, and like someone else said, he may start to emulate his behavior; although you may need to break the bond, but you have to think of a coach as a teacher and there is no way in hell a teacher would be allowed to stay in their position if they had a part-time position slanging dope.

Scenario 20 Hidden Pain

Your twenty-one-year-old son has been getting into several physical altercation of late and seems to be on the edge and very angry. You sit down and talk with him and he shares he has been hiding a secret from the family for many years; he burst out in tears and tells you he had been molested on several times from a family friend, Raymond aka Ray Ray. How do you react to this and what are you going to do with this info?

CA: Ray Ray's getting castrated today and Mama's going to jail. Don't fuck with MY babies, you will suffer.

C2: What if your son tells you to let it be because he doesn't want you to get any trouble

CA: I call the police to report this crime . . . hopefully . . . unless Mama Bear instinct takes over . . . then shit's about to get real.

C2: Is there any point where you speak to Raymond?

CA: For what purpose?

C2: Some people may want to confront him considering he was a friend of the family

CA: I would confront him, but not with any words

GG: I'm pissed just reading this. My son's father and I will be addressing some things

TF: I would get help (counseling) for my son. I would confront Ray Ray . . . I might kill Ray Ray

C2: So you address and Ray says I don't know what the hell you are talking about I like women not little boys

TF: My son would be with me . . . because Ray Ray is going to face my son. Then I would drive my son home . . . and go back and possibly kill Ray Ray's nasty lying a$$

C2: I know this could be a very touchy scenario, but as parents sometimes you might notice some anger in your sons and we just can't say he is just being a boy because sometimes young people have difficulties expressing their anger and it could manifest and come out in different ways.

TF: It is a very touchy situation! I would be devastated!! I would always wonder if I missed something. It's easy for me to say what I would do because I'm not faced with it. I would definitely get counseling for my son

CA: I agree with u TF and Thank God neither of us is facing this tragic scenario.

GG: I feel you TF. My son is 21. I'm fortunate enough that this situation isn't mine. But that "Chester" would face us.

KJP: For me this is worrisome and goes a little deeper than just a beat down . . . I'm reading the words repeatedly and smdh . . . cause us as parents need to start parenting. I know that we will never know everything that is going on in our children's lives but we should know when something like this is happening before it gets to a crazy number. I have been a stay at home mother for 8 yrs now and it is because of how I was raised . . . I wasn't raises in a daycare so I wasn't putting mine there. We are a busy society that isn't involves enough or paying enough attention to our children and many of us should have never made or had babies, so I'm placing blame on the parent for lack of involvement and I me or my husband or both are going to jail for murder!

DP: How old is Ray-Ray? If Ray-Ray and my son are the same age this could be a much deeper problem on more epic level. It didn't start with Ray-Ray. Again, parents need to parent there children. Parents need to have open conversations with their children about inappropriate touching and behavior even with family and friends. So many times we shame it and children are afraid to speak what is happening to them or their friends

C2: The son may not have shared it with anyone because he was questioning his manhood because someone was trying to take his The sad thing I have worked with boys that were molested and they went on to become sexual perpetrators themselves

DP: David - like you I worked in the field of child crimes for 15 years. I did death investigations, sexual abuse and physical abuse. I have interviewed parents of victims and perpetrators and no two stories are the same but the on common theme. Parents have got to pay MORE ATTENTION to their children. Even reading the responses of your daily questions sometimes, I hold back because until you are challenged you have no idea how you will react. Only thing that is true is whomever and where ever your faith lies is who gets called on the most.

TA: Raymond would cease to exist (it's always good to have friends in low places). My son would not ever have to be in a situation again feeling inferior to Raymond or anyone else. My job as the parent is to make sure my kids are safe and can come to me no matter what. This would be communicated to him and I would put him in therapy for as long as he needed it.

C2: Real talk real live situations that we can't be afraid to have these courageous conversations, now I am big time sports fan, but I get more satisfaction everyday discussing these scenarios because they are definitely not a game.

GG: It's easy to sit back and blame parents about not reading the signs. If you have been trying to communicate and keeping the lines open. Not being in the eye of the storm is a different view than being the person to judge the aftermath. Parents are not only raising these kids but working to support them. It's hard. Lord knows my son took me through. If he doesn't want to go to therapy after 18 we as parents cant make them.

C2: We can't blame parents for the actions of this sick twisted individual, most parents have to work and we can only hope that they are in good hands. But then again the shit is happening at schools by our trusted teachers

CA: I would blame myself if this ever happened to my son . . . that's why I would kill Ray Ray.

C2: You may feel bad as a parent but how in the world can you control every aspect of your child's life

CA: You can't. It's not healthy but we can empower our children with knowledge. Good touch/bad touch . . . boundaries.

DP: The point that should be taken it is never that simple. There is no cookie cutter answer or remedy. Until you hear the story or live the story, you have no idea what you would do. "Kill Ray-Ray" is the easy answer. You have to remember you still have to be a parent to your child when the storm passes over. David, this was a good one. Brings back some memories of scenarios and I know why I had to let it go . . .

CA: I AM SO PARANOID ABOUT THIS happening. I don't care if people think I'm totally insane. I always err on the side of caution no matter what . . .

Issue: Twenty-one-year-old son finally comes clean and tells his mother the reason he has been angry because he has been fighting the demons of the past of being molested by a friend of the family.

Perspective: Mama is going to jail because she is going to kill Ray Ray, don't fuck with my babies. Ray Ray will be confronted with my son being present, but after I drop my son off, I may feel the need to kill Ray Ray. I would get counseling for my son but I would feel bad because I would be thinking did I miss something. We need to do a better job parenting our children and speak to them; issues like this could be prevented with more parenting. Raymond would not exist; my job as a parent is to keep my children safe. It's easy to blame parents, but we also have the responsibility to work to support our children as well, you can't be in two places at one time.

Knowledge: This young man was able to survive this misfortunate situation but many young men are not able to weather the storm. I think the key issue for this young man was staying active and busy to block and suppressed this painful experience.

Action: The most popular decision would be to go look for Raymond and take his life, but in all reality ten to twelve years have went by, you can only be thankful that nothing more happen and your son was able to maintain for the most part. If only this could have been found out earlier because it's a shame Raymond is walking as a free man.

Consequences: Many things can come out of this scenario, the obvious is this young man will always have some mental scars behind these actions, also in some cases the victims can go and become sexual perpetrators themselves and finally someone could end up in prison for taking Raymond's life.

Scenario 21 Ice Cream Social

John has a child, Jane, from a previous long-term relationship. John has joint custody and gets Jane three days every week. Jane has always ask that her wish would come true of her parents taking her out on an outing together for dinner and then for some ice cream. Sounds like a simple request to make Jane happy, right? Not quite, John expresses to Jane's mom, Paula, that this will cause problems in his marriage; and right now with stress on his job and other issues going on, he can't afford to have that happen. How should this be explained to Jane?

CA: There should have been a conversation about this prior to John's marriage. Blended families are just that . . . .blended. Also a conversation should be had with Jane as well about expectations of dinner with her parents but it could something innocent and simple. Bottom line it is a request the should be fulfilled.

C2: What if Jane's mother put her up to this request and her John can't stand to be in a room with each other?

CHB: John should sit his daughter down and explain to her this won't happen and he can still spend time with her and doesn't love her any less. If he does this all this is going to do is give her false hope that they may eventually be a family again

KP: Shame on John for putting his marital issues and the stress of his job a head if his child . . . Jane should be and always be his priority . . . . He needs to do whatever it takes to show Jane his unconditional love and if going with her mother and having ice cream is it then there should be no hesitation . . . .

CA: I completely agree with you, KP

AE: I can see where tension may arise with couples if the mother and father are going to dinner with their daughter and it has to be alone. I think it's more appropriate if the spouses are invited out of respect. Whether they choose to go or not is their decision.

C2: AE said make it a family reunion if you going to do it then do it up big (smiling)

CA: I disagree, AE. You are obviously not empathetic to the child in this scenario.

CA: Oh yeah, Madea's Family Reunion! LoL;

CHB: CA all parties need to be recognized in this situation. You can't always do things the way children want without looking at the big picture. It could cause more trouble than a little bit.

CA: Well, when only one party's needs are consistently met and the child's needs neglected, then that's a problem. Yeah, and the controlling, self centered, wifey needs to get a grip! And grow up

DM: So True!! Children want what they want however; we have to make choices that are best for the situation. So are you saying that if a Child does not like his/her parent new husband/wife and want them to leave them; The parent should do it because they should always put there child first.

CA: No.

CHB: We don't know if she is controlling or self centered. Maybe the child's mother is. Like I said I wouldn't spend time with my ex out of respect for my husband and he is not controlling

AE: Well that's why they need to have a family discussion with their child and try to explain why things are the way they are. Some things are going to be different and that their new step mom and dad care about them very much. It's hard to adjust but that's why they need to be supportive and talk to their child.

NNM: Everything cannot be the child's way . . . they do not all have to agree to this for the sake of the child and it may be setting the child up for false hope. I agree with CHB and AE. I would say both whole families get together or don't do it at all, not just the two parents separately.

DM: Yes, CHB I was about to say the exact same thing. Unless it is some kind of special event the ex's do not need to be around. I have been in situation where the ex was around and said some very inappropriate things to me, about her ex that I was with. I was like WOW, REALLY are you kidding me . . . but, I was then looked at as being the bad one! Funny because they did call me Controlling for not wanting her around.

C2: So is it safe to safe that most of you are saying if you moved on than keep on moving

CHB: Yes

CA: It's all about a healthy balance, and there you have it . . . exactly why the World is all fucked up.

C2: CA what are you making reference to?

CA: Your comment about most people moving on . . . . Moving on and Meeting the needs of the child can both be accomplished? It doesn't have to be either/or . . .

C2: Well not every situations permits the joining of hands of all parties

CA: That's a problem.

C2: Problem that unfortunately is bigger than our forum, but yes that problem has been around forever

HL: Tough situation. Not really sure. Many factors go into this. Jane's age would be the sticking point. His job and how bad is his current marriage.

C2: Maybe the problem that is really wrong with the world is children have too much damn say on what goes on, back in the days the phrase was stay out of grown folks business, let's campaign to bring that phrase back. We can shift the Balance of Power back to the adults.

CA: Wrong! Children's voices are rarely heard without adult advocacy! I cannot believe that you, "Counselor Extraordinaire", would even say such a thing! Not all adults are worthy of that Power!

HL: LOL . . . ..CA, maybe they should consider using preventative measures then.

C2: Children are certainly not worthy of it considering their brains are not developed until they are 25 so their executive decision making skills are irrational as a child so that will be the reason adults need to make decisions

DM: I'll say this; children should be considered in SOME situations, but this isn't one of them. I was in a situation that concerned my living situation and it worked out well.

CA: Not all adults are capable of rational thinking…in fact; some children are better decision makers than some adults!

C2: I agree most kid problems come from adults making poor decisions

COJ: I'm afraid the winner is john's current wife. If it's going to cause problems in his current marriage then it's a no no.

CA: Well it wouldn't cause problems in my relationship! So obviously, wifey and Johnny have some issues. So now Jane suffers . . . thanks for playing. Jane's emotional well being is not a fucking game!!!!!!!

C2: I guess no matter how we slice the pie, in the game of life not everyone is going to come out as winner.

CHB: Well damn CA I felt that through the phone. Yea I definitely would keep it the way it's has been.

CA: LoL!!!!! Just making my point, woops! *point . . . and winning over here. LoL I know how to advocate and negotiate. If Johnny can't afford ice cream with his child, he's a fucking loser! Thank you. I have spoken.

C2: I don't think the issue is that he can't afford ice cream with his daughter he doesn't want to ride down that slippery slope with with his wife.

CA: Well, his lame excuse is unacceptable. Time to put on your big boy pants Johnny!!!!!

C2: Arguing at home is for the unemployed they don't have shit else to do

CA: LoL!!!! No arguing . . . just a nice little family outing for the precious cargo. Try Coffee Bean next time . . . prevents arguments! lol ;)

C2: No one wants to be arguing at home over a double scoop of Vanilla Bean Ice cream

Issue: Jane wants her father and mother to take her out on an outing for dinner and ice cream, but Dad (John) will not be able to honor this request because it will cause problems at home with his wife and at this time he does not need that added stress to go along with his daily stress from his job.

Perspective: A conversation should have been held before John got married with Jane about expectations; but despite it all, John should honor the request. John needs to show his daughter unconditional love and put his marriage and job issues to the side. John needs to explain to his daughter why this can't happen because he doesn't want to give her any false hope of him getting back with her mother. This situation could cause unnecessary stress; if you are going to do it, invite all spouses to attend as well. Children do not always get their way and need to understand they do not have a say in all situations.

Knowledge: Prior to John getting married, he was always flexible and open to Jane's entire request. Many people would consider her being spoiled; but ever since he has gotten married, everything seems to be a problem. John has done a poor job of balancing his relationships.

Actions: A simple solution for John could have been "Let me take my daughter out along with her mother, what my wife doesn't know will not hurt her, hell I am sure I don't know everything she does." Problem is solved.

Consequences: Jane having resentment with stepmom because ever since she came into her father's life, the dynamics have changed; also if John does decide to sneak off and attend the outing and his wife finds out and certainly some issues will arise and she will question the nature of the outing. Request like this can be granted with open communication and understanding from each party; if not, the ice cream can get real messy before Jane gets this request granted.

Scenario 22 Search and Seizure

After hearing about the Columbia Mall killer, we as parents better start doing room searches, and find out what is going on with these kids, checking journals, diaries, lifting up mattresses, going through drawers, and closets, to see what they are thinking. We are living in a world of hurt and pain; just remember hurt people like to hurt people.

TC: How would you feel if your parents read your diary or went through your personal items? I think children, teens, and adults have same expectations of privacy.

C2: Are you looking at the end result of death, as a child anything and everything is accessible to parents. Last I checked kids don't pay bills and I felt something was odd going on I am going to investigate point blank.

CHB: My mother went through everything I had and I agree with you.

TC: Is it unreasonable to think snooping through a child's personal items, a parent can absolutely determine when or if they are going to kill someone. Snooping to me is an underhanded way of finding out information, parents need to talk, communicate and watch the behavior of their children not invade their privacy.

TC: Why buy your child a diary or a personal journal for their deepest personal thoughts, and then read it. Why not talk to them and give them a little privacy to vent in the diary without a fear. Everyone needs a little piece of total privacy. Snooping creates sneaky character in children (and adults).

C2: I truly think you are missing the whole point of this, there is no such thing as privacy or confidentiality if as parents you think your child is at risk for hurting themselves or others,

TC: I get your point, the point I am making is, as a parent, even if we invaded the privacy of our children, it could be difficult to determine that our child could be in danger to themselves or others. If we snoop, a child hides it better (if we let them think they have privacy) we may find out more) Also, as a parent, we never think our kids could do something like that.

C2: And you certain of this because of what? So that is the exact point on why we need to intervene, so as you can see its happening so throw your theory out the window.

CA: Whenever, I see/hear about a shooting. The first thing I think is, I want to know this kid's story. Where are the Parents?

TC: No parent has an absolute theory, because some situations will have you throw your theory out the window. I don't mean to speak for every parent, I mean me as a parent.

RB: There are always signs of distress, communication and parenting is key. Personally, I'm all about it so as long as you're in my house, my right to ask, look and tell you there is a problem. I've read diaries and mine is often out, I've read text. I ask the embarrassing yet necessary questions. This I had to learn as the years have passed. Safety first, loves unconditionally.

YWB: Nope till your 18 and pay bills everything in my house is my business period, these kids are holding on to some real crap.

C2: Yes indeed but most parents have decided that they want to be friends with their children and try to make them feel as an equal to them.

Issue: In regards to the mall killings, parents need to investigate more and do more room searches to see what they can find out. Our kids are living in a world of pain.

Perspectives: Parents should not snoop around in their children's belongings. Anything in the house parents are privy to, children have no belongings considering they have not bought anything. Just because you go snooping doesn't mean you find out anything. At least investigate and err on the side of caution.

Knowledge: In this day and age, children are living with a lot of pain and hurt that they are hiding. They are not sharing this information with parents and they are taking these matters in their own hands. The problem solving techniques are not always the most appropriate ways to handle matters.

Actions: Parents need to have family discussions and talk about current events, maybe watch the news together, anything that brings the family together to open up dialogue; it's vital for the safety of our children.

Consequences: Without communication and letting parents solve things on their own, we open ourselves to potential harm, either our kids hurting someone or getting hurt. This is not a game and must be taken seriously. You do not want to be on the other end of the phone where someone is saying your kid has been murdered or murdered someone.

Scenario 23 The Creep Show

Vincent and Arthur have been best friends since kindergarten and always had each other's back no matter what. They both work at the Betty Ford Youth Drug Facility. Well one day, Arthur had the duty of escorting Denise, a sixteen-year-old girl to court. On the way back from court while they were driving, Denise asked if she can have a cigarette because she was stressed out; as she asked, she started rubbing his manhood. Arthur gave in and said on one condition, if she will have sex with him; Denise agreed, and off to Arthur's house they went. On the way back, Arthur told Denise no one can know what happened and she must request for shower as soon as they get back to the facility. When they got back, she requested for a shower and Shift Supervisor Vincent thought that was odd considering shower time was 8:00 p.m. every night. The rest of the evening, Denise was acting fidgety and weird. Vincent called her to the office and ask did anything happen at court and he also noticed she smell like cigarettes this afternoon. He questions her on where she got one from and how did that work. She broke down and said, "Arthur gave me one on the condition, we have sex." This info totally devastated Vincent because he was stuck between a rock and a hard place. What does Vincent need to do from this point forward?

MM: Talk to his friend about what he has done, if that don't work, do the next best thing turn that ass in.

MJ: Turn him in! Regardless if she is, she still is a child and is vulnerable at this time in her life. I'm so disgusted with this!!!

C2: Does Vincent have any obligations or loyalty to his best friend Arthur?

MJ: No his friend is a pedophile

MJa: Vincent should tell his friend you quit or I tell

HL: Vincent needs to do his job, he should have loyalty to his friend, but his job is primary focus. He's in the position he is in so he can protect children from people has man turned into.

DP: Wrong is wrong, Arthur should be accountable for his actions and Vincent is being a friend by doing his job. Arthur was the one not being a good friend by putting himself and his friend in that situation. Turn him in

TA: The last time I checked both contributing to the delinquency of a minor & statutory rape were felonies, so unless Vincent is an idiot he needs to turn Arthur in for two reasons. 1. His freedom. 2. His job, I don't know about anyone else but my loyalty stops at losing my freedom. Vincent's obligation is only to be a friend and when Arthur put both of their jobs and freedom at risk that obligation stopped.

Issue: Vincent was faced with turning in his friend Arthur to the authorities for having sex with a minor while out for a court appointment. Denise asked for a cigarette and came on to Arthur; Arthur took her up on the offer. Now Vincent has a decision to make.

Perspectives: Talk to his friend to see what happened, and if that doesn't work, you have to turn him in. Turn him in; he took advantage of a vulnerable child. Give your friend ultimatum, quit job or you will tell. Job is priority; he is in a position to protect children from harm. Arthur needs to be held accountable for his behavior; he put them both in awkward positions. Vincent needs to turn Arthur in for two reasons: (1) His freedom (2) His job. When a friend compromises that, your friendship is in serious jeopardy.

Knowledge: Arthur has always had a sketchy past; it's very shocking that he passed the screening to work with young people; he has always been someone who made decisions based on instant gratification.

Action: I would speak to Arthur with total disappointment in my heart; I would encourage him to turn himself in to the authorities and I would let him know I am not going down with his freakish ass. I would give him an hour to make up his mind on what he is going to do. So either he does it or I will be doing it, regardless it's going to get done.

Consequences: The first concern would be Denise obviously she would need some therapy and may need to relocate to a different facility; clearly she is still function off addict tendencies, I want what I want when I want it, hence cigarette and sexual aggression plus favors. As far as Arthur goes, I am sure this would throw a major monkey wrench in our friendship; but as you get older, sometimes you have to weed out the individuals who are not living the quality of life. Arthur, really, brother? A child come on FAM, there are a lot of women that are looking for a working man, damn not the creep show with a minor. What part of the game are you playing?

Scenario 24 Triple Whammy

Triple Whammy
Sandy's twenty-one-year-old son Rayshawn's girlfriend Sakina shared that she was pregnant. Sakina was not sure if she wanted to keep the baby and after discussing it with her Dad Freddy, they decided that it was best to abort the child because Rayshawn was not in a position to

take care of her child because he was not working. Sandy took offense to this comment about her son, like most mothers who don't want anyone to bad mouth their boys. Sandy called Sakina and spoke with her heart to heart and stated that she should keep the baby and she would help out as much as she could with caring for her grandchild. The discussion worked; Sakina decided to keep the baby. A couple days later, Sandy's cousin Kisha came over and said did you know that Rayshawn had someone pregnant Sandy said yes I know his girlfriend Sakina is pregnant. Kisha said I'm talking about the girl Lanae, the twenty-one-year-old who already has a child; she is pregnant with twins for a Rayshawn. Sandy responded by saying "Holy s——, now what will Sandy do?" More importantly, Rayshawn is caught out there with three babies on the way; neither Sakina nor Lanae know what is going on. Rayshawn has hit the jackpot—Triple Whammy.

C2: Sandy should have stayed out of it in the first place! sandy needs to talk to her son and tell him to talk to these two ladies and then let them make up their own minds.

DP: Well . . . Well 1) Sandy should have stayed out of it. 2) Why are they having unprotected sex? 3) It is ultimately Sakina's decision and she will need all the support she can get. Her father, his mother and ultimately Rashawn.

TA: Sandy needs to keep her word and help out Sakina. This one is an easy one

C2: What about Lanae? What about the scenario from this morning

TA: What about Lanae? Sandy had the discussion with Sakina and talked her in to not having an abortion. So she has the responsibility of honoring her word. That hasn't changed just because another girl turns up pregnant. That's her son's responsibility.

C2: I got you, good response

HL: The question is, will Sandy? The road is littered with good intentions, but bad results.

TA: Sandy should have been speaking with her son instead of the girlfriend.

MJO: The son needs to step up to the plate and get a job He has 3 children to take care of. That's nice of the grandmother and I hope she also does for the other grandchild.

KP: Sandy has great intentions but she is only the grandmother and will not have to deal with this child as I think Sakina will need. I think Sandy is taking the responsibility off her son shoulders. (A true sign that she has done this for him before, hence 2 girls pregnant. Sakina needs to have a discussion with Rashawn and her father. Her father will be the primary provider for this child and will effect him tremendously so his feelings need to be heard (Not that it's his decision or right to tell her what to do) Sakina needs to find out what's best for her not her so called "boyfriend" mother.

HL: KP: That is what men refer to as coddling sons and it impedes their growth into adulthood particularly being a fully functional responsible adult man. So unfortunately the cycle continues

KP: I agree HL! My ex husbands mother coddled him. It was a big strain on our relationship until I had to give him an ultimatum. I would not marry him until he stood up to his mother and lived his own life. At first she was very upset and talked bad about me to the family but he finally got to see the freedom he so much wanted and the growth he saw in himself. The family knew how she was and was glad to see that he put his mother in check. In the end he was much better for it.

HL: It will David and so many people have played an active role in allowing it to happen. I would comment farther, but sensitive souls need a break today haha

KP: I think some mothers of boys don't see the impact this will have on the girls that have these children. The roles are different when it comes to boys with children and their families then the girls with children and their families

HL: They don't see it unless it is THEIR daughter that is pregnant. Then they want to kick ass. By then, it's too late!! It's like the saying goes . . . . .'Momma's baby, daddy's maybe'

Issue: Rayshawn has two girls pregnant at the same time, one of them is pregnant with twins. Rayshawn's mother Sandy only knew about the one girl Sakina and she convinced her to keep the baby and stated she would help her out with the baby. She later found that Rayshawn had another girl pregnant as well who is expecting twins, now she has the jackpot ding ding ding, three grandbabies; the million dollar question, will she assist with the other two?

Perspective: Sandy should have stayed out of it in the first place. She needs to have her son speak to these young ladies, she should not be the voice. Why are they having unprotected sex? Since Sandy stated she would help Sakina, she is obligated to help her because she talked her out of having an abortion. Rayshawn needs to step to the plate and get a job to take care of his three children he have on his way. Sandy's actions are coddling her son and will stunt his development of becoming a man.

Knowledge: Sandy is biting off more than she can chew with telling Sakina she would help out; I hope she is not speaking about financially because she has two young children herself. Last I checked, Rayshawn had not graduated from high school, so again he will be adding to the statistics of young single noneducated parents on the welfare system.

Action: The best thing Sandy can do is encourage her son to go back to school to get his GED and get a job so he can have a better quality of life for himself and her grandbabies.

Consequences: If things continue to pan out like this, Rayshawn will have to live the life of a hustler, which puts his life span at serious jeopardy. There is no way he can afford to take care of three newborns on a minimum wage income. Usually hitting threes of something results in winning; but in this case, everyone will be a loser especially the babies.

CHAPTER 4

Health Issues

Scenario 25 Can I Hold Your Whip

TINA HAS BEEN dating Tony for a while and has been very generous with letting him use her vehicle; in fact he drops her off at work every morning while according to coworkers he joy rides and runs out her gas. This time Tony has went too far, Tina's daughter was rushed to the hospital for overdosing on pills due to being depressed over not returning back to school her senior year . . . in college because of finances, Tina has been trying to get a hold of him for over two hours but was unable to reach him; finally she ends up catching a fifty-dollar cab to get to her daughter. She ends up getting a ride home from her parents who roasted her because of the car situations. The very next day, Tony had the car again. What the hell is Tina's problem? I say stuck on stupid.

SB: It's sad how many people are "stuck on stupid"

YH: You be getting deep my brother lol, I be laughing but dat shit be true as hell, LMAO Fam :)

C2: Thanks Fam I try to keep it entertaining but make people think all the time

YH: Now you do!

MJ: Her problem is she thinks lowly of herself and thinks she has to do these things to keep man. She is afraid to be alone and that frame of mind is keeping her from thinking clearly. It might take a long time but one day she will wake up.

HL: An adage my boy once told me . . . .' When the pain of being the same becomes too great, that is when someone will change'. She hasn't hit that pain threshold yet.

MJ: Exactly HL!!

C2: It should have hit when her daughter tried to take her life and she couldn't get to her while Tony was parking lot pimping her ride out

MJ: You're right David but sometimes it takes more for some people. My mom always says it takes a brick house to fall on top of people for them to wake up.

EG: I pray not my child, Tina has work to do on herself, show my man the door without the car, loll! Hug your child and reassure her all will be well. There are too many marks in this scenario, were the child's father, how come her parents were not consulted to assist in grand child's education? Is there domestic violence accruing?

HL: I think the overdose of her daughter is a side issue. Here is why: If her daughter wasn't into drugs, then there would have been another situation that would have come up and the outcome possibly would have still been the same. I believe she doesn't care about her car, but more about him being in her life and it maybe because she doesn't value herself.

C2: The issue with the daughter should have superseded all other issues in my opinion, let's continue the dialog people, I will check back in later

KCJ: Dumbdickeddownstupidwhoknows

CA: Foot in ass! He's kicked to the curb . . . LOSER!

C2: Red flag to me is why a grown ass man doesn't have his own vehicle.

HL: LOL . . . I don't David, but I don't depend on anyone other than myself to get me to where I have to be. The reason why I said the overdoes was a side issue is that you could have put any situation and the outcome wouldn't have changed. She has evaluated what is important in her life.

C2: In that is the difference Tony is depending on Tina everyday

HL: Unless Tony is using the car to bring home income, he is abusing her and what she is giving him, but that will all come to an end if she puts her foot down.

Issue: Tina got in the habit of letting Tony use her vehicle, he would drop her at work and it would appear that he did a lot of joy riding. Well one morning, she is trying to get a hold of Tony for hours but was unsuccessful; the issue was that Tina's daughter had overdosed on pill because she was upset that she could not return back to college for her senior year. Eventually Tina caught a cab to the hospital in which she had to pay $50.00.

Perspectives: Some people just continue to be stuck on stupid. Suffering from low esteem and until she thinks better of herself, she will continue to make these choices. She will change when the pain becomes too much, you may see change. She needs to dismiss this guy and reassure her daughter everything will be okay. Clearly she is getting abused by Tony and until she puts her foot down, he will continue to play her like monopoly.

Knowledge: Sometimes people start new relationship as a way to show that they have moved on, you have some individuals that sit back and find your weaknesses and exploit them every opportunity they get, Tina has been exposed and I am sure Tony will take her for a ride that may be worse than her previous relationship.

Action: Tina should have took her keys back as soon as she met up with Tony, how in the hell could you be riding around in someone else's car and not have the audacity to pick up the phone; when you are using someone's belonging, you are slave to them, but clearly Tony knows who he is dealing with and was able to get away with it.

Consequences: Many outcomes can come out of this scenario; for one, what if he gets into an accident while driving her vehicle, guess what Tina will be shit out of luck. I am sure this will not be the last time Tony will not respond to Tina's call when she needs her vehicle to get somewhere. Sooner or later, his usage of her vehicle will impact her professionally as well as personally. The best thing she can do for him is purchase a bus pass for him; if he didn't have a vehicle coming into a relationship, he should not be blessed with one now. You can't get use to what you never had.

Scenario 26 Don't Open One Door without Closing Another

Cliff had recently lost his wife due to a battle with cancer; at two previous wakes, he ran into Gwen someone he previously dated. Cliff asked Gwen to look him up and the phone book and to give him a call. So one day she decided to do just that, Cliff offered to take Gwen to breakfast and eventually their schedules meshed. The next several months off and on they would see each other and then go a month without communicating. Gwen was growing increasingly frustrated with Cliff's inconsistent patterns. Hey, public, can you help Gwen figure out what the hell is the deal with Cliff?

WC: Hey Gwen he just loss his wife a few months ago! Give him some time.

N: Maybe he is really not ready to move on from the death of his wife. Or he needed her as a stepping stone to get back into the "dating" scene. Maybe he just is not feeling her. Can't she just call him and ask?

C2: N, good question, WC that could be the case

RHS: He needs time . . . marriage and death is hard, just like marriage and divorce

COJ: Move on. Ain't nobody got time for that. Either you're onto me or you're not.

TS: Communication is always key! He probably does like spending time with her but feels guilty for doing so . . .

HL: I don't think Cliff has a problem, but Gwen should have weighed her decision better than to take serious someone who has suffered as Cliff has.

DP: The stages of grief must be complete before Cliff can move on. Gwen met him during times of death and grief, that of his wife and the 2 wakes he was attending. He must grieve all of those. Each time he sees her or talks to her he is possible reminded of the most painful times of his life. Grief can be worse than divorce or a break up.

C2: Cliff don't go opening one door without closing the other it's not fair to that person waiting on the other side of the opening door

HL: I would agree, but I would have hoped that people understand that just because a door is opened doesn't mean they have to walk through it when not looking though it first to ensure that is what they wish to walk into. Some people want to have other clean up behind them as opposed to cleaning up themselves. Not only is that not wise, it is a way to enable someone to pass on accountability.

DP: Cliff may not have opened the door intentionally. When we grieve we look for things to replace the loss not necessarily looking for something new.

HL: Which is why grieve alone. No muss, no fuss

EG: Cliff is someone she should leave alone. Go back to the reasoning for the first break up!

C2: Also sometimes people use death as a way to receive comfort from others; it turns into a game of manipulation. The winning phrase becomes awwwww poor Cliff do you need something, I'm there for you if you need something, bingo Cliff has just won, music to his ears.

EG: A card, a scripture verse and viewing him from the side line because she had a relationship with and it didn't work so either figure out why it didn't work or keep your distance because your time is valuable!

DP: Bottom-line - Gwen is taking advantage of Cliff's vulnerability at this point and in turn she is being disappointed by his lack of emotional attachment. It is a process and until Cliff goes through the process, however long it takes someone is going to be left out. She can meet all the needs she wants as you say David it will be music to his ears but it is not equal to the loss sustained. If your dog dies and you get another one. The new dog is not the same no matter how well you feed it, walk it or pet it. By the time it is all over she will need a support group just like Cliff.

C2: Gwen should have never called first; I would have had him called me to test his interest

RHS: Let me be clear, never was there a comparison BTW death and divorce . . . . . . with both u need time to heal and sometimes having someone to take your mind off the situation helps with the healing process, and if a person is upfront with you its your free will, to jump feet first in . . . . ..you were told.

DP: I don't know if calling was wrong just her expectations

C2: At the end of the day Cliff should give Gwen an update on where he is at emotionally, going months without communication is not cool

KM: Speaking as someone who lost a spouse, I tended to be in the company of others WHEN I needed and WHY I needed. My emotions were all over the place and sometimes I may have needed my girls to be silly with or go shopping. Other times I may have needed the company and conversation of a male. Gwen should probably have taken that into consideration before trying to establish a relationship with a still grieving widower.

Issue: Cliff ran into Gwen at several wakes in the last month, they use to date years ago but cliff had recently lost his wife to cancer so he appears to be on the rebound. Cliff suggested that Gwen look him up and Gwen did just that, she called him one day and they planned to see each other. After finally hanging out, Cliff's behavior has become sporadic and inconsistent. Gwen has become very frustrated with this situation. What in the world is going on with Cliff?

Perspective: Cliff just lost his wife, can he get some time? Maybe he was using Gwen as a stepping stone, or he may not be feeling her. Gwen needs to move on, ain't nobody got time for that. Cliff could be feeling guilty for spending time with Gwen. Cliff is going through the stages of grief, and each time he came into contact with Gwen, it was death related. Gwen needs to go back to the original break up and move forward.

Knowledge: Gwen never took into consideration what Cliff was going through and only thought about how nice it would be to just have a friend or companion, a male friend to do things with instead of dealing with the pain of loneliness.

Action: Gwen should have been a friend and maybe converse over the phone; as soon as she started having expectations, the disappointment kicked in, once Cliff would have his episodes of disappearing. Always gage someone's situation before you jump head in first because if the person is shallow, you may end up bumping your head.

Consequences: When people are lonely they tend to wear blinders which cause them not to see the bigger picture. Gwen built this situation to be bigger than what it was and thought she was walking through a door of hope but what she ran into was another door with a padlock, which at the time could not be opened. "Access Denied."

Scenario 27 Following Your Dream or Following Your Heart

Tyreke was offered a full academic scholarship to Georgetown University, his dream college he always wanted to attend. That summer before he was getting ready to leave, his mother Brenda told him she has been diagnose with cancer that is spreading throughout her body and she doesn't expect to live that much longer. She wants him to pursue his dreams and go ahead and attend Georgetown, which would make her so much happier. What should Tyreke do?

CA: Honor his mother.

C2: At the expense of something happening and he's not present.

CA: If his mom is okay with that possibility, then yes.

MJ: I agree with Cheryl.

NNM: Stay with his mom . . . Georgetown will always be there.

C2: Will that free-ride scholarship always be there.

PC: He would resent his dead mother over the years if he stayed. His mother is dying, he has to live his life.

PG: He must go on with his journey, live life with no regrets, mom knows he loves her. Grant her last wish, do well

NNM: Money does not mean everything.

AS: Death is final. You only have one mom. I myself would spend the time with my mom, time that I would never get back. As far as Georgetown, I would write them and explain to them my situation and *pray* that God would open another door that I may be granted a full scholarship.

C2: Explain money doesn't mean anything to the poor, but I see both sides of the situation, and, Alicia, that appears to be a good resolution.

AA: Do what you feel is right, Tyreke. One life as we know it. There is a percentage of students that change matriculation after entering college, and there is a percentage of students that drop out of college altogether. Bill Gates, Steve Jobs, Mark Zuckerburg . . . all were dropouts. You're bright enough to get that academic full ride so although this may a tough decision, it's your decision. I'm here for you homeboy, now go out and FUTW!

AS: David, sometimes when you explain the situation especially a situation like that, the school or someone who hears about the story, may want to grant him a scholarship or funding to be used for a later date. AS.

Issue: Tyreke always dreamed of attending his school of choice, Georgetown University. He received a full-ride scholarship; there was one major obstacle—his mother shared the news she was diagnosed with cancer and was not expected to live much longer but she wanted him to follow his dreams and go on and attend college. Decisions, decisions, decisions.

Perspectives: Tyreke should honor his mother's request and attend college. Stay with mom during her time of need, Georgetown is not going anywhere. He may resent his mother later on; he needs to live his life. Continue on with his journey make his mother proud by doing well. Death is the end of time, you have one mom, cherish that time together.

Knowledge: Tyreke grew up with a close-knit family and despite his mother's wish, Tyreke felt like he has to be there for his mother. Considering she raised him as a single parent, so he has a strong bond that he refuse to break; so although his mother wants him to fulfill his goal, me knowing Tyreke, he will be right by her side.

Action: If I were Tyreke, I would submit a letter of mitigating circumstances and hopefully they can place a hold on my scholarship. Certainly graduation or attending college is paramount as a prerequisite to success but the pain of losing your mother supersedes all. I would not be able to focus knowing that I could receive that call saying that my mother has passed. I would be walking on eggshells. Once my mother is laid to rest, I would enroll in college and do what I need to do to graduate from college.

Consequences: This scenario can play out in many ways if he decides to go and she passes without him having closure; he could live a life of regrets, which could impact him mentally for the rest of his life. If he puts college off until his mother passes, he may lose momentum and other circumstances may surface that cause to lose motivation in school.

Scenario 28 Getting My Drink On

Bradley and Tiffany have been married for ten years but been together a total of twenty-five years. Bradley has hit rock bottom due to drinking and drugging. He recently spent ninety days in a drug and alcohol rehab. Bradley knew he was fighting for his life and had to get out of the streets because he was going to die. When Bradley returned home, he was already facing adversity due to Tiffany. It seems like she was drinking more than ever, she was going through a twelve pack every other day. Bradley pleaded for her to stop drinking and recommended that she get help. Tiffany stated because his life became unmanageable does not mean she needs to give up drinking, she enjoys it and he has to deal with his demons on his own. Bradley is not going to make it without his family support and especially his wife. What are Bradley's options to remain sober in that household?

HL: Get away from each other and he go seek help.

C2: Twenty-five years together that is all he knows, change is scary.

HL: If all he knows is abuse, then I'd say what he knows needs to be expanded upon. JMO.

DP: Agreed. Sounds like she needs help as well. If not, this is not going to end well. He hit his bottom and Tiffany has not.

C2: She doesn't feel like that, she is maintaining her part-time job and taking care of their kids so her job is done in her eyes.

DP: The cycle of addiction says different. The first stop to dealing with an addiction is admitting the problem. Bradley has to maintain his sobriety or he will relapse.

C2: People, places, and things causes relapse; Bradley has to leave his home. Tiffany is not respecting his illness.

TC: Tiffany sounds like a functional drunk and those are one of the worse kind because she may not ever realize she had a problem. Bradley needs to have a serious talk with her and encourage her to try to do more with her life than just being satisfied getting by. If she is not willing to change, he cannot return to their household because he needs to change his environment, meaning he needs family support and someone who understands that he wants and needs to stay sober.

HL: And that is the problem. Her story isn't through his eyes.

WC: Bradley has to do what he has to for himself first then he can try to help his wife.

COJ: Ummmmmm, so sad. Maybe he should try an intervention. A lot of times people with drinking problems don't think they have a problem. I hope he doesn't turn back into a drunk because of her.

KP: If she is not willing to admit she has a problem then there is nothing anyone can do . . . She should be willing to do this not only for herself but for him too . . . if she wasn't a part if his rehab, she cannot fully understand the effects of her drinking around him . . . for his health and sobriety, he needs to separate himself from her . . .

Issue: Bradley and Tiffany have been together for twenty-five years, but recently, Bradley has hit rock bottom due to drinking and drugging. Bradley spent time in the rehab; but when his stint was over, he returned home to his wife who happens to be drinking more than ever. Bradley pleaded for her to stop drinking, but she felt like she was not the one with the problem.

Perspective: Get away from each other and go seek help. She needs help but has not hit rock bottom yet. Bradley needs to have a talk with her; if she is not willing to change, Bradley needs to change his environment. Bradley has to do what he has to do, self-preservation first. Due to Tiffany not being a part of Bradley's recovery, he needs to separate himself from her so he can stay clean.

Knowledge: What people don't know is that Bradley has taking Tiffany to hell and back. Tiffany was always in his corner but Bradley had no respect for himself or her during the time he was out in the world. There were many nights where he did not make it home because of his addiction. Bradley literally drove her to drink, so now that she has got started she is having too much fun to stop.

Action: Bradley needs time to find himself, I don't know if he can blame Tiffany for the way she has reacted to him; in normal situations he would need to be patient with her, but in this case, he needs to run and get away because he is fighting for his life. Once he rebuilds himself up then maybe he can return to Tiffany and help her begin the recovery phase.

Consequences: If he stays with Tiffany, he runs the risk of relapsing because we all know that people, places, and things are the triggers that will cause people to use again. If Bradley uses again, he may be painting his ticket to an early gravesite. If he leaves, Tiffany may have resentment toward him for leaving, considering she was there for him all those years and now he can't do the same thing in return. Sometimes you have to put yourself first especially when it's a life or death situation.

Scenario 29 Got It Going On

Brenda and James have been together for seven years. James, after a few years, began to have health issues, like diabetes, and back problems; their sex life slowly begin to suffer, until it became barely any sex at all. Brenda is a very attractive woman and receives lots of attention from other men; she has begun to voice her complaints about not having sex as often as desired. James only response is it's his health, and it's not much he can do to change his sex drive. Brenda is contemplating if she should leave although she loves him, or stay in a sexless relationship. Keep in mind Brenda is seven years younger than James.

WC: James better get some Viagra or he's going to lose Brenda.

OW: For better or worse . . . it's other things they can do and use for that matter! Don't think she should seek pleasure elsewhere . . . it just might be worse than her current situation . . . IJS.

COJ: Sex toys may be worth a try.

YWB: A relationship is not based on sex and love ensures all things. They aren't married but some people are selfish. I know how it I'd to be sick and illness makes sex a nonfactor. She has to be understanding of his issues, but he have to also, there's too many pills like cialis and Viagra herbals and penis pumps. He better get something or his chick is gone.

DP: Unfortunately, poor health management not only can ruin a sex life but it can ruin a relationship. James really needs to seek professional help for his health issues and manage them so that he can live long enough to be with Brenda the statics speak for . . .

TS: Communication and understanding on both sides is called for here. I'm hoping they are married if they have been together that long first of all. But secondly, they both need to address each other's needs. There are alternatives to actual intercourse . . . and she would be an ass to not stick by him in his illness.

C2: It seems like a matter of time she will fold from the attention of the other men especially if she catches the right talker with gifted gab.

DP: It is actually sad, he is forty and allowing his health to deteriorate on such a level. That seems to be a bigger issue.

TS: Then she doesn't understand what a covenant relationship is . . .

WM: If it was vice versa, I wouldn't run. My girl is my best friend. We were friends before we were lovers. We established that mental connection so if the physical ever stopped (lovemaking), our bond will keep us together. A lot of relationships start on lust and then feelings start. I feel it should be the other way around. That's ole school to me.

C2: Thanks, WM, for the much needed male perspective, keep sharing my brother from North Avenue.

LN: I'm sure it's just a matter of time, even though she loves him, Brenda would need to decide if she loves him enough to go without sex. James better do something to keep Brenda sexually content, or expect troubles in the future.

HL: Character *always* shows me things are bad. The question becomes what kind of character does Brenda have?

C2: Personally, it sounds like James is sitting as a lame duck.

MJ: I'm not putting all the responsibility on her, but if she really loves him, she will stick it out and help her mate. He on the other hand needs to take responsibility for his own body. There are doctors, nurses, nutritionists, physical therapists, etc. that can help him get on the right track. He has to want it for himself though. I believe with her encouraging him, he can do it.

TA: This response is based on the fact that there was no mention that they were married. If they were, then my response would be different. *However,* since they are not married, she needs to walk. Why? Because sex is obviously important to her *and* he isn't her husband . . . nor does it sound as if he wants to assist her in getting those sexual needs met. He has had seven years to take her off the market. Since he hasn't, then she isn't obligated to stay in a sexless relationship. Love is an emotion so it has to be a nonfactor in this decision. There is no rule that because you love someone you have to stay with them. If that was the case, how many of us would be stuck in some hot mess right now! This would be a perfect situation for an open relationship.

AP: Diabetes does affect a man's ability to have an erection. If he got that under control with the help of his doctor, diet, and exercise, he should be able to regain himself. Just think, most diabetics have problems with their feet, blood flows from a man's feet to his penis for an erection; if that path has problems, *it* has problems!

C2: So in regards to an open relationship, what is the point to sit around talking with someone who is getting their back dugout by the next man?

LN: LOL, if he can't provide what's needed, than he may end up in the same position, just without his knowledge, or he should dump Brenda and get a woman who cares nothing about sex.

TA: I'm with Lisa on this one. If she stays, an open relationship has to be on the table because she will eventually cheat behind his back. At least having the option of an open relationship negates the deception. Of course, that is if he wants her to stay because those would be the two options: open relationship or break up.

C2: So what percentage of importance is sex in a relationship?

TC: I have a couple of issues: (1) They have been together seven years and are not married. (2) He is only forty and having quite a bit of medical issues, is he not taking care of himself. The sex thing is not even the main issue.

C2: Diabetes is an illness that can wear on you progressively and some of it may be out of his control and I am talking from experience, and who says you have to have a time table to be married, shit if they were married, would that change the presenting issue.

TA: David, you can't put a percentage of importance on sex in a relationship because that number is dependent upon the two people in the relationship. It will be different for everyone. That is something that should be discussed early in a relationship just like money, religion amongst other topics prior to getting serious.

C2: TA, true, each individual's relationship choice.

KM: There is no good scenario where man can accept his woman getting plowed by another man. If he does accept that scenario by allowing his woman to get plowed by another man, people better start checking the newspaper for murder/suicide.

HL: David: I'm amused by some of the response. I think it goes back to the standard of what is acceptable?

AM: Brenda needs to get a toy and a gym membership for her man. Seems like he just doesn't take care of his body. As his woman, she should feel the need to help. Running for the hills would make her a fair-weather woman. That's true. There has to be something he can do to improve his quality of life. I am a strong believer that if you love someone, you should be there with them through the good and bad.

Issue: James and Brenda have been dating for seven years but due to his deteriorating health, James has been unable to perform sexually. Brenda is seven years younger and gets attention from many; she is becoming sexually frustrated and has contemplated leaving James although she loves him.

Perspective: James better take some sexual enhancer or Brenda will leave him. Brenda should not seek pleasure elsewhere, the grass is not always greener on the other side. Relationship should never be based on sex, and sometimes illnesses cause sex to be a nonfactor that in this day and age there are many medications to help get the "big boy" working. Considering they are not married, she should leave instead of staying in a sexless relationship. Perfect situation for an open relationship. No way will any man let his woman get plowed by another man; if this is the case, look out for murder/suicide report in the newspaper.

Knowledge: Brenda use to love the dirty draws James wore and although he is seven years older, nothing ever came between them; but once his health went down, their time started diminishing. James felt like he was losing his self-worth and Brenda was at his sexual peak. James was not big on taking medications because of his pride but he realize he was losing a battle he can't win.

Action: It comes down to if James wants someone to stick around because they felt bad for him, or is he willing to let her walk to seek out her sexual pleasures. Brenda never had anyone who care for her like James, but James states he would let her go before he pumps medication into his body so he can perform sexually. If it is meant to be, it will be.

Consequences: If James pushes Brenda out the door, he may become angry and bitter because of his illness and I am sure this is going to impact him with future relationships. If Brenda stays, would the attention she is receiving from the other men lead her to having an affair? Would she have resentment toward James for allowing her to stay? If Brenda decides to leave, she may get involved with someone who only likes her for sex, but the way he treats her is nothing like James, and which she may want to return and he doesn't take her back. People, when you find someone to love you unconditionally, hold on to that love, you may never find that love again.

Scenario 30 Something Just Ain't Right

Kenny and Dolly dated when they were in college fifteen years ago, Kenny was physically and emotionally attached to Dolly but they ended up going their separate ways. Dolly ended up getting married but has been divorced the past two years; after finding her on Facebook, Kenny has been trying to hook up. Dolly decided that would be a good thing since Kenny was such the gentleman before. Kenny invited her over for dinner where he prepared baked salmon, roasted potatoes, corn, string beans, Caesar salad, and a light and fluffy lemon pound cake. Kenny also made sure he had Dolly's favorite wine, Red Moscato. When Dolly arrived, Kenny was trembling with excitement, but it all went sour when they went to kiss and Kenny realized that she was missing all of her front teeth. Should Kenny terminate this date? What would you do if this was you?

RS: Crucial . . . I think you keep the date. You spent the money. Pray to god she has dentures . . .

LFJ: If it is true LOVE he will accept her if he comfortable he will ask her about that. I believe he had the ONCE WAS FEELINGS and not the HERE AND NOW FEELINGS. He wanted her, He looked her up so was this a lust thing? ANY WHO . . . Dolly honey it's 2014 and times have changed you know you need some teeth. Ppl want artificial females so YES love you have to get some teeth. To add Yuck you kissing already. Noooo thanks to that.

C2: what's up Fam, RS how can you eat with that teethless sight

RS: I would hold off on kissing . . . maybe, Dome . . .

TC: Kenny made a lot of food, who eats like that? Missing front teeth are a deal breaker for me. But if he chooses to stay, he should find out why her teeth are missing. I am thinking drugs, violence, bad hygiene or predisposition in her family (more deal breakers).

THP: He didn't see her teeth missing when she came in the house and started talking or they just went straight to kissing if so that was a straight booty call and the dinner was a decoy . . . 15 yrs ago is a long time, now its time to get to know that person all over again. I think anyway.

C2: TC that was a great gesture the food, people eat like like that occasionally, Tisha we all know that women pay attention to details than men or maybe he was prepping for dinner when she walked in

PC: Ain't nothing wrong with a swinging door. Kenny has a place for his tongue to run to and from . . . ..All at the same damn time. Lol

AM: I'm sorry I would have been taken aback. My reaction alone may have ruined the night. Like u knows I was expecting you to still have teeth in your damn mouth why would u let me kiss u before at least warning me Gosh? I would want to know the deal with that. Did someone knock all your teeth out? Did u use crack or something?

NNM: Lol at RS, I caught that comment. You not right lol.

LHM: If you truly love and care for someone even after all of those years you will accept them for who they are, assist them without hesitation, and most of all love them unconditionally. Once they sit & talk about their lives over the years he may find out that there were health issues. Never judge a book by its cover.1

CWRG: This is hilarious! Give the girl a break. She can buy some teeth.

NNM: She needs to get some teeth ASAP, and things should be fine after that.

HL: Haha . . . I suppose that if that is his only problem, he can see if she is willing to have dental implant and offer to pay for them. Tact will be require!!

C2: You women are killing me, several points I need to make 1. The first attraction is the physical attraction, 2. women are so detailed oriented so I find it hard to believe that if you wouldn't talk to a man with leaning shoes you would talk to someone with missing teeth, now understand if you with someone and this happens that is a different ball game, but if someone is trying to get back in the game and they have no teeth tell their ass to go sit back on the bench

SB: Lololololol . . . Dave you are hilarious!!!

YWB: Ok I don't usually comment on this stuff but. How the heck someone gets to your doorstep and you don't recognize she don't have teeth! She might been hungry but she wouldn't have got in my house. CRACK ROCK. U do not need a degree to figure that out. And you didn't say he made pureed salmon . . . so I'm mad at him no date woulda occurred and no kiss woulda took place period he coulda got cleaned outta his house and his health in. 5 minutes tryin to be the man.

C2: Stated before if he was prepping that illustrious dinner than its a chance that could of been an easy oversight, let's not focus on the teeth let's look at the time he put into that dinner, that meal can woo any women out of their pants

YWB: See that's the problem trying to woo the pants off. I bet he saw the other parts just fine.

Issue: Kenny and Dolly reunited after being together fifteen years ago in college. Dolly recently divorced two years ago and Kenny found her on Facebook and has been trying to hook up, and finally because of their previous relationship, Dolly gave Kenny a chance. After inviting her over for a meal fit for a queen, everything was perfect and finally when there was time for affection and they were about to kiss, Kenny realized Dolly did not have any teeth.

Perspectives: Keep the date; you spent all that money on dinner. If it's true love, Kenny would accept her for who she is, but at the same time, she needs to get some teeth. Missing teeth a definite deal breaker, but Kenny should find out what is going on. Having no teeth makes oral that much better. She could have warned Kenny that she had no teeth; she needs to let him know what the deal is on why she doesn't have any teeth. It doesn't take a genius to figure out she was on crack, she would have never been allowed in my house, she could have cleaned him out of his house and health.

Knowledge: Dolly had been in an abusive relationship in the past but also she did have some disease that caused her teeth to decay, she was also going through some issues with her insurance. Before these set of bad circumstances, you would be hard pressed to find too many women that matched her looks.

Actions: If I were in the predicament, my heart would definitely ache for her and it would be hard to actually finish eating a meal with her because my stomach would be turning and I would be feeling guilt and shame for her, but the naughty side may cause me to skip dinner and give her some dessert to fool around with for a while.

Consequences: More than likely, this no-teeth episode may have killed the chase for Kenny after all these years and I am sure Dolly will realized potentially Kenny was living in the past and had on his mind the old Dolly. Needless to say, until she gets her grill fixed, Kenny is going to end up disappointing her like her previous husband.

Scenario 31 Trying to Reinvent Myself

Gale was dating Ralph for a short time but certain family members kept telling her he was no good, he was a compulsive liar. Gale had reached her midforties where she was looking for something long term. Ralph started off working but ran into a funk and he ended up losing his job shortly after due to drinking. Gale continued to keep Ralph around because he told her he would change. Although he had nothing to bring to the table, he continued to drink and complain stating he refused to work a minimum wage job; finally things hit the fan and Gale put Ralph out to stay with his drinking buddy, Annie Jones. Two days later, Ralph was hospitalized for a ruptured ulcer; upon being discharged, he asked Gale can he come back and stay with her, instead of the room at the homeless shelter. What should Gale do?

SF: Is this a trick question?

CF: No tricks SF go ahead and give us your opinion

DP: This does not warrant an answer David. Unless Gale is just hard up. Change her number. Send him a fruit basket for the shelter so he can have some items to trade and give him the deuces. Tell him to call Annie

SF: I agree! Why would a woman that didn't have issues even deal with this kind of shit?

C2: Well sometimes these answers are not black and white; each of us can name several people who are living this nightmare

CA: I can only tell you what I would do. It's really none of my business what Gale should do. It's her decision to make

SF: A woman that's going through that kind of crap needs someone like you to tell her that it's not normal. There are things that she could do, rather than stay with someone that's controlling her emotionally and financially. A piece of crap that calls himself a man wouldn't use her unless he was getting something out of it, so she's worth something. Right? A lot of the time, people in her situation doesn't reach out to their family, b/c they're embarrassed, or b/c their family situation isn't something they'd willingly go back to. There are other options. What state is this in, so I know where to direct her?

C2: fear of being alone

SF: Well then, enjoy being "transition guy".

C2: If everyone had perfect relationships the divorce rate wouldn't be so high

HL: Leave him where he is . . . ..

KP: Gale should help him from a distance . . . Do not let him back in but lead him to the professionals he needs to become an active and healthy person in society . . . ..She can support him through the transitions he will go through but can not do it for him . . . ..

C2: Should she really help him after all he created this mess

SF: No. Why should he be her responsibility for his bad behavior?

MM: I would have been done, compulsive liar, I am not going to be able to do that. They can be friends from a distance, but naw he couldn't stay with me.

KP: We are all human and may need help from time to time . . . No matter where we come from or what degree are problems are . . . . we by nature need to feel love and compassion no matter how bad we as humans may be . . . if we all gave a little more compassion and love for each other our society wouldn't be in the State it is now . . . ..

RS: My relationship was built on a long friendship and I married my best friend knowing that if I cannot wipe my own ass one day, she will. That love is vice versa as well. If you're not feeling that, you can be a friend for support over the phone. He doesn't need to be in your home.

Sometimes people need to hit rock bottom to make drastic changes to better themselves...

C2: Thanks for Sharing RS, well said

RS: No problem bro . . . Very interesting...

KM: Naw. She needs to let that man be a man and figure out how to get what he needs and wants on his own. At some point "helping" becomes "enabling".

HL: I would like to say that enabling someone to continually behave irresponsibillly is to enable them. That will only allow them to behave as they always have. In order to teach/help some, they have to be willing to help themselves. Even the first admission in any 12 step programs is to admit the problem. If he isn't there yet, then no amount of help from anyone will be beneficial. I don't spend resources on those who won't make good use of it. In other words, how many of us would get into a boat with a patch when it has 20 holes?

Issue: Gale had recently started dating Ralph, Gale was in her midforties and felt like it was her time to find some happiness, but with Ralph, Gale's family members felt he was not it because he was a compulsive liar. In due time, Gale realize that her family members were correct and Ralph was a fraud.

Perspective: Gale needs to change her number and walk away. Why would anyone be in this controlling situation, seek help from family members or other resources. Gale can provide support from a distance; do not let him back into your life. We all can use a little at times and no matter what how bad that person maybe, we can show compassion. Helping too much can be enabling, people have to be willing to help themselves. Ralph doesn't need to be in the home, sometimes people need to hit rock bottom to make drastic changes to better themselves.

Knowledge: Gale had been feeling a sense of loneliness and was introduce to Ralph by one of her sisters so that made her move forward; but despite that, her closest sister and oldest son felt he was a liar based on a previous conversation with Ralph. In due time, Gale realized that Ralph was full of crap and their relationship was on a downward spiral.

Action: Again these situations boil down to a better scenario process, just because someone tries to play matchmaker does not mean that is the person for you. Most people who play that role is not the model of great relationships. Tell them to mind their own damn business and they date whoever; after your fling is over, I am sure you will be the source of personal entertainment.

Consequences: In most cases, these hooks ups do not amount to anything and if you are someone who had apprehension and trust issues before, this will more than likely set you back. Never trust a man with a thick mustache, something about a man who states he has not drank in ten years but he at a bar appears to be suspect. Always consider and evaluate the source who is bringing you the info; if that person has always been solid in their judge of character, please take that consideration instead of a random stranger.

CHAPTER 5

Education

Scenario 32 All Work in No Play

MIKE A TWENTY-THREE-YEAR-OLD intern for the school psychologist program had been interning at a middle school and doing well; his first evaluation was outstanding and Mike definitely had his swag going on; Gwen, his site supervisor, would ask Mike did he want to join her them for happy hour and each time Mike would say "no," he did not want to mix business with pleasure. As Thanksgiving break rolled around, Gwen asked Mike did he want to come over for Thanksgivings to do some paperwork. Mike declined and stated that was family time for him. One day Mike had to miss his scheduled day at the school because he desperately needed to finish a paper for school; he ended up making up his day the next day, and when he went in Gwen ripped him a new one, stating how irresponsible he was and how the kids were counting on him and at this point he would not make a good school psychologist. Needless to say, at the end of the semester, Mike received a horrible evaluation. What do you think should have happened in this situation?

KJ: Sounds like Gwen took him rejection her invitations personally, and allowed her emotions to grade him. He is obviously talented, and made a mistake. God does not like ugly. She could have graded him properly, horribly not.

CA: For missing one day? Whatever, Gwen has issues, get some help girl lol

KJ: I understand that, I'm glad she had perfect attendance for her entire career.

CA: Lack of flexibility, empathy and compassion, why couldn't he just make up the day he missed?

C2: Should Mike made himself more flexible and entertained her request?

KJ: Absolutely not that was not part of the internship. She knows better.

CA: Gwen has boundary issues

MM: Would he have to do the class over, or he can take it over turn her ass in.

TA: She was wrong but I was taught to not ever give anyone a reason whether justifiable or not to fire you/give bad reports etc. He knew that paper was due long before that day. He should have pulled an all nighter and did both things he made a commitment to because he knew what he signed up for.

C2: Yes you never want anyone to control your fate, we only can control our actions so in that case Mike should have managed his time better, on the other it seems like his body of work could have granted him a past on this particular occasion,

MM: Why should sex make him pass, why do people have to have sex to get a better job? Yes she did have something on her mind, I know she was not upset over an happy hour drink. He also did not have his shit in order, he had his dream map out but again did not have his shit in order.

C2: The only thing he did wrong is not call. How many of us and probably even Gwen is guilty of forgetting to call? First of all she had an agenda, why would you ask a School Psychologist that deals with children out to happy hour? If you were so concerned about the children and expect Mike to be there on the next day functioning at 100%. Secondly why would you ask anyone if they wanted to work on Thanksgiving? These were preludes for an opportunity to have a jump off with Mike. She probably thought the reason he did go in because he was entertaining someone the night before and most likely it made her angry, because of rejections but then again if you know a person is so adamant about doing great at his job, and appear to be responsible why not give a call to check and see if anything happened.

KJP: Mike first has to do better and look at how he contributed to this happening to him and then re discuss this happening to him and Gwen and her Supervisor. Whoever bottom line to be honest, take accountability for your part and do better next time if you lost your opportunity this time. This failure may be what he needed to make him better next time around. Also it is your choice to do as you please and if you don't want to mix business with pleasure, then don't and whoever doesn't like it ole well, But they gotten respect it, whenever you are in a situation like this you need to be on point and think forward because we got some sensitive take everything personal get back at you for any little thing, kinds folks out here in this world. Always have your game tight and right.

Issue: Twenty-three-year-old intern in school psychologist was given a poor evaluation based on him rescheduling his intern schedule day because he had to complete a paper for class. Meanwhile, his intern supervisor had made many attempts to connect with Mike outside of school such as at happy hours and on Thanksgiving, Mike declined each offer.

Perspectives: Gwen took his rejections of her invitations personally and graded him out of emotions. Mike should have been able to make up the missed day without a problem; she lacked empathy and flexibility. Gwen has boundary issues but never let anyone control your fate, always handle your business. Sex should not be a prerequisite for a successful grade under no circumstances. Gwen definitely had a hidden agenda by her invitations to the happy hour and Thanksgiving to do paperwork; now seriously, who does that?

Knowledge: Mike went on to do well on his intern class and after bringing the issue to his professor, she basically ripped up the poor evaluation and stated that Gwen's behavior was totally inappropriate and she would never send an intern to that school and removed her off the list.

Action: Mike should have entertained going to the happy hour at least one time to see what moves she was going to make and just maybe he would have held all the chips in his hand after she would have got drunk and said or did something stupid.

Consequences: Gwen may have come on to Mike and something could have happened between them, which could have made their working relationship very interesting. It's almost paramount that Gwen was going to behave the way she did because she was out to get plowed by Mike and she was hoping that it took place, and since it did not, he did not passed the test.

Scenario 33 Crack the Code

Thought of the day, I have been an educator for about twenty years and each year people are writing books and doing research on how to turn challenging schools around and everyone thinks they have the magic formula; well how can this code or equation be cracked, teachers are taught to call home when students are disruptive, lacking motivation, and for various other reasons. Parents discipline them, maybe physical, to keep it real dish out a good ass kicking, students return back to school with a minor bruise, counselors or teachers call CPS on the parents, parents now being investigated, so now the trust is broken between the school and parents. Parents remove themselves from any issues their child has at school and tell teachers to handle it because they don't have time for that shit. So how can we bridge the gap with these scenarios happening every day.

HL: Good old fashion community involvement

LH: My parents didn't have to spank me to discipline me. Taking away the TV or not being allowed outside was enough for me to learn my lesson. When a student recently told me he lost social media privileges when he brought home a report card riddled with D's and E's and that was the only consequence I was floored.

NG: Well as a parent of a 15 yr old girl it is not easy at all. Since the day that child entered high school it has been hell, between socializing and the boys her grades were declining and her attitude was increasing. I am currently getting phone calls from teachers; yes I dished out a good amount of ass beatings. We've had major arguments and what I found out that works best besides taking away her phone is gathering some family members, my friends, that know and love her and they just talk to her. After the intervention they keep in constant contact with her at the moment. I truly believe it does take a village. At the present time she is working on bringing up her grades to remain in the honor program, and we still have two more years of high school then college, also I pray everyday.

KP: These days people are only out for themselves and do not care that they hurt or step on to get what they want, growing up my neighbors looked out for each other. They all took responsibility in help raising all the children in the neighborhood, if I did something wrong and I was over at a friend's house, their parents had no trouble disciplining me and telling my parents. But on the flip side we were supporting each other when we played in a basketball game, got an award at school or even if we received our report card and went on to the next grade. We were praised by all. The sense of it takes a village to raise a child is gone; we must rely on ourselves and family to give all positive feedback to our children. Be role models so they can be able to make the best decisions and live life with integrity and morals. Be available to your children, some parents want to be your child's friend. You're a parent first and for most. Not a friend.

MJ: I don't believe in beating the crap out of your children but I do believe in spanking when they're small. The system and the government have too much say and control over what parents can say or do. The system is set up to teach demonic things that parents are totally blind sided to. Unless prayer and God are allowed back in school it will never be well with the system. It is set up to dumb down the students on purpose and with all that is going on, we wonder why our children are the way they are. It's all about control and socializing everyone to conform. Many parents and their I don't care attitudes; their vicious cycles we can do what we know is right and hopefully reach one child at a time.

KJP: Today you have to be an outstanding parent just to be considered good in the eyes of most, especially your own kids. As a parent there is no checkout option that most parents opt for when things get tough. Like when CPS is called out or the law gets involved. This is when they say you have to be more involved instead of opting out of your mandatory parenting responsibilities. Do for your kids at a young age what you do for yourself now. Help them by surrounding them with like minds... Make sure they are keeping the right company, get them mentors, and get to know your neighbors. Understand that you don't have a life of your own once you have kids and you need to wrap your head around committing to a 21 year parenting plan, make sure your kids see you involved and who you know. It will influence some of their decisions making. Bottom line it takes a village to maintain the fountain you create at home. But if you don't have one set real good, life and circumstances will set it for you and yours.

HL: Discipline comes in many forms, beating is not discipline! What does the Bible speak of when it comes to the rod?

MJ: He that spareth his rod hateth his son, but he loveth chasteneth him betimes (Proverb 13:24 KJV)

Issue: Crack the code, teachers are taught to call home for disruptive behavior, lacking motivation, and any other reasons, but once the parents discipline them and the child returns with a bruise, the roles are reversed and now the parents are getting called on to CPS, which turns a teacher and parent relationship into mistrust and parents remove themselves from all school-related activities.

Perspectives: My parents did not have to spank me; they used other methods of discipline such as *no* TV or stay your ass in the house. Organizing family community meetings work best; child is getting tag teamed by several adults. Back in the days, we grew up in a community environment where all adults held children accountable for their behavior. Society has removed the power of parents and they have too much say in parental discipline. There is no opt-out rule when you have children; when the tough get going as parents, we need to step up our game.

Knowledge: The current system is not working; the mistrust is at all time high, the question remains how we can get more parental involvement. Just a thought, maybe find a way that teachers get paid over the summer by holding meetings with parents so they can come up with a game plan before the school year starts; therefore, everyone can be on the same page. I am sure this will bridge the gap toward the positive side.

Action: As a parent you can understand the frustrations many parents face when they receive that phone call at home or work; the teacher is asking that you correct the behavior and sometimes a slap to the dome does the job, but as counselors, sometimes we have to make that call, which we may not know all the dynamics to the situations and it add to the friction. Back in the day, parents did not worry about this shit because kids knew not to air out their dirty laundry because if so, when we got home, our ass was grass and our parents were the lawn mower.

Consequences: We have created division amongst parents and school; we keep saying it takes a village to raise a child, but how can we keep this trend going without a major player in the game (parents). It has to be a better way to discipline without major violence, but if a parent takes it there without readjusting a child's face, who are we to cause strive for the parents when we don't know the entire situation.

Scenario 34 Grooming at It's Finest

Tamika would stay after school to help out Mr. Walker, she would wipe down his white board, and help put up chairs, and file papers. She will receive volunteer's hours for her services. One day after completing her task, Mr. Walker gave her a big hug and held her sort of tight. He also gave her $50.00 and told her to spend it wisely. Mr. Walker asked Tamika if she was hungry and he would take her out to grab something to eat so she didn't have to worry about dinner this evening. When Tamika returned to the school building, Tamika called her mother for a ride home at 7:00 p.m. Next morning when Tamika's mother was waking her up for school she realized the $ 50.00 bill on her dresser. She asked Tamika where did the money come from and Tamika nonchalantly responded Mr. Walker. What should Tamika's mother do?

HL: Investigate

TS: Inappropriate

HL: David, I'll say something you and I can attest to, but it would be looked as jaded by others. To get an unbiased answer to this, I'll withhold my explanation until more have responded.

LN: Communication with Tamika is key, find out about her experience with Mr. Walker it appears to me he rewarded her for a job well done. Hugging can be inappropriate, but if his intentions are pure, no harm no foul, then meet with Mr. Walker to thank him for showing his appreciation and because she's a volunteer, no cash is necessary.

HL: Ok, those who are in the area of teaching, particularly males are often looked as predatorily beings when that isn't the case. One of the reasons why many men don't go out of their way to mentor or assist in many ways is because of the ways things such as this are perceived. Now, I wouldn't say that hugging is normal thing between students and staff, but how many would actually think that if this was a male to male or female to female scenario would raise an eyebrow. I don't know the teacher and his history and that would matter to me because if this is something he's only did once, then I would have a word with him (as a staff member/Principal) and let him know that it could be looked at as something that could bring bad attention to him and the school. I've myself hugged many of my teachers and never thought a thing of it. During my senior year and toward graduation, it's almost expected and never thought of it at all. Students will work harder in those classes because they actually knew someone cared. Nowadays, we have fewer teachers who care and go out of their way to not show any attention to students unless it is to correct bad attitudes or behaviors. Then we wonder why some students fail. I would love to correct some of the things I see younger females do, but the attention it would bring makes me hesitate and I error on the side of caution. If the students fail or ends up in a less than desirable situation (pregnant at that age) then I don't wonder why, I already know why. Not enough adult males in their lives providing incentive to do right and avoid wrong. Money is just an incentive to keep doing what she is doing, we all work to earn, if we show the students at a young age that learning is a profitable undertaking, maybe we can save them from the streets. Who knows ... the $ 50.00 could have been to get her a new pair of shoes for the ones she had all year. Wise handling of finances is always a good asset to have, but never taught.

MJ: I don't care how innocent his intentions were. The actions are inappropriate. The mother should have a discussion with Tamika and Mr. Walker together. You can't give the devil any room. Even the purest of hearts can be contaminated. If it doesn't stop then I would have Tamika doing her volunteer work somewhere else.

TS: I agree with MJ. My immediate thought was not that he was a predator, merely that his actions are inappropriate. Especially taking her off school grounds to get something to eat. For my own protection I would never do these things be of how the child or may interpret them.

HL: The devil interesting how hugging is compared to a devilish act. So if a male teacher hears about a male student losing his father and he comforts him by hugging him and telling him that it'll be ok, is that going to be looked at as a devilish act? Man, I'm glad that not everything is blown out of proportion before being investigated.

TS: The side hug is always a compromise to the full frontal, just saying.

HL: TS, that is understood, how many times do students who play sports go off school ground without anyone else around. I agree with your last statement, but that is why I said investigate. We are only going on what is posted and it doesn't say frontal or side. With gathering information, that can be determined. To just automatically condemn the act is a bit presumptuous.

MJ: You're twisting my words HL. It's not the hug itself. It's the confinement of it and what can be perceived of it from others. Like I said it may have been innocent, but it can be perceived as not. The position he is in, the age of the student, the surroundings they're in.

RS: I pretty much agree with most statements. I do not see anything wrong with rewarding a student for a job well done, but the reward should be communicated to mom before disbursement.

HL: MJ, I didn't twist your words, I just gave you a different perspective to consider. I said it could bring bad attentions. I don't condemn any act by anyone without investigation.

TS: Going with a student alone off grounds is never appropriate.

HL; I agree, but that is only 1 aspect of the scenario. I was talking more of the hug. I've been in situations where I needed assistance from a staff member and if I didn't get it, who knows what things would have ended. I also have known others to do odd jobs for money for staff.

C2: To go along with HL, sometimes teachers hire students as babysitters.

KP: My sister is a teacher and in this day and age they are told and have had workshops on what are appropriate actions toward students. Teachers cannot be too careful to make sure that there are not being put in a compromising situation. Mr. Walker intentions could be an innocent act and just trying to help Tamika and her mother. Going to take her to eat is out of line, he needs to keep it professional; hugging her unfortunately is not looked at as a positive gesture in this day and age. It's sad because teachers are the only people that give these children positive reinforcement and encouragement. Society and government has taken over our school system.

HL: I agree KP

KP: We have to remember, we are not in the 70's, 80's 90's... We all have to understand its different now. What we think should be done and what needs to be done are two different things. We have to play the cards that are dealt in this generation (sad but true)

HL: Agreed and shameful

DP: This scenario can be looked at on so many levels. 1. Inappropriate is the 1st reaction because of hug and exchange of money. We have put so many restrictions on innocent human interactions and made them dirty and sinful. 2, He fed her, I'm a mentor in the community and often before I can do an outing with my mentee. I have to get them something to eat. There are 12 mouths in the home. They are growing children and although there is assistance in the home a spaghetti dinner for 12 doesn't go as far as it does for maybe a family 3. So should we assume Mr. Walker was wining and dining or he recognized or need?

MJ: I didn't say report him, so I don't believe I was too harsh. The mother should have that meeting with him and her daughter and then all misunderstandings can be put to rest. I agree with RS that Mr. Walker should have communicated his intentions. See more small matters can be blown way out to epic proportions. Some precautionary measures can be something like never taking the students off school grounds without parent permission. They have to get permission slips for field trips and such. Discuss rewards with the parents. Of course a parent is going to wonder where their child got $50 from. Definitely cover yourself because people can get really crazy with things like this. Oh and don't let it get out of hand and the media gets a hold of something like that. It's a wrap if that happens.

YWB: Very inappropriate, the mother is going to handle it and I hope it does not turn out ugly.

MJo: Very well said MJ.

MJ: Thank you MJO, I just hate that the system is set up for failure. Those with good intentions can do right and those who do evil things seem to get away with things. Our babies need to be protected either way.

MJO: Amen

YWB: A teacher giving money to a student and taking her out to eat without her parent's knowledge is inappropriate period! I'm from the old school if your mother or father didn't give it to you it's a reason why. That is why you have 50 yr old men dating 26 year old girls.

Hence comes the words Sugar Daddy's in some girls mind. I would see that teacher and that school and let them know. Yes we all may need attention but keep your hands and your money away from my daughter.

MJO: Totally agree YWB.

C2: What if this teacher was moving on to another job or retiring and this was his pardon gift to her.

AS: Give the money back. Strangers, yes he's still a stranger, don't need to be giving out money.

JD: I think her mother should talk to her. I wouldn't give the money back and I would hug my child and be proud of her. I don't feel anything wrong was done here. My Principal in high school hugged me and I appreciate him to this day he made a huge impact in my life, he's the reason I joined the military, he was in the reserves and he brought me chocolate covered macadamia nuts from Hawaii so having been in a similar situations I would say there's nothing going on here, he hugged her tight? My Principal hugged me tight and when my aunt passed in the 11th grade he came to the funeral and when my dad passed a few yrs ago, he came and I was happier to see the most inspirational man I'd ever met aside from my father.

HL: MJ, see how my post are relevant even before someone post about it. Judge not lest you be judged.

JD: I mean my Principal never took me out to dinner but I went to his house for dinner with his wife and kids. I needed to see that structure; I really enjoyed spending time with him. It was a great experience.

HL: I mentioned a situation like that JD before you posted and I was said to be twisting words. I just pointed out that there are situations that we should investigate and move on from there. I don't like to convict anyone based on my perceptions of things. Facts make better judges than any emotions.

MJ: 2 totally different situations, I still stand by what I said.

HL: Not sure I follow you, but just as well.

KCJ: Maybe Tamika is lacking a male figure in her life, and he is just being kind. If it were more to it, then I'm sure she would have hid it. Maybe he knows they are struggling and that would help them out. Maybe Tamika had been speaking out loud something she wanted and by her working after school and he paid her. Not all teachers are perverted.

RC: I think the mother should talk to her daughter about this to make the teacher hasn't made her feel uncomfortable in any kind of way and also talk to the teacher give the money back and let him know she doesn't agree with his actions it may be innocent but you can't be too sure with so much going on these days.

Issue: Student staying after helping a teacher who gives her volunteer hours, and one day he gives her a hug and $50.00 for helping him out and he takes her out to dinner also as a token of appreciation. The next morning, Tamika questioned her about the money and Tamika tells her "Mr. Walker gave it to her." Now what should Mom do?

Perspective: Find out the nature of the relationship; meet with Mr. Walker and tell him money is not necessary. Society views male adult's relationships with female students as taboo so we wonder why males are dead set against working with females who are desperately for fatherly figures. Teacher actions are totally inappropriate despite his intentions maybe innocent. There is nothing wrong with rewarding a student, but it should be discussed with a parent first. Again society and government has taken over the school system and this situation can be totally innocent and sometimes teachers are the only place where students receive positive reinforcement. Teacher giving student or taking them out without parent permission is totally inappropriate; if parents did not give, it then don't accept.

Knowledge: Many of the perspectives was on point, but one particular individual's thoughts resonated with my thoughts because many young ladies need that male bonding time with males; we see it every day that girls that have poor relationships with males, we can probe deeper and find out that young lady is lacking male involvement in her life. Just remember sometimes a little hug is refreshing and it's a way of giving hope and reassurance. Our babies need love from somewhere so don't be afraid to show love toward them, they will perform at an all time high when they feel safe.

Action: There is nothing wrong with Tamika's mother being concerned about $50.00, but let's be quick to condemn this good man for caring; I am sure Tamika will always remember this moment as a kind gesture, but again Mom has the final say on this matter. I just hope she would not confront Mr. Walker in an accusatory way when his heart is in the right place unlike the corrupt minds of you wicked evil society members.

Consequences: The consequences of the relationship between Tamika and Mr. Walker could be blown out of proportion because it would be based on perception; a young girl hanging out with a man during after school hours is destine to make good faculty-room talk. This also opens discussions from the student body that Mr. Walker is the Sugar Daddy on staff, so he better be prepared for one of these hot developed girls to impose their will on Big Pippin Walker, stay tuned.

Scenario 35 Parental Ignorance

Laurie has a negative view in regards to education; she is someone who barely skated through to get her high school diploma and really had a dislike for white educators. She firmly believed that they have no compassion when it comes to black children; this was manifested by her actions with her son Lionel who took a special liking to his teacher Ms. Bailey, a young Caucasian female who recently graduated from college but took pride in building relationships with her students. Since working with Ms. Bailey, Lionel's reading level has improved two grade levels so she has been great for Lionel; but once Laurie found out she was white, she removed Lionel from the after school program. After removal from the program, Lionel's grades started to suffer again. What should we do to help Lionel?

WC: Nothing anyone can do his dumb ass mama needs help

KP: First the schools need to pull Lionel's mother in to talk to her about his digression. Second Laura needs to get a reality check. If she wants what is best for her son no matter what the color the teacher is she would leave it alone. Put her personal feelings aside and do some research on what statistics are about our young black youth, give him the best opportunities he has so he doesn't turn out to be one of those statistics. Do not be a detriment to your child's future.

TS: Does this really happen? So sad, as a teacher, I would try to discuss with the parent the same positive relationships I have with my students. So she would understand my motivation and genuine concern for the well being of her child.

EG: This mom has to understand the importance of change. This teacher happens to be white but has the ability to find in others greatness, something no one else has ever done in her life and should be embracing and continuously encouraging it to her son. This should prompt her to go back to school, get her education and become a change agent.

N: Not to be mean but she is perpetuating a cycle of ignorance and because of her struggles is setting her son up for failure. If she was a purple space chicken and her son was thriving let him stay with the space chicken. Instilling prejudice in children should be a crime.

EG: You're on fire with your response so how can we encourage her to better herself and allow her child to continue thriving.

N: I would tug at her heart first by asking her to look at the types of struggles she had and ask if she wanted better for her son and encourage her to sit on some of the sessions to make sure their was nothing "wrong" going on. If that didn't work the next conversation would include a civil rights conversations and black people holding ourselves back. If that didn't work I'd break out some bible verse. After that friendship over I refuse to be a part of willful ignorance.

C2: At the end of the day when you are making a decision for a child you ask the one essential question. Is this in the best interest of the child?

DP: This is definitely difficult and if all efforts fail to get Laura to invest in her child's education, I would get the authorities involved, call it being a snitch but people have fought long and hard for these opportunities. The consequences of having another ignorant person walking around are inexcusable, depriving a child is a form of abuse and although it seems extreme the consequences for the life of the child can be catastrophic.

EG: DP, is there any laws on the books for ignorance lol?

DP: Not for ignorance but there is for education deprivation to a minor. Too bad there aren't any laws for ignorance. Thank God we can protect Lionel.

HL: I'm not sure what can be done in terms of legal help from anyone who isn't the father. Hopefully he is involved and he makes sure his son receives the proper education he was getting. As far as his mother, I want say what a self centered cretin she is and in serious need of a reality check about the lack of education and how it negatively impacts African American Males.

AP: His mother needs an outreach program to help educate herself along with her son.

ALM: She's selfish it's a problem to be racist enough to hinder your child's development. I guess if she feels that strongly about it there is nothing anyone else can do. Maybe she should go to Sylvan and find a good black tutor.

COJ: Not much you can do unfortunately Lionel has a nut bucket for a mother, sad situation for the kid.

Issue: Mother had experienced a total dislike for the education system and due to her anger and struggles in life, it left her very close minded. Her son Lionel had been receiving tutoring from a young Caucasian female who Lionel responded well to and his grades made a drastic change for the better. Once Laura found out she was white, she wanted to pull Lionel tutoring.

Perspective: Mother's dumb ass needs help for standing in her child's way of being successful. School needs to become involved and show Laura the data and the gains Lionel has made since being part of the tutoring program. Teacher should reach out to the parent to explain that she wants to build partnership and explain all the good things Lionel is doing in the tutoring program. Laura is demonstrating actions of ignorance and her behavior is criminal potentially putting her racist views on her child. Maybe the authorities need to get involved because this is a case of educational neglect.

Knowledge: When parents have bitterness toward education, it does not matter who the teacher is and there is nothing you can do to change it. We can only hope that we can work to change the mindset and just maybe by finding or seeing happiness from their child that may be the deal breaker, but if not, they may continue to be stuck in their shit. Remember hurt people like to hurt people so sometimes our children have to pay for choices we adults make and that are real talk.

Actions: If that was my son, I would sit down with Laura and find out what the hell is her problem and check her about the poor experience she had at school does not have to be Lionel's experience; and if she does not get it together, it may be better that he resides with me. As much as a jerk I can be, I don't play around when it comes down to schooling I want the best for children, the ultimate goal of parenting is to put your children in a better position than you are in. If you see them doing better, you need to do better.

Consequences: The way this scenario played out, Lionel is headed down a dead-end road but hopefully by someone confronting Laura and giving her back the crap she is giving out something that will hit her on her head and wake her ass up from the nightmare she is living. We all go through shit in life but it's what you do to get out of these jams that matter. I have been through hell and back and I refuse to lose, and the one thing I can't stand to see is a trifling parent not helping their children prosper in an already difficult world to live in.

Scenario 36 Respect and Protect

Timmy and Rebecca's garage was ransacked last week when they returned home. Which led Tim to go purchased a gun to protect his family; meanwhile, Tim Jr. was getting bullied in middle school by a bunch of eighth graders. This led Tim Jr. to watch closely on where his dad placed the gun, Rebecca was apprehensive about Tim bringing a gun into their household because of all the horror stories she has read about and seen on the news. I guess we should never question a woman's intuition because two days later, Rebecca received a phone call from the assistant principal from Mile High Middle School John Filmore stating that someone needs to come pick up Tim from school and he will be expelled for the reminder of the school year for category 3 offense, possession in or use of a firearm on school property, which goes up to a one year expulsion. Who is to blame for this situation? How would you handle this situation if it was your child?

HL: Apparently Tim didn't take gun safety courses. The number one rule for being a fire arms owner is the make sure they are secure. The lack of awareness on Tim's behalf is possibly why Rebecca was more apprehensive. The father and son both need to be more aware through education about the dangers that guns presents.

KP: Wow how irresponsible of Tim!!! This all falls on his shoulder!!! He wanted to be a protector but he didn't follow the rules. He needs to pay the price for being a negligent father and then sit down with Tim Jr. and explain to him how his actions were a result of a lack of communication. Explain to him the ramifications of such actions and then kiss his wife ass.

KJP: Anytime there is a gun in the home. It needs to be secured properly. After that step is taken conversations need to be had about guns and there dangers and what they are to be used for. This will also need to come with teachable moments all the time, if it were my child I would explain how disappointed I was and get counseling and help them to understand that there are consequences for everything we do, and help them to be more responsible and understand all that could have went wrong and why they need to be thankful no one got hurt.

Issue: Tim purchased a gun after someone broke into his garbage, he felt like it was needed to protect his family. His wife was apprehensive about bringing a gun in the household, meanwhile Tim Jr. was being bullied in school so he was watching closely where his dad kept the gun and took it to school for self-defense. Later on that day, Rebecca received a phone call from AP stating that someone needs to pick Tim; he will be expelled due to bringing a firearm to school.

Perspective: Apparently Tim did not take a firearms safety course to learn about security, and he needs more education along with his son, Tim is irresponsible and he is to blame entirely for his son's suspension and he needs to talk with his son about his lack of communication and the ramifications. A serious conversation needs to be held about firearms and consequences and everything that could have went wrong with this situation.

Knowledge: I guess I can understand where Big Tim was coming from when he purchased the gun, he wanted to make sure he bust a cap in someone's ass who was bold enough to come and mess with his shit; but at the same time, he should have sat with his family and explained the situation and emphasized that no one should ever touch the gun unless it was for extreme measures. Due to the lack of communication, his son will need to spend time at an alternative school, which sets him back from regular instruction in regards to taking foreign languages, physical education, and honors or GT-level courses.

Action: If I were Big Tim, I would find out who these bullies are and I would have a heart to heart conversation with them and their parents so they would know I am not playing around, and if they keep bothering my son, I will see that someone ends up permanently disabled; but before all of that, I will see if I could appeal the expulsion or at least reduce it down because my son has been a model student and has never been in any kind of trouble, so please reconsider this offense.

Consequences: The consequences to my actions could lead to more drama if the bullies' families take an ignorant stance and buck against my request; so I am sure Rebecca would be pissed with all the bravado I am displaying, but I could not have my son living in fear. I am pretty sure the expulsion will hold up unless my son reported it to the school personnel and nothing was done about it, and guess what, that could happen in some schools; never a school I work at, that is for sure, because I can't stand no bully unless I am doing the bullying and I would only do it to make a point.

Scenario 37 Summer Loving Happen So Fast

Your sixteen-year-old daughter who will be a rising senior in the fall ranked #3 in her graduating class who will be expecting to get several full-ride scholarships to college. Michael, twenty-two years old, just recently graduated from college with a Bachelors in Business Management, started fooling around with Page. Page had a crush on Michael since she was very young. Page ends up getting pregnant and now college may be pushed to the back burner. How are you going to handle this life-changing situation?

PC: If page is the name of my 16 yr old daughter then Michael will be enrolled at the University of Heaven for the Fall Semester.

CPM: Statutory rape, jail, and abortion, still going to college in that order.

CA: Isn't it illegal for a 22 yr old to have sex with a 16 yr old child? So Michael is a pedophile

KJP: I would be upset and very disappointed because I know I taught her better, but supportive. Page will continue with her education as long as she can until she has the baby and then I will help her out as day care, until she gets her degree. In the interim she and I will device a plan for her future that she will sign off on and if she doesn't I will go back to my original gangster thoughts. Let me know when you are moving in with Michael and I hope you caught a good one that is gonna take care of you and the baby. I'll babysit from time to time but call me first to see if I am available. I would let her know its okay if you made mistakes and learn from them but since you didn't, you gonna learn today.

CA: This is very complex family meeting time.

KJP: What I am teaching my kids early is have fun but don't get too involved and when you want to take it a step further make sure you know who raised him/her cause everyone is a product of their past and if you can't get along with his family friends and alike he's probably not the one. As far as my husband I can't speak for him but since he cares I know Michael would have to know that and hopefully thought twice about knocking our daughter up. I believe in mistakes, I don't believe in stupidity. So even though I would be upset I would for sure make sure she is set up for success and if Michael was my son he would sure man up and take care of his responsibility and we would help out when we can but I'm mom now and when I become a grandma I will show my difference and I would like to address though that I probably would have known about the crush… so that relationship would have been monitored from jump. I keep mine really busy so the only socialization they get outside of school is during sports; otherwise they are consumed with homework, so I'm not really sure how Michael wiggled his way through.

AA: I like this one David Glover, hits close to home. Daughter is 17 entering senior year lots of holes in this scenario as well, but nothing to make light of, as for an abortion there is nothing more precious than life. I can't by any means demand to end one, especially if I can't carry life but only initiate the process. That's her decision but I will definitely bring it up, because science has granted us that option. You have the ability to do whatever we can and as we grow you see that life has infinite possibilities. Life is by no means over, but my daughter threw one hell of a monkey wrench in her shit if she did get pregnant. This is going to have me go home and reinforce what's important to my girl. Birth control, promiscuity, and definitely the morning after pill. Clearly not enough marketing goes into lamb skin condoms for males. Anything is possible I've understood one thing as a parent, that they have the ability to control their life, but you will put chains on my life in that process. I love my kids with all my heart, but you going to have to live your life, and if that means having a baby at 16 or 17 then that's the life you live. I still love you regardless.

CA: A 22 yr old man having sex with a 16 yr old girl is nasty eww and more eww fucking disgusting.

AA: But it happens, a lot isn't right but this is not far off from what happens. 22/16 can be a sheltered 26/20 still has not yet developed.

CA: If the 22/16 scenario is hasty and ew I would love your take on homosexuality another time, another David Glover scenario. 2 consenting adults is a totally different story, not even comparable scenarios. A 16 year old is not legally able to consent in this scenario; the laws in NYS define this as 3rd degree statutory rape.

AA: I get it and it also against the law to smoke weed, so now let's move on from law and talk reality. It happens more than "ew" is all I'm saying and this scenario is not far from reality.

CA: You are comparing apple to oranges

AA: And apple to oranges aren't eww

CA: A child and an adult having sex is eww

AA: So your 16 yr old girl is pregnant and tell you its from a 22 yr old and you say "ewww", "ewwww, I'd rather it be from another 16 year old?

CA: My daughter wouldn't have the opportunity to get pregnant, since she is my responsibility until she turns 18, its called parenting.

AA: That lock and key approach

CA: It's called being present, presence

AA: Let these kids live a lil bit, your not going to be everywhere with your girl, and as soon as you shelter the shit out of them and they give you all the parental accolades. Valedictorian and Harvard bound; it can turn on you in an instant.

CA: I completely agree with you, it's about healthy boundaries and healthy balance of work and play. This scenario exemplifies unhealthy boundaries.

DP: What if it a 22 year old woman and a 16 yr old boy had sex and she got pregnant? Less than 50 years ago women married men twice and sometimes 3 x their age. I'm not saying its right or wrong, we allowed society to label an age for consent and now everything is rape. Truth be told two 16 yr olds having sex in certain states is considered rape and both children can be considered sex offenders for life and conviction. I agree a conversation and proper parenting is essential to prevent mistakes on all levels.

CA: Gender irrelevant

Issue: Sixteen-year-old girl who is ranked #3 in her class who is expected to get several full-ride scholarship ends up getting pregnant by a twenty-two-year-old Michael, a recent college graduate.

Perspectives: I will be kicking that twenty-two-year-old ass for getting my child pregnant, I would support my child, but a plan needs to be created and once she deviates from the plan, she needs to rely on Michael. I have no right to want to take a life if my child decides to keep her child, I would love her regardless; but before that happens, we will discuss preventative measures. A twenty-two-year-old and a sixteen-year-old is fucking and totally inappropriate. Society has dictated situations like this when it came to calling it rape, but these situations were happening a long time ago when men were impregnating women three time their age.

Knowledge: People know that this happens more than often; the only difference is instead of the twenty-year old having a bachelor's degree, he typically has his certification in street pharmacology. Complicated scenario with a lot to consider. Situations like this are usually based on the values of the parents, also you have to look at Michael's role in this, and does he have feelings for Page or did he watch her evolve from a little girl with a crush to a young lady that has filled out and has become irresistible.

Action: If Page was my daughter, I would be devastated with all the potential scholarships going down the drain. Michael and I would need to have a man-to-man conversation. I need to see where was he going with this relationship with Page, does he have a girlfriend already? I don't know if I would jam this young man up, but my interrogation of him would be pretty intense.

Consequences: This can play out in many ways but talking to Page would be imperative; finding out her perception of the situation would be huge. I simply need to know what Page's game plan is; does she think she is ready for this challenge? What does Michael's parents say about this issue? This situation would be a hot mess. The ultimate outcome that keeps playing in my head is Michael leaving town after landing a job or his college girlfriend showing up and my little princess going into a deep depression.

Scenario 38 Sweet Appetizer

Dr. Stewart, fifty-five-year-old professor at Grambling University had to make a quick stop at Wal-Mart to pick up a few personal hygiene items; as he was walking through the store and walking ahead of him was this curvaceous young lady that had Dr. Stewart borderline drooling. If anyone knew Doc, he was someone that still has swag, he did not look his age, he still walked with a dip, dressed nice, and was well kept; young and older ladies marveled at his attractiveness. When Doc went to check out, that young lady was the cashier. They stared at each other with amazement, she said, "Oh my God, it's Mr. Stewart, my old high school world history teacher, you were my favorite and I use to have the biggest crush on you. I was a child then but now I'm a grown woman." Patrice was very forward and wrote her number on the receipt also on the note saying "call or text me and trust me you will not be disappointed." Do you think Dr. Stewart will be wrong for taking Patrice up on her offer?

COJ: Do it!!!! She's an adult now, age aint nothing but a number

DP: Nothing wrong with it

KCJ: How many years have passed since he was her teacher? He needs to check to make sure he's not violating any code of ethics; Personally, I wouldn't date anyone old enough to be my parent, but to each his/her own, or young enough to be my child.

TS: I have been teaching for 18 years, and my grown (and not so grown) students ask me out all the time. I always say no, very strict rule for me. In my mind they are still fifteen and it would just be wrong. Age isn't an issue, but violating the teacher relationship is for me.

HL: No, he wouldn't be wrong, but he might have an issue with professional relationships and I'll say this much, I was a bit older in high school than the average student and my physics/biology teacher was just out of school and was very easy on the eyes. I don't think she would even think about it and she and I are much closer in age than this couple.

KP: If he is only looking for some sexual stimulation then why not, she is willing. If he is looking long term then he needs someone who can stimulate his mind intellectually and who has some generational commonality.

TS: You are right on. If there's more than 15 years, sex is their only commonality. Too far apart leads to different levels of intellect, no matter how mature she may be.

JE: Age difference is not the issue. What Dr. Stewart should be hesitant because of the difference between their socioeconomic status, As much as I would love to say that financial/job status difference shouldn't matter when it comes to love, fact is they most often do. Not saying that it should be out of the question but when faced with this type of difference anyone should proceed with caution. There are many people out there who have ulterior motives and someone could get hurt. Even if he were to say this is only a purely physical relationship he is still human and emotions can kick in at anytime.

LN: Say it JE, Add that too major age difference, this could be very bad for the professor, I see him getting his heart broken.

KM: No, I don't think he'd be wrong to call or text her. They both are consenting adults, but the professor might want to keep that on the low low. If he would date a former student who appears to be the same age as his current students. It may become an issue with his colleagues and people in power at the University.

HL: Rule of thumb when dealing with someone in any relationship that might include sex, only deal with someone who has as much to lose as you do. That way you are assured of them keeping their mouth closed about it. That doesn't mean I advocate for him to do it, it is just a word to the unwise. Now, with that statement in mind, how many of you **REALLY** think she is worth it even for an orgasm or two.

C2: This situation probably happens more than not, its all about KYP (Knowing your personal) if someone loves to run their trap, loose lips sink ships. Keep your actions between 2 adults.

LH: I can't imagine being attracted to one of my former students. Somehow, I think there's a fine line that you don't cross, no matter how old. Now, had one of my former students been LL Cook J, I retract my statement.

Issue: Patrice ran into former teacher; Mr. Stewart was currently a teacher who currently works for Grambling University. Patrice used to have the biggest crush on him and once they established a communication, she let Mr. Stewart know that she is a grown woman so she wrote her number on his receipt. What should Mr. Stewart do?

Perspective: She is a grown ass woman; age is nothing but a number. Dr. Stewart needs to check into the policy to see if he has not violated a code of ethics. This is just morally wrong, I would never date a former student. If Dr. Stewart is looking for sexual stimulation, go for it; but if she is looking for something long term, then their age will make a difference, they are on two different levels. Dr, Stewart needs to consider the difference in the socioeconomic status; you just never know if someone is trying to job you. Two consenting adults but how would this leak if it gets back to his colleagues. The essential question is would Patrice be worth the couple of nuts he will be getting, is it really worth it.

Knowledge: This situations happens on a regular basis, many man Dr. Stewarts age fall victim to visual stimulation of a nice juicy ass and they think about the fifty-year-old glad trash bag, somehow it does not compare so they are chasing the younger women and the younger women are honored to be dealing with a stable professional older man.

Action: If I were Dr. Stewart, I may touch basis with Patrice by having a nice dinner with her to see where her head is at and what her hidden agenda is and why she wanted to connect with me. If we have a good time, who knows former teacher may spank that ass around later on.

Consequences: As was mentioned earlier, the down side of becoming involved with Patrice is, what if she turns his old ass out? You become hook but at the same point she is not satisfied, or she becomes too needy, Every turning around she is in your pockets looking for something. That is why the initial date you need to put everything on the table and if she fits your measures then put her on the table.

Scenario 39 When Enough is Enough

Malik, a tenth grader who has been raised by his mother and grandmother, was always to be respectful to women no matter what. Well one day, he was pushed to the limit by a young lady named Hennessey. For whatever reason, she felt like picking with Malik. He was called all kinds of mama's boy, gay slurs, and bitches, but Malik maintained his composure while Hennessey tried to provoke him into fighting. Whenever Malik was in trouble, he always heard the voice of reason from his mother and grandmother and that would get him through. Hennessey continued to carry on with being verbally abusive, with her classmates cheering her on. Eventually Hennessey spit in Malik's face and he shoved her to the ground. At that point in time, the teacher finally intervenes, and some of the student's video tapes the incident. Hennessey threatened to get her brothers Cornelius and Christopher to handle Malik. Hennessey's brothers were gangbangers so Malik feared for his life. How can Mom and Grandma get Malik out of this hot water? What are some of the other issues that need to be restricted?

KCJ: 1st of all she shouldn't have spit in his face. She's lucky all her nasty ass got was pushed to the ground; He should have brought this to his mother's attention earlier. As a parent, I would of have politely went up to the school, and requested a meeting with Hennessey, her parents, Principal and others. If that didn't resolve the situation then, I'll just keep that to myself. As a parent of a bullied child I can tell you, strong words of encourage can nip it in the bud.

HL: There are many dynamics at work here; I don't believe that anyone should be made a target by their parents. That puts children at a disadvantage to stand up for themselves. Allowing not only promotes an increased confidence, but it build character by allowing them to learn and discern what is right or wrong either morally or otherwise.

2. I feel in this day and age, young males are being emasculated by women who think behaviors haven't changed from when they were younger promoting them to tell boys not to not meet a threat head on when confronted when potential harm particularly when it is done by girls/women. This is a no win situation for boys/men because they're going to be looked upon as weak and feeble by society thereby setting themselves up for more destructive situations later in life. Part of being a male is a physically ability and when that is neutered, males becomes ineffective at protecting themselves. Now, that doesn't mean that a boy/man has to fight at every turn or when a situation escalates, but it would be advisable that he knows how to handle himself in situations that could lead to a physical outcome. Being a punk or being bullied is something that no child should ever be forced into becoming by parents.

3. Avoidance is another tool that his mother and grandmother should have taught him. Being that the acts of bullying were known about, they should have made it a point to be proactive in his defense as opposed to telling him to turn the other cheek.'

4. Reasoning with bullies is like reasoning with a rock. Sometimes they only understand force and if that isn't projected, then they mark that person.

5. Street justice is cruel and there may not be much they can do other than to move Malik to another school district, but that may not solve his problem of being able to be bullied.

6. Karate classes would do him a world of good. The disciplines that the martial arts teach go beyond fighting and younger males gain a measure of many things that will serve them well in life and in situations like this.

MM: Wow spitting in the face, SMH, well I think the normal reaction for most peeps would have been beat the bricks off of anyone who does something so disrespectful. I'm not saying a woman ever deserves to be hit by a man, but we women do know how to push the limits, throwing telephones, setting cars on fire, running guys down with cars, destroying things. These are extreme cases, but this young lady needs to meet her match. He could of did more than just push her down, he could of beat her ass and look like a bad guy. I do agree with with HL. @ Some point he needs 2 learn how 2 defend himself. The sad part is . . . . Hennessey feels the need 2 treat him like this 2 get a reaction probably because he doesn't pay her any attn @ all. Then she provokes him, he reacts & now she's gets it lol @ . . . But, she'll probably start liking him more jus because he put his hands in her! Sad sad sad truth!

HL: Never looked at that angle and you know what; I've seen that happen haha!!

MM: It happens way 2 much!

MJ: Wow what a scenario to come back to. Where to begin? First, let me say I do not condone anyone putting their hands on anyone else. However, she deserved worse than that. Maybe not by him but sooner or later you reap what you sow she probably told she probably told some lies to amp up her brothers and now Malik has to defend himself AGAIN!!! I would file an incident report so that it's on file. I'm stuck on whether or not he should file a police report. He does have the video for proof, but sometimes the cops won't be of any help. He definitely needs to stay away from her, even if she tries to communicate with him and avoid females like her at all cost.

MM: But she's going to need her brothers a lot (who will end up in jail or worse) & that's when she'll calm her lil ass down! Because she's going to end up with a man who treats her just like she treats others & then reality will set n & she'll b filing the police report against her boyfriend or husband! Happens all the time, so sad!

MJ: Exactly MM

C2: Everyday our young people are faced with decisions to make like Malik its unfortunate that he has to go to school in fear, who the hell can learn like that, people we have to do better

EG: Malik should have wiped his face and turn the other cheek- Matthew 5:39 Never hit a women try and convince them of their worth in the earth!

HL: It's worse when teachers allow these types of things to happen!!

MJ: I sooo agree with that statement HL

HL: Trust me EG.There are ways to convince women without hitting that discretion is the best move for them!

C2: EG her mama should teach her self worth, most people would say if you kill my dog I am going to slay your cat

EG: Yes it is HL that's my statement, don't hit a women their role is of the weaker sex and protection should be applied instead of your fist. David, yes your right but then one would have to view the home environment, you said she has brothers that gang bang so discipline from a male figure seems to be out of the question. It appears their is no adult supervision in the home so society will have to train up the children for good or bad

CHB: I really have issues with this type of situation because I have been here before. My son had an issue with a girl at school and she punched him and ripped his shirt . . . .next time she brought something to school to cut him and was kicked out. At that point all I can tell you is I let him know she revoked her female pass.

DP: I think woman take advantage of men and their respect for them. At this point, I would have kindly instructed Malik to hit her in the throat and while she tried to catch her breath, to walk away. She wouldn't ever spit again. The lack of respect for herself and others is tragic. So many incidents like these are being posted on the web of girls fighting and having such lewd behavior. The lack parental intervention is alarming because if parents were actively involved this would not be so rampant. The girls are the aggressors and we are still teaching our young men to turn the other cheek. There is a problem . . . .I'm not sure if there is a quick fix.

MJ: lol although I know it's wrong I'm actually agreeing with you DP lol

EG: DP, love the post and I agree with you and feel like behavior is taught so it's so important to demonstrate to our children proper behavior and correct them when they are wrong even correct ourselves when we are wrong.

KP: In our schools there has been a big emphasis on bullying. They are teaching our children to walk away and tell an adult right away. The teaching does not stop at school. It also has to continue at home. Parents are counting too much on the school to raise there children. Patents are not involved enough!!! Yet they blame everyone else for the issues their children have. Mom and grandmother must get involve and notify the school . . . . . . Malik needs to be taught that no matter what he should never lay his hands on anyone . . . .if he does he is not any better then the bully!!! Knowledge is power!! He will need how to deal with his peers in a way in which he won't lose his dignity and maintain his "man" hood.

EG: KP: is pushing dialog something that's becoming a lost process . . .

CHB: KP, I called my child's school twice with no response. I then went to the principals office and introduced myself as the the parent that has been calling him and he won't return my calls. It was like a big joke.

The next time the principal seen me at a game he rolled his eyes at me. He's gone now. Thank goodness.

HL: I know of a situation similar to this in which the school permitted behavior that led to a situation and the principal didn't have a problem backing up the teacher telling the student not to tell on another student. Despicable behavior such as these needs to be eradicated in schools!!

CHB: I believe it HL. The principal at my son's school had the nerve to tell me his mother would have never come to the school for him for something like that. You can imagine my response and why he would roll his eyes at me when he seen me.

C2: The anti-bullying campaign is not aligned with parent and community beliefs, many kids are taught if someone put their hands on you, you better smack fire out of someone s ass and it doesn't matter who it is

MJ: That's true David. I hear parents tell their children "you either beat their** or I will beat yours"

HL: Not completely sure about your situation CHB, but I honestly think this a situation in which a male's presence would be received differently than females. I know it sounds sexist, but I think a 6' 220 pound male coming into a school with a (_._) chewing look would be 'feared'. It seems to me that a lot of schools officials don't look at women in that same light and that is terrible.

KP: CHB that's unfortunate . . . but we as parents have to have persistence . . . change has to start at home and as much as the principal ignored you . . . all the more reason for parents to keep pushing back!!! EG you are correct . . . dialogue is like a foreign concept now . . . digital age has taken over . . . Kids and parents do not have conversations anymore . . . ..Hence all the the issues this generation is having!!

AMS: The bible says turn the other cheek two wrongs don't make a right

HL: AMS, Only if that same rhetoric was applied during the crusades.

AMS: Amen

Issue: Malik finally got fed up and shoved the hell out of Hennessey after he was called all kinds of gay slurs, bitches, and everything under the sun. Malik was a very respectful young man who was raised by his mother and grandmother, but when someone spits in your face, at what point do you finally lose it, but of course you may be faced with retaliation.

Perspective: Arrange a meeting with this young lady's parents and if that did not work maybe I need to have a conversation with Hennessey. Parents should never put pressure on their children to fight. You should never encourage a man to hit a woman, but at times, there are ladies that cross the lines. Maybe a police report needs to be filed on this incident. At a certain point, females lose their female pass so an ass whooping is necessary. If you want to act like a boy, than I will treat you like one.

Knowledge: This situation really sucks for Malik because more than likely he will be living in fear and because Hennessey's brothers have gang ties; this may be the time for Malik's mother to transfer him to another school, because trust me, those losers will be coming after Malik's throat.

Action: It may be time for mom to get Malik's father or an uncle involved in this matter and maybe they can force someone's hand, so that Malik can be left alone. In certain districts, community mediations are held to bring families together to solve the issue, but trust me you have to have a strong mediator that is running the meeting or else it can become Jerry Springer City.

Consequences: Some way, shape or form Malik, may have to run into Hennessey's brother, hopefully they will have mercy on the young fella. If the community meeting is held, hopefully it ends up in a truce. The last option Malik may need to handle her brothers by all means necessary. Sometimes if you cut the head of the snake, the rest will follow.

CHAPTER 6

Work Issues

Scenario 40 Disappearing Acts

YOU GET YOUR homeboy or home girl a job working with you and for the first year everything is going well; he or she is well liked on the job. Suddenly for two straight weeks, they are a no show, no call; your employee continues to ask you about his or her whereabouts, you don't know because they didn't have the decency to notify you. They eventually get fired and shortly after you find out that he or she stop attending because they were having relationship issues at home. Does this change your outlook on your relationships with your friend?

MJ: I would say so because they didn't communicate with you and that makes you look at them in a different way. In addition to that your reputation may or may not be on the line now.

TA: There is no excuse so no it would not change the outlook for me. Regardless of what is going on at home it only takes 60 seconds to make a phone call/send a text to give you a heads up.

MJ: So true TA but everyone doesn't think like that. Calling would be my first thought, but I guess we don't know the entire situation.

C2: So TA where does that leave your friendship it shouldn't matter 2 weeks is crazy, I look at it as they said f me and the job

MJ: That's why I said your reputation may or may not be on the line.

TA: That friendship would be downgraded to an "association" but that's why I only have 3 friends. A real friend would not ever do that to a friend. I keep a small circle to avoid these types of potential problems in my life. My friends wouldn't go 2 minutes, 2 hours or 2 days without saying something if they knew that it would potentially have a negative impact on me . . . 2 weeks is just unacceptable, period.

CG: If your friend was too embarrassed to even tell you they were having relationship problems, then where did your relationship lye in the 1st place? Did u pick up the phone & ask "hey what's going on, you haven't been to work, something wrong? Yes we are responsible for our own actions & maybe this person did go about this the wrong way, but obviously this person was so consumed about other things it effected everyone around them. This is obviously a major problem & as a friend I'd be trying to support my friend by helping them to move on from this toxic relationship! Or get them some help!

CG: I would be upset & feel a little betrayed but I tend to be empathetic & try to understand they may not have intended to handle it that way. You don't know what they were going through. Like you said a whole yr of things going well then all of a sudden things change. Doesn't sound like a person that would just skip out on a friend like that?

CA: Communication skills are the issue here or lack of them, to be exact. It's causing problems with employment, significant other, and friendships. I would call this person to discuss my concerns.

KJP: No . . . Let them know how u feel and help them through their issue and see how it goes from there.

C2: So you are left picking up the pieces and looking stupid in the face on the job, it seems to me that work would be a safe haven from arguing all day at home

KJP: Taking things personally is one of the reasons so many of us have relationship issues today . . . as long as its not impacting you and your pockets . . . .let the person know where u stand and keep it moving. Harboring things and holding grudges causes health and relationship issues all day everyday. #weonlyhavecontrolofourselves

CG: It's funny because this exact thing happened at my job, not to me personally, but a girl that caught her boyfriend cheating was devastated! She just stopped coming. But what I didn't appreciate is how they bashed her on how she handled it. At that point it's not about you or anyone else. People were taking upon themselves to take it personal. When it's truly not!

C2: look it at like this you remain friends with that individual, there is a difference between personal and professional relationships, that person would lose the professional relationship we had and I doubt if he could get a reference from me moving forward, my name is gold and I refuse to let someone turn it into bronze.

CA: How about silver? LoL

C2: There is a silver lining to that lol

CG: And your are right as far as the professional end of it. You know now, that life situations get in this person's way& ultimately can affect you. But if your already stuck on how you feel& how you attend to go about it, w/out any possibility of being swayed to asses it differently Than why ask for an opinion? I hope this person is not your fb friend. Because what could have been handled between two adults is now out there to be judged by complete strangers. If they can't handle a relationship issue, I'm sure this just puts the icing on the cake.

C2: These are critical thinking scenarios that we have an open discussion about base on our opinions, perceptions, and life experiences, there is no wrong or right answers, CG slow down and relax

SF: Of course it would, b/c when you recommend a friend for a job it's your good name that's on the line.

RHS: sure would

C2: Tell me more RHS talk to me

RHS: Put your big panties on and handle your business the correct way, period! I have tons of days I wish not to come to work due to home issues but I have to pull my GIRL PANTIES on, and keep it moving . . . sometimes you feel better once you get away . . .

C2: RHS That would be my logic no need to add to your demise by losing your job which creates another issue

RHS David, your right, ya taught me well @ B.Stratton . . . ..Mr.Socks, LOL

David Glover RHS You were such the firecracker there but extremely intelligent.

Issue: Your homeboy/home girl who you got a job based on your merits, suddenly stop attending work for two weeks as a no show, no call. Your employee continues to ask you concerning his whereabouts but you have no idea. Eventually your friend ends up getting fired from the job. Shortly after, you find out he or she stop attending because they were going through relationship issues.

Perspective: There is no excuse for his behavior; a simple call takes sixty seconds, to keep you informed. Everyone doesn't think like that and we don't know the entire situation. Maybe the friend was too embarrassed to tell you about what was going on, and by the way, did you attempt to call your friend. As a friend, you should be supporting your friend to help them get out of their bad situation. Communication skills are imperative; it appears that it's causing issues at work, home life, and friendship. We should not take these situations to heart as long as it does not directly impact you.

Knowledge: What I know from this scenario is that his relationship really started having serious issues due to jealousy from his partner; he was doing well on the job, went from work study to part time, all the way up to full time status with benefits, so of course, he had swag going on considering where he came from professionally. This would annoy his partner because suddenly he went from wearing jogging suits to shirts and ties with a dab of ladies' killer to spare. His partner was jelly and would do anything to bring his confidence down a notch and hopefully he would lose his job, which he did.

Action: If I were this guy, first of all I would have showed up at work considering my homeboy was working so hopefully that would have took some of my toxic thoughts from home away. If I would have missed a day, it would have been to check my partner's ass to let her know I am making changes for the better and I need her support; and if I can't get it, we will need to go our separate ways. You should never let anyone take food off your table or money out of your front pocket.

Consequences: Either my partner would have gotten her shit together or let me free and someone else would have appreciated my talents and just maybe I would come up on an upgrade. The bottom line is that we need to be each other's biggest cheerleaders; if not, maybe it's time to opt out for free agency and just maybe someone else will be willing to give you a long term max deal.

Scenario 41 Empty Bed

Empty Bed
Cyrus, a fifty-year-old housekeeper at Susquehanna Memorial Medical Center, was very well liked around the hospital mainly because he knew his music. I don't care if it was country, R&B, hip hop, jazz, blues, or rock, he knew his music and he loves engaging people in these conversations. Many of his colleagues thought he would make an excellent music history teacher at a community college. Cyrus never pursued that interest any further; he has been working at the hospital ever since he graduated from high school, he also still resides at home with his parents. In a recent conversation, he shared with one of the

nurses that he never had a girlfriend and he remains a virgin to this day. The nurse asks was he interested in her helping him find a girlfriend, Cyrus agreed with excitement. On the outside, Cyrus appears to be socially awkward but he has a heart of gold on the inside. In a situation like this, should his dad be blamed for not schooling his son so that he can enjoy the enrichment of companionship? Certainly it's a father's duty to teach his son to become a man and to enjoy the fruits and labors of being a man; do you agree or disagree, talk to me.

TA: This one doesn't make sense to me. Why should his dad be blamed and how do you know it is his dad's fault? He is 50! At some point he needs to be responsible for himself and I'm thinking that was about 30 years ago. Being socially awkward isn't a manhood issue, so putting on his dad isn't fair to either him or his dad in my opinion.

KP: Seems as if his parents might have kept him a bubble. Not teaching him all aspects of life. Laying pipe is just one if them but what about his ability to function without his parents. Seems as if he is dependent on his patents for everything. His parents seemed to have held him back from living a life of a true individual. He is now 50 and is stuck in what is his "normal". Unfortunately I think him finding a girlfriend who will understand or put up with a man who is not self sufficient and has lived his life in a bubble I don't see it happening.

C2: TA, true I don't have all the ins and outs but this is the info I got and to me like KP said so how Cyrus remained in that bubble to long and to be honest he may never experience sex or love which saddens me.

MJ: I am disturbed by this. Not having a girlfriend isn't the big issue with me. The fact that he still lives with his parents and is 50!!!! That is just wrong on so many levels!!! However, before I get too harsh, I have to ask if this man is mentally impaired at all. It's a valid question because if he is then I can see that he has to be cared for by others. Or get assisted living like at Aspire.

C2: He has some social challenges

MJ: I don't have the expertise to answer this question appropriately then.

Issue: Fifty-year-old housekeeper who happens to be socially awkward. Shared with a nurse that he still was a virgin and that he never had a girlfriend; his interest is solely music over the years. When asked if he wanted her to find him a girlfriend, he was totally fine with that; currently Cyrus still resides at home with his parents. Should his father be the blame for his lack of male development?

Perspectives: His dad is not responsible for this; his job is to instill confidence in his son. At some point, Cyrus needs to be responsible for him, being socially awkward is not a manhood issue. His parents have kept sheltered in a bubble, which in turn he has been missing out on many of the essentials things in life, him finding a woman may be unrealistic at this point. I am disturbed by him not having a girlfriend, but he is fifty years old and still living with his parents. If he is mentally challenged, there are programs called Aspire.

Knowledge: Cyrus is a very nice young man who I assume that may be touch with Asperger's Syndrome so he is very socially awkward and can strike up a conversation about music and talk about an hour straight discussing the history and all the genres of music. It is highly unlikely he will meet someone unless he attends some programs or different events. His days more than likely consist of work than home.

Action: The reality is sad that someone's life is so structured and his parents have not taken him off the nipple to give him some freedom to grow and develop as a man. I hate to see what will become of Cyrus if something happens to his parents. I really think he needs to transitions into an independent living facility or at least attend a weekend program where he has the chance to socialize with others that may be at the same level mentally or some of the same interest. I think he could have taught a History of Music class at a community college, he is that informed or has that much in sight on music.

Consequences: More than likely Cyrus will grow old with his parents and remain America's most oldest virgin; I don't know all the family dynamics, it may be one of those situations where the rest of the family may say it's not our concern so they stay out of it and leave it in the hands of his parents until something happens to the parents and they have to deal with the fake ass Barry Gordy.

Scenario 42 It's All About Me

Milton and Shelby have been dating for six months, all along Milton has been working doubles three to four times a week as an X-ray tech saving up to pay for his nursing classes; on Valentine's Day, Milton forgot to get a gift for Shelby because he was working, which also happens to be his birthday. Shelby was so pissed that she ignored Milton's phone calls for the next several days. Did she overreact? If I am not mistaken, don't you think Milton's birthday should have superseded V-day?

SS: His birthday was definitely more important. Especially since he was working so hard for what could possibly be there future. Which makes me ask what did she get him for his birthday ok?!

C2: Shannon, she did get him anything her focus was V-day

HL: Milton should read the tea leaves and get out while he isn't committed to marriage. Anything else on his behalf would be a fatal error in my opinion.

C2: She couldn't see the big picture extremely single minded focused

HL: Which is all the more reason for him to leave her and that mindset alone? Go be with someone who values sacrifice and hard work. This female clearly doesn't.

C2: HL, I wonder how many women would speak to their real feelings not their FB feelings and side with Shelby, will the Real Slim Shadies please stand up (lol)

C2: Or maybe deep down he did not get Shelby anything because he is trying figure out who the hell is Valentine????

TS: If the birthday stuff wasn't there I would be irritated I didn't get a card or any kind of acknowledgment . . . which would have been communicated and a simple "I'm sorry" would have sufficed. But her forgetting his birthday trumps that to no end. I would have had dinner ready for him and the Valentine's gift would be after for both of us.

MJ: Birthday trumps V-day. She definitely overreacted. If she would have answered his call she would have found all this out. Selfish!!!

C2: TS, this goes back to Herbert's point from previous post, women and their expectations, just assuming and knowing she would be getting a gift, or better yet maybe feeling a sense of entitlement.

TS: Without the birthday consideration . . . it would depend how I felt the rest of the year. If he always made me feel special, Valentine's is just another day . . . I'm not one to ask about gifts though. Physical touch and quality time are my love languages . . .

JS: What it all boils down to is Feb. 14th is the worst day to be born if you're a guy . . . lol

MJ: lol at JS

MM: She should have understood that he's been working doubles all week and the fact that he hasn't gotten any sleep played a major factor. Because of his schedule they could've celebrated both V-day and b-day at a later time. It's not that serious! She could've @ least called to tell him happy b-day and V-day or text if she thought he was tired.

C2: my girl, lol, MM always can count on you to break it down

MM: Yea she's really closed minded. It's only V-day. It comes twice a yr, just called something different. If I were him I wouldn't answer her calls. His hard work will pay off and he'll get the women who admire his sacrifice later. She's not the one

MJ: Right MM . . . or she could have brought him lunch or sent him a text . . . anything. Small gestures do big things.

MM: The fact that he's busting his ass working like a damn slave . . . .. Should have made her do something big plus it's his b-day . . . .. She should have cooked him dinner, rubbed his back, etc . . . ..I'm sure, had this been planned out . . . It would been a g

MJ: yeah but if she was really into him instead of herself she would have realized what was going on before the day even arrived. This never would have been an issue.

MM: Exactly MJ . . . . . . She would have known his schedule and they could've planned to do something @ a later date and time . . . . Peps have to stop being so 1 sided.

HL: its comments and expectations like those Tonya, that men like me, kick women who think like that, back to Venus!!

HL: I let perspective mates know from day 1 that the only holiday I celebrate is Thanksgiving. Like Cool Moe Dee said . . . 'If it ain't tax, I don't pay that'

MM: Lol, well u not kicking me anywhere. I'm here to stay! U ain't go jus get a $2 pancake, bust yo ass all week and call it quits lol now deal with it.

HL: I don't do breakfast either unless she stays the night. So I guess it's something I don't have to deal with haha.

MM: HL and I'd NEVER eat at a Denny's'!!

YWB: Nope

C2: Sometimes people minimize others actions to cover up the nothing that they are doing.

Issue: Milton has been grinding hard to pay for his nursing classes and on Valentine's Day, which happens to be his birthday; he forgets to get Shelby a gift. Shelby is pissed and ignored Milton's phone calls for the next several days. Doesn't Milton's birthday supersede some made-up holiday?

Perspectives: His birthday was more important and considering he was working so hard; by the way, what did she get him for his birthday? Milton needs to get the hell out of the relationship fast and hurry. If the birthday equation was not there, I would be irritated as a women but considering it was his birthday, I would have had a nice dinner ready for him and the V-Day gift would have come after. What it boils down to that being born February 14 is the worse day a guy can be born. Shelby should have understood that he has been working hard and could have forgotten; these days could have been celebrated at a later date, trust me it's not that serious.

Knowledge: In some situations women can be so selfish when it comes to this superficial crap like V-Day, Sweetest Day, Christmas, and Mother's Day. Holidays that are created to boost the economy and the expectations they have for men that they will not live up to themselves. Shelby was flat out wrong and this scenario, Milton was working to save money to enhance his career and was not thinking about spending money because that is what the norm would do. I spend my damn money when I get good and ready to spend it, not because it's placed on a calendar.

Action: If I were Milton, I would let it ride out without contacting her. Personally I would call for a week straight if I cared for her, and if I didn't hear back from her, I would consider our relationship over and start putting my next plan together. If I decide to go back to Shelby, it will be on my terms and my slogan would be "Get in where you can fit it."

Consequences: The consequences to my actions are if Shelby falls back and start dating someone else, and my canine instincts kick in and I want to mark my territory but she objects. I am sure most decent looking women can find a man with Sucka stamped all over his face who would go for the bullshit that Shelby tried to pull; the question is will she respect this man in the long run, probably not. Keep in mind when you have the "It's all about me" mentality, then essentially you should remain by yourself that way; it's a guarantee that it will be all about you.

Scenario 43 It's Getting Hot Up in Here

Daniel and his supervisor have been flirting with each other for over a year; Daniel is a single thirty-two-year-old, while Aleya is thirty, but very unhappily married but will not leave her marriage because of her two young children. One day, Aleya mention that she had a dream about Daniel and woke up next to her husband sweating . . . bullets. She never gave Daniel the details of the dream just to keep him in suspense. Daniel decided to write Aleya sexual erotic letters at least twice a week; eventually Aleya became addicted and her desires became so strong for Daniel. One night when Daniel walked Aleya to the car, before she got into the car, he grabbed her gently and started kissing her. After this kiss, they became very close friends and Daniel became her confidante to listen to the stories about how her husband was cheating and paid her no attention. Eventually Daniel and Aleya confessed their love for each other and continued to fool around at work, but nothing happened outside of work because of Aleya's paranoia that her husband would find out. Sometimes the work is where you spend the most of your time. Have you ever grew an attraction for a coworker? How did you cool down that heat?

EG: Grass is always greener so you think until you get over and it needs to be cut as well. Ye are of God, my little children, and have overcome them: because greater is he that is in you than he that is in the world. (1 John 4:4 ASV). Excellent post Dave, putting the devil on notice!

C2: Thanks E, always trying to give the people something real but entertaining

MJ: Well it might be too late to cool down because now they might have soul ties. The grass might be greener but that's way more mowing she has to do now. It's not love either . . . its fleshly desires . . . lust. Oh and the husband, even though he's doing his own dirt, will eventually find out. Whatever is in the dark will eventually come to the light. I do understand where she's coming from though. I've been there and it took a whole lot of praying and divine intervention to get out of it.

C2: How did the divine intervention work?

TC: If Aleya wasn't married, it would be all fun and games. Unfortunately she is, unhappily or otherwise. They have already gone too far and now all they can do is decide who is going to quit and leave the job. That is rule #1 of a workplace situation, someone will have to find another job.

C2: What if they are both satisfied with their positions and finding another job is not an option due to the lack of jobs

MJ: I asked God to remove him from me and He did. That person no longer works with me or lives near me. I didn't have enough strength to do it on my own. I wasn't married, but I had a strong addiction to that person and that was bad enough. It took a long time, but now I can function like a normal person and that stronghold is gone. Yes TC, can't play with the enemy must put your foot on his neck-Joshua 10:24

TC: David - IDK what to do about that. My mother always said "Don't s*** where you eat" I take it one step further to include, I don't date anyone that lives too close to me, works with me, goes to school with me or is close to my family. Because I am not wiling to quit my job, move, change schools or not be close to my family

MJ: I live by that now TC but I had to learn the hard way. Thank God I'm not a knuckle head anymore

C2: So where would you meet a decent partner, if not at work, school, maybe at a bowling alley, donut shop, or piggly wiggly.

TC: David - I have found the easiest way to meet someone is being third wheel with a girlfriend and her boyfriend. He will get tired of being cock-blocked and hook you up. No effort involved

MJ: Ha! I didn't even think of that . . . I might try that. Thanks for the tip.

C2: You are a professional cock blocker wow

MJ: hahahahaha

HL: Yes. With a shower afterward, SMH@some of the replies . . .

KP: Never dated anyone at work . . . I'm a supervisor and I feel it would compromise my authority and my integrity . . . .I just keep them as eye candy!!!!!

HL: KP: Best that way!!

Issue: Daniel and Aleya have been flirting around with each other for over a year; Aleya had a desirable dream regarding Daniel with her husband next to her. Aleya decided to plant the seed to Daniel to let him know he was in her thoughts; this led to Daniel to draw up inferences and he started writing Aleya erotic letters. Soon after, they begin to share kisses and personal conversations during work hours, but never outside of work. Aleya always made sure to leave this passion at work due to her being worried her hubby would find out.

Perspectives: The grass always seems to be greener on the other side; it's the devil at work. Sooner or later, her husband will find out; whatever is in the dark will eventually come to light. They have gone too far and now one of them needs to decide who will quit their job, don't shit where you eat. Rules of dating never date anyone that lives too close to you, coworkers, classmate, or someone close to your family. Dating someone as a supervisor, you would be compromising my authority and my integrity. Keep them as eye candy.

Knowledge: This situation never amounted to anything because of Aleya's inconsistent behavior and her willingness to take risk outside of work. Eventually Daniel relocated to another state and they talk periodically. They plan to get together when he came to visit but nothing ever jumped off although she eventually left her husband. So Daniel had to take her for what she was—a bullshit artist.

Action: If I were Daniel, he was better off just walking away from this basket case; I think he was more caught up in the fact that he never got the goodies and clearly it was something he wanted, but is it worth to compromise his heart? Being they no longer have to see each other, it makes it that much easier.

Consequences: If Daniel would have got with Aleya, my concern would be she was going to eventually get back with her husband and that would have left Daniel hanging out to dry. Sometimes we want what we can't have; even when you get a sample, you may have to be satisfied with just that because in cases like this, someone will get overcooked, and if you keep playing with fire, someone surely will get burned.

Scenario 44 Pimping Pastor

Scenario: You are doing your weekly errands; you are on your way back from an in service and decide to stop at a Target you don't typically don't go to; as you are walking in, you see your pastor holding hands and kissing on another women that isn't his wife. Do you return back to that church, do you say something to him at the time you witness his actions, or do you say who am I to judge and keep it moving?

JLO: M.Y.O.B!!

AB: Now that's deep I got to get back at you but that one that's a shame Give me a minute.

JP: That's why I skip church altogether. Don't need to complicate my life further.

LN: Walk up and say "Hello", how is Mrs. doing? See you in Church Sunday? Will you be preaching this week? I'm going to need to have a meeting with you after church, and then take a picture.

EG: Tape all you can then you approach him in a respectful manner and calmly share your disappointment in his action but it seems unlikely this scenario would be reality because just like the dark and perverted world he would have tried to conceal it to the best of his ability being in the open is unlikely. Then you allow him to address the church on his own or you assist him by doing it yourself. Provide him with the same grace God has provided you but insist he step down for the better movement of the church. Leaders have a protocol written in the word concerning behavior 1 Timothy 3:1-7 no one is above approach. Then start the search for new leadership and the rebuilding of the torn congregation.

KLC: -it, the devil knew scripture and how to use it to his advantage- Jesus in the wilderness . . .

EG: JP, don't let man allow you to miss out on the best thing that ever and will ever happen to you.

C2: EG I like your take on this but I disagree with this not being realistic because what if his mistress got tired of being in the dark and wanted to be seen in the sun light.

KM: I would ask if his side piece has a sister.

JP: EG, I'm a product of Catholic Schooling all of my life. Elementary, HS and College. I have been to church thousands of times; however what has the Catholic Church taught its parishioners over the last 10-15 years regarding how they handle corruption and scandal?

EG: Dave, she understands her role upon taking it so you have to play that part but God would send the Holy Spirit to speak with her and the preacher any way, the question is who would listen and repent showing Godly sorrow. That reminds me of Isaac and Rebecca, they had Essua and Jacob. Rebecca wanted to circumvent God's will-read Genesis 27:1-41

EG: Jerry, great example of how man has profited off Christ but never provided those who were follow them Him in an intimate way. Lets time you start an authentic relationship with your Father in heaven and read the manuscript of life and you will find your destiny in the earth.

EG: KM, spoken like a Pharisee, why don't you hang Him on the cross? Again!

BP: Walk up to them n says hi pastor n First Lady as if it was his wife. Then if she'd said I'm not his wife then Opps I know you're married sorry. N keep walking see yawl.

MMA: That happen to me I was working at I hop in N.C. and I seen the preacher man with some one else. And to answer the question I don't know I didn't tell on him I said the lord will take care of that . . . MYOB!!!!!!

AA: I expect it

C2: Aaron why do you expect those actions from supposedly such a powerful, influential individual

AA: Because I don't give him that power. Anything is possible, and that scenario is not far fetched at all

C2: Understood brother

EG: AA, man disappoints but God- and hope maketh not ashamed; because the love of God is shed abroad in our hearts by the Holy Ghost which is given unto us. (Romans 5:5 KJVDA). Know Him for yourself so you can show yourself approved!

SG: Hypocrite. I'd probably not confront directly, but let him know I'd seen--and never return to that church again. (If in this hypothetical scenario I even went to church. Hypocrisy is one of the reasons I don't.)

AA: You better go get sum God girl!

EG: I'm with you AA; I am encouraging all to find a personal relationship with God. My plea is that we go beyond our finite thinking . . .

SG: No thanks.

MJ: Who's to say this man was placed as Pastor by God? He might have placed himself there and gave himself a title. Yes everyone makes mistakes but the Matthew 7 says in verse 18 A good trees cannot bring forth evil fruit; neither can a corrupt tree bring forth good fruit. 19 Every tree that bringeth not forth good fruit is hewn down, and cast into the fire. 20 Wherefore by their fruits ye shall know them. 21 not every one that saith Lord, Lord shall enter into the kingdom of heaven; but he that doeth the will of my Father which is in heaven. Pastors are held highly accountable for their actions and if they're not bearing any good fruit I wouldn't be sitting under their teaching in the first place. All I would do is let him see that I see him and walk away. I would pray for him and let the Lord deal with his sin. I have my own issues to fix.

TC: The Pastor is still just a man, he is not perfect and I don't expect any pastor to be. I would speak so that he knows I saw him and Sunday we will pray and repenting together because we all sin. The pastor is not the one who is supposed to teach you how to live, so don't follow his or anyone else's example, that's what the Bible is for.

Issue: You were out doing your weekly errands; after leaving service, you stop at Target and guess who you see—your pastor holding hands and kissing on another women who wasn't his wife. What should you do?

Perspective:

Mind your damn business, that is why I don't do church altogether, don't need any unnecessary drama. Make sure you speak, ask will he be at church next week, ask for a meeting and snap that picture. Insist that he steps down from his position at the church. Ask if his side piece has a sister since we know that she gets down like that. I come to expect things like this because I don't give him that kind of power.

Knowledge: This pastor is known for this behavior, but no one has ever said anything because he is a powerful man in the community; but no matter how much bad he does, he does so many great things with the youth, so people tend to put the blankets over their eyes and keep it moving. Does not make it right, but who are we to judge, a freak will be a freak. Hey, the man likes women; it could be several other scenarios, such as liking other me, or little boys, so this should be a sign of relief.

Action: I would keep it moving because like someone else mentioned, he is a man, he is human and I don't hold him high on a pedestal; he just happens to be someone who delivers a good word. When you start worshipping people, that is when you become devastated when they disappoint you. The only person who you really trust is yourself because that is all you have control over and sometimes we can't even trust ourselves.

Consequences: If everyone continues to turn their head, what kind of congregation are we really building, something based on lies and deceit? What about his poor wife, what about her? She knows what is going on; she chooses to stay because of the glam life and the financial security. The problem many of us have is that we are always in others business, and if we used half of the energy on us, we can work on making us a better us. Pimp on player to you can't pimp anymore; just remember sooner or later this will bite you in your tight high wasted suit wearing ass.

Scenario 45 Show Me the Money

You have been married to someone for over seven years; depending on your situation, your man had recently got a promotion on his job so you two had been looking to purchase a home, but suddenly you received a phone call stating that you have been offered a job as a nursing supervisor at the biggest hospital in the ATL offering you forty thousand more a year, this means you will need to relocate. Your husband refuses to leave because he hates the south and also because he just got a promotion, so he tells you moving is not an option for him or you. Do you stay or leave?

TG: Marriage is about compromise . . . . Weighing out the pros and cons . . . Hating the south is an excuse . . . money pays bills . . . not convenience . . .

C2: Tee so what would you do?

TG: I'm going to go get my 40000 a year . . . I want to be successful too not a moocher . . .

C2: So you leave based on your selfish needs and throw away everything you have built with Leroy

KP: Money only buys happiness for a while . . . if you and your mate r happy now r u willing to give that up for 40000 a year for a lifetime if happiness

TG: What if I were the one always making sacrifices . . . been there done that . . . making many sacrafices entitles you to be selfish sometimes . . . marriage isn't about "I AM MAN HEAR ME ROAR"

TG: NOW IF I'M HAPPY WITH YOU AND THERES NO FINANCIAL BURDENS . . . I PROBABLY WOULD STAY

C2: It's 40000 more a year; currently she makes 50000 now this raise would push her salary to 90000 a year

KP: Conversation, communication, compromise

C2: KJC, he doesn't want to leave what's to talk about, he doesn't want to ride on his woman's coat tail

KJC: Smdh @ ride coat tails.

C2: He is clocking 60 gees, you and he have no children but he has one son from a previous relationship that will be a junior this year

MR: Stay!

MJ: Forget about your "feelings". Both parties should pray and see what God says about the situation. If you're in the will of God then no matter what you will do you will prosper.

MMA: Well it sounds good on both sides south is good, if two people love each other they will work it out . . . i had to leave the south cause i didn't have back u and i have to start over it's hard being a single black woman, with a child and know good help im just saying, who and who need to talk...Because I wish I could have it like that word@ god is good . . .

C2: @MR why stay? @MJ That sounds good in theory but decision need to be made in a short turnaround@ MMA you are a strong sister that knows how to soldier things out I am sure it will all work it self out

MMA: Thank you and you will work it out to . . .

CA: Where does the son live?

C2: With her mother but spends a lot of time with dad

CA: The son lives with his Mom nearby his father and stepmother?

C2: Yes they all have a great relation ship as well

CA: What about his son? This is a crucial time in his life. He needs his Dad.

C2: So stay or leave

CA: Why was this person even applying for jobs out of town? This doesn't make any sense to me . . .

MMA: Will the dad have a job when goes to Atl.

CA: How far is Atlanta from where they live now?

C2: It was a personal connection her Aunt gave her s job lead

C2: MMA he doesn't have one he will need to apply. They currently live in VA

CA: What are the reasons the father doesn't want to move? Besides the ones listed in your question . . .

C2: He hates the Deep South, he just a promotion himself, his son is a junior and high school and his mother is elderly and lives alone

MMA: Now wait he will have to apply, so he will leave the other job and move to a different place with no job . . . then he will have to go in to savings to keep up and so he still be the man in the house?????

C2: Yes Maya exactly how do you feel about that?

CA: How is there relationship/marriage? Is it solid? If yes, then I'm staying. This is a good man with his heart and morals in the right place. Done deal, I'm sorry imp not a selfish woman I'm a loving woman and this is not right, even though she going to be ballin but in the mean time in between time he is a man and he has pride . . .

C2: Engaged to be married summer of 2014

CA: Is the relationship on solid ground?

C2: Yes had been solid until this offered has been put on the table

CA: Is she happy in her career in Virginia?

C2: She is okay but her goal is to become a nursing supervisor

CA: Okay. Is it possible for her to become a nursing supervisor in her current city?

C2: Possible but not guaranteed, ATL offer will give her a 10% increase every year

CA: Okay and what about her relationship? Will they maintain a long-distance relationship or break up? What city in VA? I'm calculating the cost of living differences.

AH: wow dat wuz deep I would follow ma hart

C2: As far as their relationship I don't have the answer, they currently live in Richmond

AH: wow

CA: The money is significant but cannot buy love. Personally, I would stay, if she loves this man. Money only buys more stuff. LoL :)

C2: What's up AH how are you? Stay or leave

PF: Sounds like an open door blessing to me. I think she should take it and he stay where he is until he finds something as well. Her blessing may be an upgrade for their future and if she misses out on that because he just doesn't want to move, it may end up causing strain on the relationship

C2: Patrice good point if she declines it and their relationship turns sours will this constantly is thrown up in Leroy's face.

CA: Why would she do that if she's making the decision to stay? She would be mad at herself then, not him.

PF: Naw . . . .it would be at him because she would feel like she only said no because HE didn't want to move. That's reality. You would think she would be mad at herself but it would come out on him

CA: Yeah but he's thinking about his son and elderly mother not just himself. Well if she feels that way, then she needs to just move because that's ridiculous.

C2: CA it may be difficult for some to balance between career goals and family. Does Leroy need to think about moving moms down and have LJ (Leroy Jr) maybe apply to colleges when the times come in ATL?

PF: That's true.

CA: I think a family meeting would be a great option to discuss all of the options.1

C2: We have to make all situations a win win and many times that is the problem we don't balance shit out

C2: Yes and that's a great idea a family meeting with all parties involved, in fact that would be nice for most families to have a meeting monthly to catch up and parents can provide supervision on certain topic areas with their children

CA: That way they can creative problem solve together to create the best resolution possible. :)

TM: EG should answer this question

C2: I am sure he will, but I would like to hear your opinion

PG: Dave you be trippin moral you stay because your united as one and money can be the root to all evil, ghetto ass wife leaves for money but guess what her ass will suffer!!!!!!! Love ya, The LOVE of money is the root of evil . . .

PG: thank you understood

C2: Physs remember these are scenarios that open up wonderful dialogue, why do that woman have to be ghetto because she is chasing upward mobility

PG: you looked wrong this is what most wives will do. when united in marriage let him lead he is to carry the house hold not what is brought in its what is done with it if his job is done all is well no need to t chance the dollar

C2: Unfortunately this is a new day and people think totally different it's about that mighty dollar

EG: The only response to this scenario would should be-And the rib, which the Lord God had taken from man, made him a woman, and brought her unto the man. And Adam said this is now bone of my bones, and flesh of my flesh: she shall be called Woman, because she was taken out of Man. My opinion is that folks do not believe on God to help them through situations. Everyone tends to look toward society standards to dictate how their life should be and ultimately turn out. If you are a true believer know that God sets you up and puts you down. And if you are disobedient, he will put you down as fast as he lifted you up. Degrees and all. And know that most times what looks like a great opportunity may not be so great.

CA: Could be a test . . .

EG: Not a test if it does not line up with His will for your life, God needs to be consulted on this scenario-couple in prayer!

CA: So then it's a temptation.

CA: Okay . . . yes . . . that makes sense Eric. :)

EG: Gen 3:1: Now the serpent was more subtle than any beast of the field which the LORD God had made. And he said unto the woman, Yea, hath God said, Ye shall not eat of every tree of the garden? Who are you listening to?

C2: Who said God's will didn't direct her to ATL

CA: Did they pray about it yet?

EG: God's will brings peace not strife. Because as the male you have been selected (Adam)-And the Lord God said, it is not good that the man should be alone; I will make him a help meet for him. Therefore shall a man leave his father and his mother, and shall cleave unto his wife: and they shall be one flesh. (Genesis 2:18, 24 KJV)

Issue: The wife has been offered a job in ATL as a nursing supervisor at the biggest hospital making 40,000 a year; the only problem is that the husband just got a promotion himself and he hates the south. He states this is not an option for you or him. Does she stay or go?

Perspective: Marriage is a compromise weighing the pros and cons, I am going for my forty thousand more a year. The question is if you are willing to give happiness away for forty thousand more a year. They need to pray and see where God leads them in the future. If she loves her man, she will stay and realize money does not buy happiness. Open blessing for her, take it and he stays where he is at until he is able to find something.

Knowledge: Forty thousand a year is life-changing money and an offer that comes once in a lifetime; this offer needs to be discussed with strong consideration. But in the same breath, I understand a man will be a man in sometimes that comes with being a very close minded. If he puts his pride to the side and opens his eyes, he would see a better future for both.

Action: If I were the man in this situation, I would look at the market in my profession and see if a transfer is possible. I would also consider if she is going to be someone that lets money change her because I don't want any bullshit once we get there about she is carrying me because she is making more money. The house issue has to be looked at closely because it may be much cheaper to purchase a house in Atlanta, and you will get a better bang for your buck.

Consequences: This is a very tough call because if she turns down the offer and never gets an opportunity like that again, then I am sure this will come up on a regular basis. Situations like this are tough for many men because to follow your wife for a career move may appear that you giving up control. Situations like this can't be rehearsed, it's something that test your strength of your relationship, values, morals, and beliefs. If money is the basis of growth in your relationship, then the choice is made; she will be leaving his ass on the next plane and she does not know when she will be back again. Men, if your woman has an opportunity like, this please don't shoot it down without any consideration; there is no "I" in team, do what you expect your wife would do for you.

Scenario 46 Time for Myself

Wilbert was a carpenter and work many long hours, and some days or nights, he just needed some time for himself. One evening, he was working late, he decided to stop at the local bar and grill for a late dinner in a couple of cocktails; his wife text him a couple of times but he just did not feel like replying. Sherry (wife) decided that she would drive down to the bar and grill; as Wilbert was walking out, Sherry came up to him going off on Wilbert, calling him a fucking liar and he is the biggest bull shitter because earlier he stated he was coming straight home, mind you she had been out with her friends earlier. This was Sherry's second episode this month; on a more serious note, Wilbert was getting tired of it. Earlier this month, Wilbert had decided to order the Mayweather vs. Maidana boxing match as a way to unwind after a long workday. Sherry got the bill and she confronted Wilbert and asks who the fucked ordered this for $69.99? Does Wilbert need to re-evaluate his marriage? And why don't women give men the necessary space they require when needed?

HL: Yes he does, Control? I'm not sure why anyone doesn't want to allow for their mate/partner to have some time to unwind.

MJ: He should have told her he was going to the bar. If after that she still went off then she would have been totally wrong. I say this because he told her one thing and did another which made look suspect. Now I do admit she overreacted as women do sometimes and she could have handled that differently. Although he works he could have told her about the fight. They do pay bills together. I think this relationship has a lack of communication and these inviting problems.

TS: Communication is the key I wouldn't have an issue with my man stopping at the bar but it appears like he is being deceitful if he isn't giving her the courtesy of letting her know and that goes both ways. It's not that he went but that it looked like he was hiding something.

C2: Considering she was running the streets with her friends, why in the hell does he have to report to her when he steps out.

HL: Lol, sometimes in order to cover the obvious, the other angles are left to the wind. I wondered how she knew he was where he was? If he was actually trying to be deceitful, then why go where he could easily be found? Appearances are deceiving and that is why one should ask before out right condemnation of a person. He giving her his whereabouts would have has been met with the same hostility. That has been shown. The best way to drive a man away is to nag him unnecessary. She is well on her way to do that.

TS: But she tells him she was going out? If so she should expect the same courtesy. Again the issue shouldn't be that he went out but that the communication might not have been open and honest.

HL: Let me ask you this question. Is it necessary to know where your mate is at all the time? If so, then should have answered the text, if not she is out of line.

TS: Of course not but he said he was going home and didn't. Then didn't answer texts. Lies of omission are still lies. A good woman doesn't need to know where her man is at all times but common courtesy would be to at least let someone know when you won't be home. Like I said this goes both ways. Yes she overreacted severely but he was inconsiderate.

HL: I don't overlook his behavior, however that shouldn't give anyone carte blanche to behave that way.

Issue: Wilbert was a very hard worker and at times like to have time for himself; the problem is when he does not communicate with his wife, she loses her cool and goes off. Is this necessary, her reaction.

Perspective: She has control issues. He should have told her his plans; he told her one thing and did another, not cool. Communication is the key to at least have courtesy to let her know his plans. The best way to lose a man is to keep nagging him about things. Due to his lack of communication, it appears he was hiding something.

Knowledge: One of the pivotal factors is that I believe that Wilbert had cheated on his wife previously; but because of that, does that give her the right to behave like this and will she always treat him like a big kid because of her insecurities?

Actions: Wilbert has a lot to think about in regards to his wife; if this was me, and because I messed up in the past, I would let her know when I need time for myself, but it will mean just that, I need my time alone especially if I had a long and grueling day. If she could not accept that then our situation would turn into us needing time away. Not to minimize her feelings, but when you decide to take someone back, the trust has to begin somewhere; if you can't take it, and you faced with irrational thoughts on the regular basis, it may be time to go separate ways before the tension builds up and something physical takes place.

Consequences: If you two decide to stay together, it will be times of rough patches, but the intermittent explosive behavior would need to stop because who's going to tolerate that behavior. I would really be concerned for Shelly's mental health because if Wilbert is not where he said he was going to be, that will be a trigger for her to go off. If Wilbert decides to leave Sherry, I believe that she would make his life a living hell; so in the grand scheme of things, Wilbert needs to change this thought process to "Time for Myself" to "Time for Sherry."

Scenario 47 Three Way Split

Twenty-year-old Alexa called her dad to complain about her mother Cathy and stepdad Mason. Alexa's issues was that she wanted to move out and get her own apt. Her dad asked what is going on at home. Alexa is a full-time student at community college and works three days out of the week bringing home 325 dollars every two weeks. Well recently

Cathy has told Alexa she will have to give her more money toward bills, in fact they will split the bills down the middle three ways between Cathy, Alexa, and Mason. The ironic thing is Mason does not have a job. Her dad was upset and didn't think this was fair; Alexa asked her dad not to say anything to Cathy, how much would you expect, you're twenty years old to pay? Should her dad say something to Cathy on the strength that his daughter is getting taken advantage of by Cathy and Mason?

DP: Do I really have to answer this? Really David . . . .FRFR

C2: Yes you do, this is not cut and dry

DP: I know everything is not black and white. So is Mason on disability or incapacitated in any way that he cannot work or contribute? I mean Alexa for the most part is still a dependent and possibly because she is in college dad could still pay child support until college is complete. Some parents make their children pay as a life lesson but not to support the household and sometimes every mouth has to contribute out of necessity due to financial hardship. I guess the real question is does Alexa not know enough about the situation to know that her $$ is important to the maintenance of the household or does she know that her $$ is not needed and is wasted.

C2: Mason lost his job due to drinking on lunch break, I would say 200 a month is suffice for Alexa to contribute, in addition Cathy has 2 other kids by Mason, Mason needs to step his game up

DP: Definitely. Mason is the problem and has a problem. Then Alexa anger is justified. She looks to her parents to support her and her siblings and be responsible. Mason let them down. Cathy should be expecting Mason to be a man, and cover his responsibilities as a father, now Alexa is at a crossroad, either complies with what's being asked of her my mother, or is a responsible young lady and gets an apartment of her own, especially if dad is willing to help.

LN: If you're over 18 and you're working, you will be subject to a contribution, it's based on how much they earn, they will never leave the nest, if it too easy and free to stay

TF: It's okay for Cathy to have Alexa contribute to something in the household, to teach her responsibility . . . .such as a cell phone bill, car insurance or a utility bill. Mason being the "man" of the house should be doing way better than what he is doing. How does Cathy expect Alexa to split the bills 3 ways when it's only 2 of them working??? I can certainly understand Alexander being upset that she has to pay and Cathy is supporting her man!

TF: Yes the father should say something but he needs to be prepared to help his daughter get her own place.

TC: Hmmmmmm good one. Good for Alexa for being a full time student. She should not have to contribute as much as her mother and stepfather. Maybe she should move in with her father. Good for her for being responsible and holding down a part time job while still being in school full time. Her lazy butt stepfather should find a job. Lazy sucka.

HL: As long as it is a true 3 way split, I don't see much harm. I would if I were her father) see how much she can do on her own and be willing to subsidize her living on her own.

HL: Or Alexa could find someone as dependable as her, move in together and I'm sure she'd discover that 1/3 is better than 1/2

C2: HL, Mason isn't working, Alexa focus should be on school, I thought the goal is to put your children in a better position than you are, Cathy and Mason need to step their game up.

HL: Mason's lack of employment is not the issue. Here is why:

1.Mason has the ability to get a job. With the income he would be earning, it would NOT offset what she would have to pay IF the bills are indeed split 3 ways. My advice to Alexa would be to see the bills, do the math and look for a place and roommate who would be willing and is responsible as she is. This will teach Alexa an invaluable lesson about dealing with men who are not able to maintain employment as well as money management. An indirect result of her mother's choice can turn out to be a huge benefit to her when she chooses a mate. All lessons learned as young adults aren't always clearly visible. She will reflect back on this time and realize it was a blessing in disguise. Mason and Cathy may need to become better role models, but Alexa will have to deal with the realities of paying more than 1/3/ of home expenses one day. Better learn while she has a safety net of only 1/3. Call me tough, but if children aren't taught as a young age, then I'd say someone is doing them a disservice.

C2: Just maybe Cathy does not want the best for Alexa, and deep down she is jealous and wants to make it hard for her

SF: I understand the lesson that we're supposed to make this a better world than what we found it, and that our offspring deserve special consideration for getting a leg up from us, but in this day and age, where people that do their best sometimes find themselves in circumstances where they have a hard time finding employment that pays a living wage after years of paying into our system, it hits hard.

At the same time, when my family was doing fair to well, and I got my first job, I was expected to contribute, b/c it wasn't all about me.

In this case, she has to consider the costs that she'll rack up living there, compared to what she would have to put forward living on her own, with a roommate, or roommates, and figure it out from there. It would be nice if they could give her 6 months to save up for what she needed without them, because that is fair.

TC: It is a good idea for children (well an adult) living in the household should contribute something but the first thing her mother needs to do is get rid of the dead weight. Her dad should not get involved unless he is willing to let his daughter live with him. What goes on in their household is really none of the dads business.

C2: Even if his daughter is getting drag down mentally with their comfortable being uncomfortable attitudes

TC: As a parent, that is a sensitive area, telling another parent what they should or should not be doing in their house, where you don't pay any of the bills. Alexa is an adult and she needs to tell her mom what she is comfortable paying. As her daughter, she should not be expected to pay a third of the bills because there are 5 people in the household, at the max she should pay is 1/5 of the bills. Mason needs to be a man, as a women and a mother I am not comfortable with a grown man in my house not providing for his family, I couldn't respect him.

HL: How did you get 5 people? I see only 3.

TC: In David's comments he stated that the mom and step dad have 2 other kids.

HL: Ah, I see, but do you really expect two children to pay bills?

TC: No but I expect their parents to take care of them not their older sister

Issue: Two adult's parents not doing what they supposed to do instead of teaching their daughter responsibility by letting her give money toward household expenses, Cathy (Mom) decides they will split everything in 1/3; the problem is Mason is not working. Alexa is upset with the proposal and calls her dad for money to move out. Should Dad confront Mom about this matter?

Perspective: Is Alexa's money a necessity to the household expenses or it is being wasted. Why isn't Mason working? Cathy needs to tell Mason to step up his game; maybe if Alexa's dad can help, maybe Alexa will be better off finding her own apartment. If you are eighteen, a contribution is required, if not, you will never leave the nest. Alexa should contribute something to the household such as a utility bill. As long as it's a three-way split, this should not be a problem.

Knowledge: The bottom line is Cathy does not hold Mason accountable; if your child is attending college fulltime that is the golden ticket does not make her pay one third of the household bills that is added stress that she does not need while attending college. Put the pressure on your man, why are you letting him off the hook, are you really that damn desperate? Our jobs as parents are to build up our children and not tear them down. One minor bill is reasonable for a twenty-year-old to pay.

Action: If I were Alexa, I would see the availability of living with her dad because this environment she is living in is toxic and I strongly believe they are going to continue to milk Alexa, which will eventually impact her studies. It's always adults that make poor decisions that impact their children. Alexa, run as fast as you can to get the hell away.

Consequences: I am sure if Alexa left, this would cause a hardship for her mother's household; but the truth of the matter, the hardship falls on Mason who decides he wanted to start happy hour early at work. Once he got fired, he showed Cathy his loyalty was not to his family obligations. Word to Cathy, Alexa is not your damn man, tell Mason to clean up his shit he created and cheers to that.

CHAPTER 7

Friendship Issues

Scenario 48 Don't Hate Participate

DON'T HATE PARTICIPATE, Doug was given an opportunity to join an online business; he was someone who did it the right way, went to school has a bachelor's and master's degree, he has climbed the ladder slowly but surely but never felt that was enough. Doug hates to be shackled by any job and wants to create wealth; he ask three buddies to jump in the fire together. His boys was hesitant and declined because of fear of change. Doug decided to go off on his own and linked up with some coworkers and now each one of them are making a residual income of three thousand a month extra income. Doug's savings is growing steadily, he is vacationing, living life to the fullest, is stress free as current job, and is projected to hit six figures in the next six months. If you were presented with this opportunity, would you take advantage of it?

LFJ: I sure would tell Doug I want in

JE: Depends on what type of business it was. I wouldn't sell out my morals and beliefs for wealth. There also must be some type of intrinsic motivation, that's why the corporate world and I don't get along very well. Pure, profit driven purpose is a breeding ground for corruption therefore a turn off for me.

C2: Legitimate business just benefiting off the trends and demands of what people are looking for now a days

JE: If it involved some sort of consumer products probably not, never been interested in that. Only if the work was fulfilling, purposeful, heuristic and not monotonous. Never would I decline out of fear of change though

C2: I agree with you totally about the work has to fulfilling and purposeful if not than there will be a lack of passion

HL: It depends on the amount of time and other resources I would need to contribute.

C2: Strictly promoting through Facebook and word of mouth or other means of communication

AMS: Yes I would

Issue: Friend of yours brings a business opportunity to you that you can make life-changing money to travel and save. You decline, Doug implements the business with some coworkers and the business soars with success.

Perspective: Count me in I, want monetary growth and satisfaction. As long as it is legitimate and fulfilling, then I don't mind. Depend on time and other resources. Not into business with consumer products, does not do it for me.

Knowledge: People are presenting with opportunities on a regular basis or they know someone who is starting a business, they simply are not willing to grow and develop for the betterment of their family. These people you need to walk away from and associate with individuals who are about that life. It does not matter if you have known them over twenty years; if you don't have anything in common, it's time to walk away point blank.

Action: If Doug came to me with an opportunity, more than likely I would be all over it, considering he is a credible source. Most people I know are not risk takers and are comfortable being uncomfortable. I want to become financially free and experience the good life so I am willing to take chances for greater results down the road.

Consequences: It's a fifty-fifty thing you give something a shot; if it does not work, you keep plugging along until it gets to the point when you have no fight left. If you never decide to take risk you will continue to get what you may have been getting, which is nothing. Let's be honest, every person that ends up wealthy is someone who took chances in life and because of that things worked out for them. Life is too short and just because you drop to your knees and pray does not mean that a pot of gold will land before you. If you want it, then let's go out and get it.

Scenario 49 Homie Lover Friend

Olivia has turned your life around, where she used to be wild and do things without thinking; but ever since her daughter came into this world, she has made a complete change, everything she does is for the betterment of her daughter. At this stage of the game, the dating thing does not work for her based on all the uncertainties that come with it, so she says she will pass on that. Meanwhile she has been connecting back and forth one of her homies that they had some dealing off and on over the years. She is ready to reconnect with him because of the safety issues, she knows what she is getting from him. Now of course she has needs to be met and he always fulfilled those needs and I am sure he will relish the opportunity to have her again. What are the pros and cons of having a homie-lover-friend?

MMC: Finish the story. I want more.

C2: You have to answer the question presented

AB: Someone always catch feelings.

C2: There will always be feelings good, bad or indifferent

MJ: Pros is that she can trust him and knows him. The cons are that she can't have that type if relationship with a new child

AB: I believe you should always be open with communication and put everything on the table in the beginning. Therefore, both parties know where they stand.

KP: If her goal is to have only a sexual relationship then why not . . . she needs to make sure she is being very discrete when in comes to a homie lover friend and not let her daughter learn of or see this guy

TA: Pros: No strings attached relationship that is liberating because she gets her needs met without all the extra responsibility of a "traditional" relationship; Cons: Not having exclusivity, which means what the other person does (or who they do) when they are not with you isn't any of your business. Women often get this line blurred more than men so she is playing with fire.

Issues: Olivia has grown and matured since having her daughter; back in the days, she was loose and irresponsible. She is not into dating because of the unknown, but she does have a homie that they fooled around every so often and they reconnected. She knows he will service her, so that is her game plan, what do you think?

Perspective: Situations like this, someone will eventually catch feelings. She knows and trusts him but their relationship can't go any farther. Put all fifty-two on the cable before they start back up, and addressed expectations. Relationship is okay but she needs to keep it from her daughter. No added responsibility but can get her needs met, needs to keep everything in perspective and don't lose control because her homie-lover is not committed to her.

Knowledge: These two live out of state and the frequency of them seeing each other may not be that often, they known each other for years since they were younger and I believe they can handle boundaries with each other. Over the years, they always had some closeness but they never took it to the commitment level; I am certain that their homie-lover friendship will work for them.

Action: Sometimes when people get older and they established a mutual agreement between themselves and children are in the equations, it's easier for themselves and children are in the equations; it's easier for them to be involved with someone they already know instead of getting caught up in the dating game, which is risky business. Women that work full-time and full-time parent simply don't have the time to be getting to know some potential freakish jerk, so homie-lover will be just fine.

Consequences: The consequences can be that by Olivia continuing her relationship with her homie-lover she has packed it in for marriage due to her mindset because once she gets deep into her forties, her body and sex appeal may go to the waste side unless she works out to keep it tight. What if her and homie lover hook up this time and they realize enough of this foolishness, let's make it work out this time, that would throw a major monkey wrench in Olivia's game.

Scenario 50 Johnnie Blaze

Scenario discussion: Tierra has been dating Johnny for about a 1 ½ months. In the past when she was invited to her friends for a social get together, she would be the only one dateless; this time she has decided to take Johnny, while there Johnny was standoffish, rude, and did not socialize much but he damn sure got his drink on. Due to his behavior, Tierra was the laughing stock amongst her circle. My question is when you are dating, how long do you wait before you bring someone you are seeing around friends and family?

HL: My comfort level with that person. That will vary

C2: Talking about the variations brother HL.

TA: When it becomes a long term relationship. I don't bring anyone around my family if he isn't long term.

ALM: For me my inner circle are not that judgmental. They want whats best for me. I would bring him around them as soon as we have confirmed having interest in each other. That way i can see how he reacts around my people and so i can get their honest opinions of my potential suitor.

C2: TA how do you know when that long term is legit

C2: Well ALM that is not the case for everyone's inner circle, and why does their opinion matter.

ALM: Their opinions matter because when your in the middle of a situation you have one perspective, but those on the outside looking in may be able to see things you didn't. Not to mention following your heart sometimes goes against your brain's standards. I ultimately have the final decision but i do take into account what people who care about me have to say.

C2: Okay I just like to keep the dialogue going, good response

HL: Sorry about the posting, then running. I had to get to the salt mine.

First thing is am I just dating this person for a short time or am I looking forward to making this person my wife. If I am dating for company, then them meeting my family isn't an issue. I'm more than willing to allow my family to know my circle. Second, if I am looking to marry this person, then it will be months before they meet my family. Odd some may think, but I've discovered that in order for me to advance any relationship to that level, I have to be sure that person is going to stand up to all those things I want in a mate and that is daunting. I'm very demanding, unyielding and won't take short cuts on things that I deem mandatory. Some women say they want x in a man and Y, but when presented with those items they claim they want in a man, it become clear that they really don't.

Issue: Tierra had recently started dating Johnny the past 11/2 months, so when one of her friends put together a get together, Tierra decided to bring Johnny because typically she is the one that is dateless; well Johnny was rude, standoffish, and a lush. After the event, Tierra's friends made sure they let her know. Which bring me to the question of how long do you wait before you invite someone around family and friends?

Perspectives: Depending on how comfortable you feel. It has to be a committable relationship before that person is brought around my peeps. I would have no problem bringing them around my inner circle because I want another set of eyes to give me feedback on my new friend. I value my inner circle's feedback and sometimes you may get caught in the person, but your circle sees something different. If it's a random date, it does not matter if she meets the family; but if it's my potential wife, I have to make sure she lives up to my expectation and she is ready and not just talk.

Knowledge: Tierra was a nice intelligent young lady but she had poor judgment in choosing guys and many times her friends who were real critical teased her about her selections; but this time she felt she had a winner in Johnny, but again there had to be a breakdown in the screening process, and also sometimes the people we are closer to sit back and wait on your demise. Choose your mate and friends wisely or you will continue being the laughing stock of the party.

Action: Sometimes we have to know our surroundings and get a feel for our environment before bringing Johnny Blaze to a big major get together, do something on a smaller scale engage with him in politics or a controversial conversation and see how he handles the heat; if he shows his ass on that level, let him go. Also as we get older, we have to figure out who our real friends are and I can tell you this opposite attracts does not work with friendships. Look for individuals who have something in common with you, stop rolling with flocks of people when you get a certain age; if you have three or more people that you call your bestie, that is a recipe for disaster.

Consequences: It's the same ole movie if you keep doing what you are doing, it always boils down to choices. Every circle of friends has someone they consider the weakest link and they are waiting to crack slick on you for social relation issues or they find flaws in your dressing game. If you feel you are the target, it may be time to do a spring cleaning and febreeze yourself away from them and focus on people who truly care about your feelings.

Scenario 51 Last of the American Virgins

American virgin, Brenda, thirty-eight, and Larry, twenty-nine, have been dating for one year. Larry is a virgin and wishes to wait to marry before having sex. Brenda is very sexual, enjoy sex on a regular basis. Larry has proposed and Brenda has reluctantly accepted; her biggest concern is having a man that she has to teach about sex. One night they are out at a bar with friends celebrating a birthday. She meets a random guy and sneaks off to the men's bathroom to have sex with him. They are caught by one of Larry's friends so instead of accepting responsibility for her freakish behavior, she blames Larry for it because of his unwillingness to have premarital sex, stating that if he would have gave her some, this would not have happened. What should Larry do about his horny-ass fiancé?

DP: Larry should think about marrying his fiancé because sex is a small part of the relationship. If she loved him then she should have waited until the marriage. Show him that much respect to let him know that she truly loves him for him.

LFJ: Be mine. Lol I'd take a virgin ANY DAY! She should've appreciated the man. He is a virgin and wants a marriage Jackpot. Some males want sex and No Commitment Ever. Larry should leave her ASAP.

COJ: Excuse me ding dong Brenda. This is exactly why 38 yr old women should want NOTHING to so with a guy who's 29!!!!!!!!!! Please end the relationship and move on to the next. Find yourself a ma n in his early 40's. Just my 2 cents.

DP: Well . . . She doesn't respect him enough to wait then I would say she doesn't respect herself enough either to be worth it. The issue is Brenda and her level of self worth because she is measuring it by the fact if someone wants to have sex with her.

LHM: Abstinence is beautiful and wanting to wait until you're married living life according to the Bible is a blessing!! If Brenda is unable to accept his lifestyle and his way of living then she should never have agreed to marry him. She wasn't blindsided she knew exactly what she was getting into!! Larry needs to find him a virtuous woman who shares the same morals and values as he does. You know what they say . . . once a cheater always a cheater . . . BAM!!

KM: Kick her to the curb. She knew what she was getting into when she accepted his proposal. If sex is what she wants/needs, she should be with someone who isn't compromising his values by giving it to her. And Larry should find a virgin who shares his beliefs.

C2: KM where are the Virgins at?

KM: That's a good question David lol

C2: If they are around they are hidden very well consider this generation is dropping it like it's hot in elementary school

CA: I'm a virgin. lol

LH: She's having sex with a random guy? She's nasty and he can do better.

KA: Fire Her ASAP!!!!!!

CA: Drop it like it's hot! lol

KP: If Brenda could not respect and honor Larry then he needs to let her go!!!

Issue: Larry has been dating Brenda for over a year. He is a virgin and wants to remain that way until he gets married. Brenda is very sexual and likes to have it on a regular basis. Going into their engagement, there are several issues that stand out. She is almost ten years older and she is sexual and he is not. One evening, they went out together and she decided to have sex with a random guy, and one of Larry's friends caught her in the act in the men's bathroom. Instead of taking responsibility for her actions, she blames Larry. Should Larry call this engagement off?

Perspectives: Larry should reconsider marrying Brenda; she does not respect his values. She should value him as a virgin; it's rare and unique, so precious. Brenda needs to find someone her own age; stop being a cougar! Living life like it supposed to be is a beautiful thing and clearly Brenda does not value that premise. Larry needs to find someone with the same value system, lick Brenda to the curb, no respect for self or Larry.

Knowledge: I am concerned when individual's hookup and are together under false pretenses; again if you don't have the same value system or beliefs, it typically will not work. Opposites do not attract, throw that theory out the window. Relationships with more things in common have a better chance of making it. It's done; she violated Larry in front of his boys, no turning back. Larry, you are setting up yourself for hurt and pain.

Action: Larry needs to get out; it makes me wonder what the connection was in the first place. What made him say this is the one I want to marry? I guess the quickest way to screen someone out is to bring them amongst friends and something usually comes out. Larry found out the hard way and Brenda's true colors came out; he needs to bow out this relationship before her random sexual encounters become more personable such as her sleeping with one of Larry's friend in their bed. These situations can result in serious violent acts; hello, have you ever watched the ID channel or Fatal Attraction?

Consequences: I am sure Larry will hear it from his boys, which the pressure will be on him to walk away from this relationship. Nobody wants to be with someone who is viewed as a hoe, but if he decides to stay with her, then Larry may need to consider relocating; but again, a hoe will be a hoe no matter where they go. Decisions, decisions, we make them based on our hearts so at the end of the day that is what we need to go with and you can live with it because it's your decision.

Scenario 52 Marriage Over Friendship

Sometimes friendships don't last, Derek and Kelly have been friends for over seventeen years and during those times they had a few moments between them, but nothing too serious. Derek was more of a mentor for Kelly as she moved up the professional ladder. Derek gave her the blueprint and she followed it and her career took off. When Kelly started dating her soon to be insecure, controlling husband, Ralph, things change between Kelly and Derek. One day Derek left a message from Kelly's phone joking with her, something they both did to each other, and Ralph got the message and called Derek up going off without Derek getting in a word. But at times Derek felt like he was going to have to step to Ralph and kick his ass, but he was more of a professional to behave like that; the last straw to Derek and Kelly's friendship ending was the fact she got married, Derek did not get a personal invitation. Kelly sent the invitation to Derek's mother who lives in another state. Derek felt like he deserved better and he did not attend the wedding and has not spoken to Kelly since then, which was over eight years ago. Is Derek wrong for feeling bitter?

MH: Yes and know but honestly Derek is dealing with mixed emotions

C2: MH talk to us about those mixed emotions

MH: From my standpoint the way I see it Derek is bitter toward Ralph and saddened by losing the friendship he and Kelly once shared! Had it not been for the joking message everyone would still be fine! Just my opinion!

C2: Just to add to the scenario, Ralph was envious of Derek from day one because Kelly spoke highly of him

MH So this definitely would spell out Derek's vindictive feelings toward Ralph, and not in the least bit is Derek wrong for what he feels about Ralph simply because he was envious of the man from day one and it's not Kelly's fault

C2: They had a few moments

COJ: We'll as far as I'm concerned I don't believe in friendships between people of the opposite sex. Not close friendships anyway. Not unless both people are friends with that person. Causes too much confusion too often. So, once you get married or are in a monogamous (spelling?) relationship you must put your mate before your friends (especially friends of the opposite sex). Just my 2 cents.

C2: COJ even though Derek was a great friend and help her professionally I feel he could have got a personal invite to the wedding

HL: NO. For Derek it is a simple as K.I.M.

C2: Herb please explain let them people know

SIW: Hell no! I would a probably felt the same way knowing me because I love hard no matter friends or fam! So if u allow someone to come between what we have I'm going to feel some type of way

HL: If someone is going to allow their mentor to be pushed aside in that manner, then the only choice is to allow it to die on the vine. She has shown him what he meant to her. The situation between him and Ralph is immaterial. She took their professional relationships for granted and fails to understand how her success is based on his advice. To add insult to it, she invited his mother which to me is a direct power move to show him how highly she thinks of him. Those are the type of things that leave an indelible stain on a person. When anyone has professional success, then very first thing they do is allow for the acknowledgement of those who help them get to where they are. I'm sure most of have seen acceptance speeches. What are the some of the first things they do? Thank those who gave them their first chance at success. She violated the cardinal rule. I hope she is able to flourish without him because once word of her betrayal spreads (and it will be her own fault), very few are going to want to work with her let alone give her any advise. In the cut throat world of Corporate America, one needs every advantage they can get. Not only did she lose an ally, she tossed a friend on the scrap heap.

KP: Kelly should have encourage a friendship between Derek and Ralph from the beginning . . . the dynamics between a man and a women that are only friends is hard to keep the boundaries as such . . . due to their few moments And the years of friendship he formed an emotional connection to Kelly of more then friends. A line that Kelly didn't cross . . . Ralph's insecurities probably came from Kelly who shared her and Derek's close relationship stories. Unfortunately Derek needs to let Kelly be . . . If her husband is jealous and controlling she will get sick of it soon and Derek will be the first person she calls . . .

HL: And if I were Derek, I would politely say I can't assist you and hang up. That is how betrayal is rewarded!! A relationship between those two would never work. Derek doesn't need Ralph, but without Derek, she isn't where she is. So who needs who?

KP: True HL but if they both care about her then maybe they should have come to a common ground . . . .

C2: A piece that I will throw in is Kelly damn near beg Derek to invite her and Ralph to his party for receiving his Masters degree and despite Derek dislike for Ralph he did it for Kelly.

HL: KP: Have you ever known a controlling male to ever share his woman for ANY reason?

C2: People there will always be more to the exert but this is why we have the open dialogue. KJC what's the difference I think with the reception you have more idol time for potential convo with that person you are running from. How many people really stand there and do that crap, remember these are real scenarios

KP: You are correct HL . . . She has set the tone and has allowed her husband to control her . . . . She will be regretting giving up a person who been such a pivotal part of her success as well as true friend

TC: In my opinion, when you enter into a serious relationship with someone, you have to cut off all your old relationships. So if they had moments regardless of how close they are, he had to go they can't remain friends. Everyone involved should have that understood and as a friend he should have supported her decision otherwise he is not a true friend anyways.

C2: Personally I would not make it a habit of cutting back people who have helped me grow professionally, these are part of the reason I put food on my table, can you use your husband or wife for a reference?

TC: Sometimes I think you have to make a decision whether to grow professionally or grow your relationship

C2: It's called having a nice sound balance professionally and personally if one outweighs the other that is a recipe for disaster

HL: David: I have discovered that those who advocate cutting off all ties with people have never formed relationships worth cultivating and that is sad. To have those professional connections can lead to other jobs as well as advancement in companies when a merger occurs. To allow them to go by the way side because of someone who is unable to deal with just a professional relationship is just about the most self destructive thing for a career.

C2: Yes it's an interesting dynamic, sort of like not respecting people that put things in place for you, could not be something I would do, I believe in paying homage to people who went to bat for me.

HL: Like biting the hand that fed you.

TC: I agree with that but that's not the case in this scenario because they have had "moments" so this is no longer just a professional relationship. When someone has a "moment" that relationship can never be seen as just professional and it is only fair to the person you are involved with to cut off (or at least scale back) that relationship.

HL: Seeing as it is not spelled out in the scenario, define a 'moment?

C2: A moment a few kisses here and there and everywhere lol.

TC: I wouldn't feel comfortable if my boyfriend/husband had a close female friend that they have moments with so I wouldn't stay close to a friend that I have had moments with.

EP: Ppl ppl she chose Ralph too marry. . .end of story. Pal help each other every day and far as the invite she kept it real she sent it too the mothers house to invite the family so it wouldn't be any problems between her and her man. She loves Ralph . . . sry Derek . . . .

C2: Are any of you alarmed about Ralph going into her phone checking her messages, down the road can we say future ass whooping from the control freak

KP: David if she had nothing to hide then why it is a big deal he looked at her phone? As for the ass whooping . . . .if he gave her one then he has done it before . . . .she made the decision to marry him. You should always keep friends in your circle that are a constant reinforcement to your life . . . To make you become a better you, loyal, honest and will always have your back . . . misery loves company . . .

C2: Why look through it we shouldn't get in the habit of snooping, hey should guys go through dairies? In fact when ladies are writing why not read it to your men for grammatical errors and sentence structure

KP: I agree David I'm not saying it was right . . . just saying that if the dynamics of their relationship was built on trust and honestly then the need to go through the phones wouldn't be a necessity

C2: But remember from the scenario he is controlling, so he has tendencies to control every aspect of her life and more than likely he will alienate Kelly from all friends and family

HL: David: They don't see it so no need to impress that upon them

KP: HL: just because some don't emphasize on certain aspects doesn't mean they don't see it . . . some may feel that certain aspects of the scenario are more important then others . . . Some do not need to be impressed . . . .

HL: Point well taken. That is the problem. Most will never be able to understand how a professional liaison is just as important as a mate and at times, more pivotal to success than a mate. I'm not here to beat anyone over the head with that. I just speak to what I believe. I will never tell anyone they are right or wrong for their beliefs.

KP: This is a great forum that David Glover has created . . . A tool to enlighten people of different backgrounds, race, religion, gender, sexuality, ect . . . The hope is that this scenario will teach, educate, and open up the minds to take in the knowledge adoptions of our society . . . So HL I respect your comments and all of the participates that have commented on David's scenarios . . . We all can learn something from someone . . . Thanks David Xoxoxo

C2: KP thanks for your daily support and you said it best in regards to the vision and mission of the discussion group, keep doing what you are doing xoxoxo.

Issue: Derek and Kelly been friends for fifteen solid years and he played the mentoring role, but at the time they shared some moments together, Kelly ended up hooking up with Ralph who was very controlling and jealous hearted. Ever since getting with Ralph, Derek and Kelly's relationship grew a part and Derek felt betrayed because no matter what, he always looked out for her professionally and personally. The straw that broke the camels back was when she got married to Ralph and instead of sending Derek a personal invite, she mailed him one to his mother's house who lives in a completely different state.

Perspective- Derek has mixed emotions and doesn't care for Ralph but misses his friendship with Kelly. I don't believe in friendship between opposite sex once you are married. Kelly took her professional relationship with Derek for granted and kicked him to the curb. Kelly should have encouraged a friendship between Ralph and Derek instead of shunning Derek out. Sometimes you have to make a choice grow professionally or grow your relationship. She chose Ralph, people help each other every day, and she sent the invitation to Derek's mother out of respect for her husband.

Knowledge: Every so often, you find someone who takes you under their wings and put you in a position to grow professionally. People tend to get it twisted to underestimate those relationships, who in the hell would want you relationship wise if you have nothing to offer other than a cute face. Derek was a friend first even before the moments happen between them, but to betray your allegiance to him, it becomes a character issue. I hope Ralph is fulfilling her professionally as well as personally.

Action: Personally, Derek should have seen this coming from a mile away, but it does not minimize what he felt about his perceived betrayal; I am sure he will think twice before he takes someone under his wing again especially if they will not value his friendship. But again, it's the game of life; you can put a lot into something but you never know what you will get out of it. At the end of the day, you have to enjoy the memories you shared but at the same time think to yourself, the hell with them.

Consequences: Like the old saying goes you don't want to get into any habits of burning bridges, you never know when your actions will come back to bite you in the ass. Keep your circle small and tight and stay loyal to the people that help you grow personally and professionally. I am one who understands that with growth comes help with people who have done it, many idiots only think about the here and now. Sometimes you will lose friendships and relationships for doing the right thing, but it happens.

Scenario 53 Reunited and It Doesn't Feel So Good

Scenario: Savannah and Walter run into each at the high school reunion; they have not seen each other in over twenty years, but during high school, they always had a playful crush on each other. Neither one of them are married and during the weekend festivities they begin texting each other; one thing led to another and I will leave it at that. Savannah lives in Florida and Walter lives in Delaware. One weekend, Walter has a business trip in Florida; Savannah was very accommodating while he was there and of course things spark over between them. Six months later, Savannah and one of her home girls come to Delaware with the expectations that Walter would reciprocate Savannah's hospitality; Walter had to work all weekend and never shows face although he did make time to connect with his homeboy. Savannah was terribly disappointed in Walter and decided to cut him off. Do you think Savannah is overreacting?

GG: No

C2: Come on Gerri you have to give me more explain yourself open up the dialogue

GG: It was a yes or no question. No one likes their time wasted. If it wasn't a good time to visit he should have said something.

AF: Since you didn't mention if they communicated and she told him that she was coming up to see him then things might have been different. Cause if he knew than maybe he wouldn't have been working and being a no show. So, she should just write it off as a been there done that will never entertain that again experience.

C2: What if he told her he would be tied up

MJ: If he told her he would be tied up then she shouldn't have made the trip or expected him to show.

MJ: Exactly. I agree with you AF

EB: how tied up could u b. was he tied up all day and all night. If he made time to see his other friend and he was so tied up why couldn't he make time to see her? Its sounds to me as though there was a woman that he was with that he may have failed to mention

KM: first I would like to start by saying I would never be in this situation, but women always want to cut someone off. they always want to change the rule of the relationship to fit them instead of leaving things like they are and let them slowly progress . . . I'm just saying . . . .. her ass is literally and figuratively wrong!!! How you like those apples?

EB: no KM . . . No rules were changed he was wrong. If he made time to see his boy he could've made the same time to see her.

DP: Savannah get over it. Don't take sand to the beach. You went with your girlfriend obviously not to see Walter. If it was trip specifically for Walter she would have went solo. So go out with your girlfriend, meet some new friends and when Walters free check your schedule. It is not that difficult.

C2: Great way to look at DP, Savannah was trying to do way too much, best solution come up next time dolo, and make sure Walter has a free schedule

Issue: Savannah and Walter run into each other during their high school reunion; during the weekend, they begin texting each other and one thing led to another. Their contact became more frequent, which led Walter to spend time with Savannah when he was on a business trip to Florida, in which she was very accommodating. Unfortunately, when Savannah came to Delaware with one of her girlfriends, Walter was unavailable due to his work schedules so that really pissed Savannah off and she has been done with him since. Did Savannah overreact?

Perspectives: Walter should have told her before instead of waiting her time. Write it off but never entertain doing it again. If she told him he would be working, she should not had any expectations. He had time to hang out with his boy, he could have made time for Savannah that is straight bullshit. Women always want to change the rules of the relationship to fit their particular needs. Let thing be as it is, it's a process. Don't bring sand to the beach; why in the hell did she bring her girlfriend with her if she was trying to see Walter?

Knowledge: Sometimes people try to have best of both worlds wanting to hang out with their girlfriend but having Walter at her leisure. If the man had to work, you have to respect his hustle because that is how he eats; but if I am not mistaken, Walter did attempt to see Savannah, but after she was lost sightseeing, she had an attitude. What is crazy, the two had crazy chemistry and it has all been thrown away because of the common theme "a lack of communication." Now I am shaking my big damn head (SMBDH).

Action: Certainly, this could have been handled differently by both parties; if I were Walter, maybe he could try for a remake of that weekend with one of the stipulations "is no girlfriend included," also he must make sure he is totally free that particular weekend. Savannah needs to stop being stubborn and take accountability on this matter because it's just as much the blame as Walter. If Walter wants Savannah back, he may need to bite the bullet and fly her in.

Consequences: Now the downside to this all is that two people who use to have crush on each finally connected, mind, body, and soul, and due to one mishap, may run the risk of connecting in another fifteen years, and by that time they may not be able to relight their fire they had before. People, remember time is not forever, we spend too much time griping on the little things in life. One essential question you need to ask in regards to relationships, are you better with this person in your quality world or not?

Scenario 54 Snitches Get Stiches

Snitches get stitches; Marquis was on his way home from Habib's Corner store at 10:20 p.m. where he was purchasing some snacks for his ninth-grade field trip tomorrow. As he was walking, he saw Lamont, Patrick, and Rod running out of Mrs. Ruby's backyard who happens to be the community block leader. They were wearing mask over their faces but took them off; as they approach Marquis, they were breathing heavily and all said "what's up" to Marquis and gave him a pound and ran off. Marquis thought it was strange that they were coming from Mrs. Ruby's backyard but didn't want to over analyze the situation. The next morning when he got out of the shower, he heard his mother scream out "Oh my god, who would do this" and she broke down and started crying. He went over and said, "Mom, what's wrong?" She stated it was just reported on the news that Mrs. Ruby was found dead in her house by her daughter and if anyone had any details please report it to the homicide unit. Oh s——, what should Marquis do?

TS: Talk to his trusted guidance counselor.

C2: I don't know if he is going to the average counselor unless it's the Great David Glover

HL: He has nothing to tell actually as odd as it may seem. He could say something, but to say they took part in the crime would at this point would be speculation on his behalf.

C2: Do you think he should mention something to his mother that would be a major break through

TS: He absolutely should say something! For the safety of the other people in his community.

C2: What about his fear factor of retaliation

TS: It's still the right thing to do . . . .

C2: Sometimes morals are thrown out the window for some when your life is at risk

KP: He should definitely tell . . . .tell his mother and go from there . . . .his mother has to make the best decision for him and her family . . . .Speculation or not those kids may have more info if even they didn't have anything to do with it . . . sad that he may have to fear retaliation . . . . But is his fear more great then a lifelong heaviness in is heart?

C2: Many of the youth today don't look past tomorrow so that lifelong heavy heart theory may not factor in his decision

KP: Absolutely true . . . That's why mom needs to get involved ASAP . . . . After a while he will start demonstrating some out of the character behavior . . . Mom hopefully will notice and question his actions

MJ: He definitely needs to tell. It's the right thing to do. It's the right thing to do. That's the problem these days; no one wants to do the right thing. If it were his mom, he would want someone to do it for him.

C2: Does anyone wonder why this 14 yr old was out at 1030 pm, his ass should have been in the bed

MJ: That's a good question but for all we know his mother could have sent him. It's not a shocker to me anymore. I see teens and preteens out at midnight all the time. Or I should say I hear their loud mouths outside my window. The cops patrol all the time yet it still happens. For me, my children have and will always have a curfew until they are18 or out of my house.

MS: We need to make your scenarios a graphic novel website

HL: I'm going to tell a story I want people to pay strict attention some of the things I say . . . For me, this scenario is closer to home event than people realize. I've been in a situation in which I had a friend shot by people who were trying to rob him and a few friends. He was the only one of the group to be shot (2 others got away without harm.) Now, no one ever told the police what happened and it has less to do with fear of retaliation, but more self preservation. Being that we spent more time on the block hanging out, we didn't know if the people who shot him would be back. My boys were into the street life and knew what came with it. Now, it is a know fact that the police aren't in the business of solving crimes the right way, but more along the line of finding someone to fit the crime. The complete opposite way of how it should be. This puts honest people in a terrible situation and makes coming forward a huge risk when we know how police departments target people for their own gain. So it isn't a question of should he come forward, it is a case of how can he without HIM being put at the scene of the crime particularly if his mother him and not aware of their rights. The police could very easily put him on the site of the crime at a time that makes it convenient for them to have a suspect. So to inform the authorities is one thing, but to understand the potential risk he is taking with his own freedom becomes a bigger issue. He could come forward anonymously, but if he is ever called as a material witness, then he'll be forced to testify. IF he isn't able to say with 100% certainty that they did anything (mind you they didn't say they did anything), he would be the center of attention for no real gain. The streets are hard enough to walk, play or just be a normally male in without putting yourself in a bad situation.

Submitting the info anonymously would be his best way to avoid that, but a trial will be required if his peeps are indeed charged with a crime. No right or wrong way to go about it, but the IMPORTANT question becomes is what would you say if this was your son and how do we teach the youth when the chance is worth the risk? Mind you, his boys could have played a prank and someone else could have been responsible for her death.

Issue: Marquis was on his way from the corner store purchasing snacks for his field trip tomorrow and he ran into three of his friends who were running out of Ms. Ruby's backyard; they all greeted him with a pound but he noticed they were breathing heavenly. The next morning, Marquis heard his mother scream out "Oh my God, who would do that to Ms. Ruby?" She explained to Marquis that Ms. Ruby was found dead and the homicide unit is asking if anyone has any details. What do you think Marquis should do?

Perspective: Talk to his trusted guidance counselor. He has nothing to tell at this point, it would just be mere speculation. He should say something for the sake of his community. He should tell his mother and take it from there. These boys may have more info to report, plus he does not want to live his life with this on his mind. He should tell it's the right thing to do; no one wants to do what's right. If he tells he can definitely putting himself in the hands of the law and we know they don't always solve things how they should be handled.

Knowledge: In this situation, it was a gang-related activity and those three boys were part of the gang and they were initiating another young man who had to kill someone to get into the gang. So as we can see, this puts Marquis in a horrible situation; it's the case of being in the wrong place at the wrong time, not an easy situation for a teenager to be in, but let's understand every day our young people are faced with these challenges.

Action: If I were Marquis, I would probably share this info with my mother but I can't say when it would be, but more than likely it would be shared with one of my closer friends. But yes I would be worried about retaliation, so situations like this is not a game because our young people are not solving issues with their hands; they are packing heat, so that increases the fear factor. One of the best options would be to tell mom so she can pack up your shit and get the hell out of dodge.

Consequences: I am sure once the boys find out it has hit the news scene, they will be stepping to Marquis on the hush-hush tip that he did not see them or else. It may get dicey for Marquis when the police start looking at surveillance tapes and they identify from the store cameras that he was in the area during that time. The best outcome for Marquis is that these boys are caught up before they get to him with their threats. No matter how this case plays out, someone has lost their life and if caught, these boys or whoever will be in jail a very long time, such a sad situation.

Scenario 55 So Fine You Blow My Mind

Tyrone posted a picture on FB as he was getting ready to attend a work function; his friend Tammy commented on the stat on how good Tyrone was looking and she and Tyrone went back in forth sending compliments to each other. Sheila, Tyrone's girlfriend, responded on the stat asking who the hell is Tammy and why is she sweating you Tyrone, and she needs to get on her own man to compliment. Who was wrong in this scenario and how would you have handled it?

WC: Tyrone should have just said Thank you and left it at that.

C2: Or Tyrone could have told Sheila to stay off his page and he will talk to her later

TS: First response is best . . . nothing wrong with a compliment. Sheila shouldn't jump on someone for that. And he def should NOT talk to Tammy on the side . . . .

HL: This is expressly why I don't deal with women who have Insecurity issues. They allow that to cloud their judgment and behavior. IMO, there was no need for her to react in such a manner.

NNM: Tyrone should have said Thanks and kept it moving. No need for all the extra compliments.

C2: What is wrong with some friendly flirting by Tyrone it's an ego booster

NNM: He needs to flirt when and where his girl can't see it.

TS: And not lead Tammy on either . . .

C2: Hey Tammy came at him first, she knew exactly what she was doing

TS: By giving a compliment!?

MMI: She should find a less attractive BF . . . .insecure!

HL: David I've always noticed a trend in these types of things . . . .women will ALWAYS say what man shouldn't do, but will NEVER say that a woman over reacted. I wonder why?!? Then we wonder why there is no accountability among them. Damn shame.

C2: Any women on here brave enough to challenge Herbs notion? Lol

C2; that compliment could have been the feeling out process

C2: Okay so here is the compliment, "Damn Ty you are looking so damn good, I wish I was your lady of honor tonight, ummm ummmmm.

MJ: That is not lady like if that was the compliment

HL: David: I'll be waiting, but I don't' think it'll happen.

HL: And it's not my feelings, it's what I have seen on your post.

MJ: Just thinking about this burns me up. That was definitely a feeling out process. Why do females have to do that? It's so trashy to me. A suitable "compliment" would have been "That is a very nice pic Tyrone" or something along those lines. It's not lady like to chase after men. It makes a female look desperate and trashy!!! And we wonder why men call us hoes and bs UGH!!!

C2: MJ what would be a correct indirect way for a women to let a man know she is interested

NNM: The man was wrong because he should not have went back and forth with the compliments. He should have said thank you and that is all. He knew his girl in his Facebook friend. How would he feel if he were in her shoes? There is a respect factor. And she should have not gone off on FB; she should have talked to him later about it. She will get better results if she approaches this calmly instead of going off.

HL: David^^^See my point!! LMBO!! More man blaming

MJ: A nice compliment as suggested above or something similar. I'm not saying a woman has to be docile and never speak to a man but we shouldn't be leading a man, who by nature is a hunter, into something like this. Of course he is going to take bait and of course the girlfriend is going to get jealous. Women are emotional creatures by nature. Now a "that's a nice pic" is not offensive but the earlier comment that started it is down right hoish . . . . Yes I know that's not a real word.

NNM: HL, the woman did overreact, but that does not dispute the fact that he should have handled it differently. Are you disputing that fact?

HL: NNM: A man is going to be a MAN! She has two options:

1. Talk to him and let him know how she feels.
2. IF the situation happens again and he does not behave differently, then she has a decision to make. Stop making gray out of black and white. It just makes things easier.

Facts, I never dispute, but intelligence I will question why is it no tused I NEVER blame a female for a situation I can handle differently. That is what a mature responsible person does IMO

C2: HL you might be in for a battle my fam NNM is no slouch, she can handle hers all day long

HL: LOL . . . I don't doubt that, but she already confirmed my point

HL: When a woman says what a man should do, she is in effect saying that he shouldn't have done x or y. It's not cognitive dissonance, but it is damned close.

NNM yes, we are in agreement HL :)

CHB: He was wrong. She was also wrong but not for checking him but for the lack of tact. She could have checked him in a less confrontational way.

NT: I see it as compliments from one friend to the other. If it was that deep it would have been some in boxing going on. He or she didn't have anything to hide. The girlfriend does have the right to check especially if she feels disrespected. Compliments ppl. We all get them its you as an individual do with it.

C2: So basically if you need to walk around on egg shells than maybe Tyrone will be better served unfriending Sheila

HL: Maybe, but I always ask: if a person behaves like that, then why bother dating them? They'll cause more issues then they are worth.

CHB: Respecting someone shouldn't be walking on eggshells. If that is how he feels . . . ..yes Tyrone should unfriended her and Sheila needs to find someone different.

C2: Herb do you mean Sheila's behavior

HL: Yes I do. This could have been a person with whom Tyrone has that type of rapport with and if that is the case, then why would anyone want to have a mate who behaves in an unnecessary way when a simple chat would solve her problem? I understand her point and it is valid, but how a situation is handled speaks volumes about a person's ability to deal with conflicts that could be potentially destructive. I mean just imagine if this was a coworker (higher up) and they were at a fund raiser or employee party and she acted like this in person. How do you think that would go over? I'd say not well.

CHB: HL I do agree that Sheila did not handle it the best way. Heck I would join in the conversation and gave both of them compliments. I'm sure that would spark a conversation later and we could have discussed my concerns.

C2: People what if Tyrone responded this way because he is not use to getting compliments from his woman

HL: Uh oh!!! Women . . . speak on this!!!

MJ: Then he needs to solve that issue before creating a new one.

HL: So when a person receives a compliment, they are wrong? That is the premise of this. Interesting . . . .

MJ: No they are not wrong for receiving the compliment. They are wrong for going about it disrespectfully. For example I wouldn't say to David . . . damn D you're so sexy . . . let's get together. Stuff like that will open doors you don't necessarily want opened. We should close open doors before opening new ones. Now if I said something like David that's a very nice suit, then that's a simple compliment and a simple thank you would suffice. If he/she would want to take it further then they shouldn't do it on a public forum. I'd like to add this applies even if they know each other extensively because then it gives room for other people to add stuff to it and offenses will come.

HL: I would agree, if SEXY had been mentioned, but it was not. Without a clear comment, it borders on bit of conjecture.

MJ: David said that Tammy said to Tyrone "Damn Ty you are looking so damn good, I wish I was your lady of honor tonight, ummm ummmmm"

HL: We could both speculate on what that means, but as long as he didn't take her up on it, then he did nothing wrong. Inappropriate if his girlfriend didn't like it or was upset by it, yes, but she could address that.

Issue: Tyrone posted a picture on FB where his friend Tammy responded with a compliment; they went back in forth giving compliments until Sheila commented and asked why is Tammy constantly giving her man compliments. Who do you think was in the wrong?

Perspective: Tyrone should have just said thank you and left that conversation alone. This is why I don't deal with insecure women; they let their insecurities cloud their judgment and behavior. If Tyrone is going to flirt, don't do where his woman can see it. Maybe Sheila should find a less attractive man if she can't handle him receiving compliments. It's not ladylike for women to chase after men. There are boundaries and a certain level of respect that has been violated.

Knowledge: Maybe Tyrone went too far, but when you are someone looking for attention because you are not receiving it from your partners, these situations happen. To avoid these situations, give your other half necessary compliments and remember not to put your business on social media because you basically exploited yourself and let the next person knows you have flaws in your relationship, which people will take advantage of if you give them an opportunity.

Action: Issue could have been solved if Tyrone would have took his flirtatious ways somewhere else instead of on FB for public viewing; he simply got caught up during a time of weakness and now he has to deal with Sheila nosey ass, and like previously stated, she showed off and now she is the weak one, and Tammy has the upper hand because she knows Tyrone's attraction is mutual so the next step is to text him to resume the conversation. Certainly Tyrone and Sheila need to have a conversation because her aggression she demonstrated on FB will have people questioning Tyrone on why in the hell is he dealing with that loose cannon.

Consequences: Based on this scenario, I think Tyrone will follow up with Tammy because she seemed to make him feel good emotionally and Sheila seems to be controlling pain in the ass and her ways will push Tyrone away. Again, Tyrone may have been wrong but Sheila could have conducted this matter totally different by conversing with Tyrone later during a private conversation. In situations like this, even though your partner may be easy on the eyes, remember to never let them blow your mind or gasket that you make yourself look like a damn fool.

CHAPTER 8

Loyalty

Scenario 56 Baby Boy on the Run

HOW MANY OF you have dealt with Mama's baby boy? There is a married couple Stan and Brenda; every time they have an argument, Stan runs and tells his mother everything Brenda doesn't have her mother to talk to and she won't tell her friends because she doesn't gossip about her husband of course. Stan's mother is going to take his side and in turn cause more strife in their relationship. Jodi the friend of Stan who happens to be the person that usually listens and guide him through the process, this time she didn't stick up for him and called him a mama's boy and told him he needs to man up. Jodi allowed him to do this when he wasn't married but refuses to allow anyone to tell her anything bad about another member of the church. Now their friendship is strained because Jodi didn't take his side. What is the presenting problem in this scenario and how can this be rectified?

AL: Stan needs to stop being a baby and keep his mother OUT of his marriage, Jodi is showing tough love by staying out, and Stan needs to learn to fix things in house. Everyone doesn't need to know everything.

DP: There are 3 people in a marriage...Husband, wife and God. No where is mother, friends or the street listed? Keep people out your business even your mother.

C2: Unfortunately mothers have been a safe haven for many men so we might be preaching to the choir on that one.

AL: my soon to be ex husband doesn't have a relationship w/ his mother but is closer to my mother so whenever there was an argument, he called my mother, this particular situation hits home . . . people need to understand that not everyone has the best intentions for your marriage which is why it needs to be protected and Stan needs to man up and figure out a way to work it out w/ Brenda in a way that doesn't require a "group" perspective

KP: There is so much you tell your family or friends when you are in a relationship/marriage . . . The more you tell the more people will form opinions about that person with only hearing one side of the story. Not fair and you are putting your other half in a bad light. Stan needs to communicate with Brenda instead if his mother . . . or his friend . . . Jodi handled it right and should not get involved . . . Stan needs to handle his business with wife and only his wife. If he needs advise or just need to vent . . . Go seek a professional . . . third party with no ties to him or his wife

C2: Depending on the race some ethnic groups may be apprehensive about sharing issues with a random individual

KP: David I have found that to be true . . . the more intimate the issue . . . . the more apprehension there is

HL: Jodi took a stand that she should have taken long ago, but she may have chosen the wrong thing to do IMO. Stan has to find a way to deal with his marriage as an adult and stop running to others to take his side. Brenda likewise may wish to seek some advice from someone by talking to a person who will give her guidance. No person is an island unto themself.

C2: If only if half of us applied that theory of keeping everyone out of your business, I know this not to be true because if so Facebook would not be a GPS to update everything you and your family does, keep everyone out your business. I know it not for everyone but a great deal of people

KP: I'm amazed about how much info people give on here!!!! They need to use it more for networking and good ole communication!!!

C2: True indeed, if you let everybody know what you doing than when its time to talk you don't have shit to talk about

HL: This is why very little of my personal life hits Facebook. Only those who know me or those I wish to invite in are permitted in.

KJP: The common thread is Stan only going to people and listening to folks that support his nonsense. How to rectify is Stan will have to come to the realization that his behaviors are pushing others away and he'll need to take responsibility for what he losses . . . Until that happens nothing will change in any of his relationships for the good

Issue: Stan and Brenda are married, and like any couples, they go through their issues. Stan has the habit of running to this mother every time something goes wrong in their relationship. Unfortunately, Brenda does not have anyone to turn to accept friends and she does not believe in gossiping about her husband. Stan's mother usually takes his side, which causes more issues in Stan's relationship. Stan's friend Jody use to be his go to person who will keep him on track, but since Stan has been married, she refuses to listen to one member of the church talking about another member. This becomes an issue with Stan, so how do these issues get rectified.

Perspectives: Stan needs to man up and keep everyone out of business including his mother. People need to understand not everyone has the best intentions for your marriage. Stan needs to learn to communicate with his wife. Stan and Brenda can use someone who has no connection with either one of them. Stan continues to go to individuals who co-sign his bullshit that makes the issues lopsided.

Knowledge: Stan's way of handling things is counterproductive in their relationship because it drives a wedge between Brenda and his mother because her opinion is biased, and anytime Stan does something, his mother takes his sides so it appears that he is never wrong. This essentially drives Brenda away from his mother and which this upsets Stan because he claims he wants Brenda and his mother to become close.

Action: Stan needs to sit down with his wife and communicate; if this can't happen, he may need to think about separation because it's unrealistic to think his wife will continue to put up with his crap. Clearly these two are not happy with each other. The one thing is for sure is that Stan will not his ties go with his mother as far as interference with his marriage; so basically Brenda is a lame duck sitting and waiting for Stan's mother to tell him to return home and he can help her with bills that have fell behind.

Consequences: Stan will more than likely continue to struggle in his marriage and along with any relationship in the future. His mom needs to take him off the nipple so that he can grow and work out his marriage; these actions are part of the reason many men struggle in becoming men because their mamas either act like they're a child or his women. Which is a totally gross relationship between son and mom? Baby Boy on the run better learn to run into his woman's arms or he definitely will be spending more time with his mother because they will be roommate.

Scenario 57 Daddy's Little Girl Angry World

Terri is a thirty-five-year-old woman who appears to be full of anger and rage. Many of her closest people think that her anger has built up over the years due to her father leaving her at an early age. Terri over the years has been extremely bitter to any males she was involved with, often badgering them with downright disrespectful ridicule. Terri's relationship with her mother is very poor and strained, although her mother will give her the skin off her back, Terri never reciprocates that love. Terri has two daughters who now are depressed at times because they don't feel they can say anything to their mother without her responding back in a nasty mannerism. Her daughters often complains to their grandmother stating "I don't like my mother." How would you help bridge the gap of love between each of these individuals?

TS: Therapy . . .

C2: That is stating the obvious but that only works if that person wants help if that person happens to be black, we don't typically seek resolution in the form of therapy, who wants to air their dirty laundry out to a random tight khaki wearing stranger

TS: Could be pastoral counseling . . . but therapy is sometimes for you to learn to deal with those we can't change . . .

C2: Pastoral counseling is no different if that person is not into church, then that no good slandering back stabbing preacher will serve Terri no good

TS: Then I guess they are all screwed!

C2: The reality of this situation every day we have angry individuals walking around whom refuses help from others because of a lack of trusting relationships, so we live in a world of screwed up individuals

KP: Daughters need to keep the communication open with their grandmother . . . She seems to give them the love and positive encouragement they need . . . and also is in the same predicament as Terri's daughters seeking the love they so desperately want . . . if Terri cannot have a healthy and loving relationship with either at least the 1st and third generation can stay close and connected.

KM: Sometimes you can't change situations you can only learn to cope with them. Although there's nothing like the love from "you're" mother, those girls may have to accept "motherly love" from "someone else's mother" (grandmother, aunties, women in the church and community

HL: THERAPY!!!

SBC: Therapy is not always the answer. It just doesn't work for some people. I would have to agree with KM. Find other alternatives to the missing love by searching out encouragement from other close relatives or friends because the fact is some people just don't want to change.

HL: SBC: You are right, but any talking is therapy and it doen't have to be professional. So with 'll say again . . . therapy.

Issue: Terri is a thirty-five-year-old woman who suffers from anger management due to the abandonment of her dad; over the years, her anger has been displayed during relationships with men, coldhearted toward her mother and two daughters. Her coldness toward her daughters has led them to depression. How can we put the pieces together for this family?

Perspective: She needs therapy for sure; daughters need to keep that close relationship with grandmother. Daughters need to accept womanly love from aunts, church members, and community involvement. Some people are reluctant to therapy especially certain ethnic groups.

Knowledge: Terri was treated like a princess when her dad was around; once he left, she became bitter and cold-hearted. Does not know how to talk to anyone and struggles with realizing who has her best interest at heart. Terri can be a nice young lady, but most people don't have the patience to penetrate the wall she has up so typically no one wants to be bothered accept good ole mom who she treats like shit most of the time.

Action: Terri may need to reach out to her dad and find out why he walked out of her life. This conversation may require her to cuss him out, but whatever works for her. I doubt if she would seek out counseling and would only think, and say I am not speaking with a damn complete stranger. I am concerned for her two daughters because as each day goes by, her daughters heart increase with malice and I am afraid the vicious cycle will continue.

Consequences: Too many times our family dynamics are destroyed because of Dad's walking away from their responsibility. The impact is tremendous; the hurt and pain that is caused, it's unfortunate how generations are affecting years down the road. Too many times we become adults and take on the attitude of "Screw him, I don't need him, and he has not been in my life all this time so who needs him now." I learned that the hard way I was prepared to get everything off my chest; one Father's Day, I called for his number and no one responded. I said "oh well." My dad died four months later; I never got the chance to say what I wanted to say for all these years. If you have a scorn relationship with your dad and he is still living, get everything off your chest before it's too late; we are all on the clock, tick tock tick tock, and time is not forever.

Scenario 58 Go with What You Feel

Go with what you feel; out of the blue, Dante messaged Asia on Facebook. It was his way of flirting with her to see where she stood. Recently, Asia had lost her significant other, so she had droughts maybe of loneliness but she seems to do well fighting it off. Dante begin to come at her heavier and strong; he told her how much he wanted her and made her have visual thoughts, which usually got her hot and horny for Dante, there were times he had her trembling with weakness. She wanted him and he wanted her. Her big issue was that she was good friends with Dante's brother (Eddie) and felt liked Eddie had developed feelings for her over the years but nothing came out of it. At times, she felt guilty for her attraction with Dante and told him; Dante brushed it off and stated, "But you want me and I need to have you." What should Asia do? And should Dante step off?

CA: Is this passage from some cheesy romance novel?

LH: Was Eddie making moves as well? Because if he wasn't, then he missed the boat.

C2: I don't think Dante knew about the moves Eddie was making, Eddie never said

C2: CA real talk real shit, real-life experiences, I guess if it's not your world it's not idealistic

AB: Maybe Dante needs to speak with Eddie and get his perspective.

C2: Maybe Eddie perspective doesn't matter the fire has been lit

MJ: She should go with whoever fulfills her all the way around. Shoot it might not be either one of them.

C2: Asia may need someone to take her to a euphoric state where she needs to go and it sounds like Dante might be the front runner for that pleasurable task

HL: Decisions, decisions . . . .

MJ: If that's all she wants. If not EPIC FAIL.

C2: Let's be honest unless you are a women that has stop putting out work and you are single and comfortable with yourself its nothing wrong with a tune up by someone you are connected with

MJ: If that's all the person wants then no. However, many women think that might fulfill them but only ending up feeling empty inside because that's not all they really wanted.

C2: If that is what she wants for the time being is it so wrong, what if she did that and been there in a long time relationship and she is looking for that one guy to explore her desires with no strings attached

MJ: I'm not disputing that. That's why I said if that's what she wants. Your stat wasn't specific as to if that's all she wanted or if she was giving in to her flesh.

C2: She is a human with needs that is all I know, I don't know all the specifics if I did what would be left to talk about

MJ: Lol true

C3: That is the beauty of the scenarios, we can draw our own conclusions but never know the real outcome, I only give the presenting issue.

MJ: no explanation needed . . . I've been on the other end before

C2: The truth of the matter sometimes a woman may need the cobwebs knock off the goods and someone has to play the role of the broom

MJ: Bahahahaha that's the best explanation I've ever heard! As you was Mr. Glover!! You are hysterical!!!

C2: I wish I could take the credit but these are words from Asia

Issue: Dante messaged Asia out of the blue to see where she stood relationship wise. Asia had recently lost her significant other so she had droughts of loneliness; the awkward thing is Asia had a good friendship with Eddie and it has grown for years. Asia could not get Dante out of her mind; she was mentally and physically attracted to him and they wanted each other badly. What should Asia do?

Perspectives: If Eddie did not make any serious moves, his lost. Dante should speak with Eddie to get his perspective. Go with the person that fulfills all of your needs and wants. If she is just looking to be satisfied sexually or will it turns out to be something else. Sometimes a person just needs their needs to be taken care of by someone they care for strongly.

Knowledge: Dante and Asia have had this silent attraction for each other for years but never acted on it, just the eye contact said enough between them. Two people undressing each other with their eyes. Sometimes situations like these is compared to destiny or could it been love at first sight. Nevertheless, I think these two will follow-up on their feelings because it's something they have been waiting on for years.

Actions: If you feel a certain way, sometimes you need to make a move, you only live once; too many times, we sit around having Waiting to Exhale sessions about what we should have done and years passed you by, sometimes you have to take the bull by his horn and go for it. It's now or never, baby; don't speak about it, be about it. I know many people who have lost out on opportunities in their life and they are still hurting.

Consequences: The best thing about this situation is that Dante may have made moves without consulting with Eddie, but again if you worry about the next man, you will be setting yourself up for failure. Now many may say Dante should back off, but who are we to say what is in someone's heart. I have learned to be amongst the uncommon and nontraditional, so I will not fault Dante for following his heart especially if he cares for Asia. I have witnessed too many people die over the past ten years and I think many of those deaths had to do with poor choices and not going with their heart. So I look at the game of life, we have limited opportunities to win and conquer what we set out to do.

Scenario 59 I Need That Earned Income Credit

Mark has not been pretty much been a deadbeat dad when it came to his daughter Brazil; she has been on this earth for three years and he has seen her a total of seven times, but despite it all, Mark had the audacity to ask Brazil's mother Michelle if he could claim Brazil on his taxes and if Michelle would be willing to help him type of a paper he had due for class. If ever there was a time for Michelle to be the apple of Mark's eye, then certainly she should honor his request. What are you thinking?

WC: Michelle would have to be one desperate ass woman to do all of the above!

C2: Or just maybe it's a way for Mark to finally be the dad that Brazil needs in her life

WC: Mark's a user . . . only thinking about Mark not Brazil.

C2: Isn't that is how the world is built self preservation first everything else secondary

WC: Not when it comes to your kids if you're a real MAN!

C2: What determines someone to be considered a real man, would Mark's ability to survive be a characteristic of being a real man, the definition of being a man is open for interpretation

C2: Before I shut it down for a view hours peep this before being a man sometimes you have to see a man to know what it takes to be a man, it's the principles of teaching, demonstration, imitation, correction and repetition.

SS: That's a joke right

C2: SS you can't make this shit up.

SS: For Marks sake I would hope so. Okay I'm done

C2: Real talk, real scenarios, real-life experiences, this is the world we have created

SS: I don't know what world you're living In but I want no parts if.Nite nite :)

C2: This is not my life this is others life please don't shoot the messenger

SS: Shots have been fired lol

C2: I wear a vest keep firing off and make sure you pack a lunch

SS: So funny that you feel you need a vest. I'm harmless and I never eat lunch, HA

C2: Okay I got you, its all good

EG: Mark you don't have to take the sins of your father-Exodus 34:7; Michelle there is still time, repent turn your situation around. No to the tax issue and no to the assistance on the paper because you're only helping out another household and that is only going to inflame the situation, if you so desire court has ways of getting your country support. Michelle know your worth in Christ and build from there excepting nothing shorter then marriage, a house/yard, a car(two), vacations, picture taking and church participation. Be the example in the earth you have been called to be.

C2: In Michelle heart, she may do what you don't expect her to do and that is making her boo Mark happy, in reference to Mark doesn't hate the player hate the game

MJ: I'm speechless! I can't get over the fact that he had the audacity to ask for anything at all!!!

TS: I realize you are playing devil's advocate . . . But really? I don't think Mark is still her "boo" . . . at least if she has any self respect he isn't.

C2: TS, stop every day we have individuals going through this tom foolery to keep someone around even though it's clear that person does not want to be present

MJ: I agree that that happens David but I'm with TS on this one. He CAN'T be her boo.

KM: Wow . . . . Looks like Mark only sees his daughter as a tax write off. And not only is he neglecting his responsibility as a role model and example for her, he's attempting to take money from the mom that could be used for her by claiming. That's selfish and inexcusable and he wouldn't even get a chance to finish the question before he got a door slammed in his face or the dial tone in his ear.

C2: KM maybe the 7th time he came to visit was an overnighter and he asked that question while Michelle was plucking his chest hairs

MJ: LOl David that's just silly

C2: You ladies think you are stating the obvious instead of thinking outside the box, things happen

TS: I would go to my goodie drawer before dealing with Mark's "tom foolery." I would much rather be without a man and have a nice tax refund!

KM: Haha Mr. Glover

MJ: Is this her only child? Does she have other children she can claim on her taxes? If she does that's the only way I can see even the dumbest woman allow that to happen.

C2: 3 children

MJ: Well I guess desperate women do desperate things . . . ..

TS: you are correct that some women sacrifice their self respect for the hope that some man will love them. What they don't realize is that someone already does . . . God! We all must find our sufficiency in Christ before we can truly be in any healthy relationship.

MJ: AMEN TS!!! My heart goes out to women like this

HL: I loathe these types of immature men. Will create a life and have nothing to do with ensuring this child will have a chance at a decent life. Pathetic at best, but then, he has the unmitigated gall to ask about claiming her on his taxes. On his school work, he should never ask anyone to his work. He needs to take a typing class and do it himself!! She should flat out tell him NO!!

HL: David: You do have a point in regards to not having an understanding of what a man should be. If he hasn't been shown, it'll be a difficult task for him to do, but not impossible. He created this reality and he must learn to deal with it head on. I have a list on my profile entitled 'Rules to Being Human" and one of those rules address things of this nature. This is his stepping stone to manhood and responsibility. He must now step up to that challenge. The number of children she has is irrelevant. He knew going in what her situation was. He should have chosen wiser and made sure he didn't create a life he didn't want. Besides, the 'hood' is full of lessons if he just opens his eyes, he would have a road map of what and what not to do.

Issue: Mark has little or nothing to do with Brazil but had the audacity to ask Michelle if he could claim Brazil on his taxes and for her to type his paper, he is a bold man, I give it to him.

Perspectives: If Michelle does this, she has to be one desperate ass human being. Michelle knows your worth with Christ; don't give in to helping another household. If Michelle has any respect for herself, this is not an option. If Mark asks me that question, he would get to meet "Tone" dial tone or the doorknob would hit him where the good Lord split him. He needs to take a typing class and be told flat out no.

Knowledge: Michelle took a risk on Match.Com and it backfired. Of course she got a beautiful daughter out of the deal, but that is one more mouth to feed along with other expenses. She needs to be held accountable as well; if you lay down with dogs, you will get fleas. I can't emphasize the screening process enough and if how a better job was done on this process it would alleviate a lot of mishaps.

Actions: Michelle definitely should have rip him a new one when he asked about claiming Brazil, but again there has to be a reason he was bold enough to ask Michelle, which makes me believe she thrives for his attention more than she leads on. Maybe she needs to start having that question of giving up his parental rights if he doesn't have any plans to coparent his daughter. Maybe he just plain and simple maybe too involved with his other family and he just can't dedicate his time to Brazil. Nevertheless, Michelle needs to prepare being a single and continue to be the best parent she can be.

Consequences: Basically she is on borrowed time right now until her daughter get to the age of questioning her father's role in her life and why he doesn't he come see her and does he love her or ever loved her. That is when the challenges begin, so I hope Michelle will be prepared to face the music because it's definitely coming. A night of passion can lead to a lifetime of pain; moral of this story—KYP (Know Your Personnel).

Scenario 60 No Brazil No Dancing

Remember the story involving Mark who asked Michelle could he claim his daughter Brazil who he has nothing to do with and only seen her about seven times in three years, also he asked Michelle could she type his paper for one of his classes; well he was back at it again asking to take Michelle out dancing in Canada, failing to mention anything about Brazil. Michelle responded back by saying once Mark shows he wants to be a part of Brazil's life, she would consider. Do you think she should give Mark another chance? Or should they be discussing Mark giving up his parental rights?

PC: When you know the nature of the beast it's easier to deal with.

TS: She needs to give up all thoughts of having a romantic relationship with Mark and focus on what is best for her child . . .

C2: So are you saying she knows he isn't shit and her expectations are low so she will get what she can

PC: She knows exactly Who Mark is and any attemp at making things work is exactly what she is looking for and should embrace. The best way to avoid getting bitten by a rattlesnake is to avoid all snakes. Why try an determine what kind of snake it is.

C2: What if Mark being in Brazil's life 50% of the time is better than the .0006 % he has been involved so far

PC: Well whatever she decides to do either way she is right. She has to live with those choices of hers.

TS: Haha! I think I'm in "avoid all snakes" mode right now . . .

CW: Hmmm, I think I would only entertain the idea of mark developing a relationship with Brazil nothing more.

COCKTAIL CONVERSATIONS BY THE CONTROVERSIAL COUNSELOR

C2: If she had love for him before Brazil that will always be a factor

CW: Being in love and having love for someone are different. But ur rt its definitely a factor.

TS: Love yourself first . . .

C2: So when we say love yourself what does that look like because if you don't eat right and you drink and drug it although you may think you love yourself essentially you are doing harm to yourself

NNM: They should be discussing Mark giving up his parental rights.

C2: That is very harsh NNM why would you end all hope for Baby Brazil

NNM: Not really when you think of all that goes into caring for a child full time. He has only seen her 7 times, and sounds like he has no intention of doing more. That's hurtful and sad.

TS: Why would that be ending all hope for her child? Better than getting her hopes up when he is only around once in a blue moon . . .

C2: Do you not believe in miracles, Mark is not dead so there is a chance

NNM: No, he has had chances. How many should he get?

C2: Until he gets it right

NNM No, he has had enough. I'm going through something similiar now.

TS: Until he gets it right?! Smh . . .

NNM: I don't get any second chance. As the active parent if I don't do for my son, no one will. He does not get a choice to not take care of his child.

C2: Okay you ladies are cutthroat I see but I understand

COJ: Da hell???? Why is her name "Brazil ?" I'm mad at that. Carry on . . .

C2: COJ really the baby can't help the name focus on the issues at hand

COJ: Okie dokie back to the issues at hand. Who has custody?? Mark needs to work on being a father before anything else. How old are these people anyway???

C2: Michelle is 40 and Mark is 41

NNM: Yea, he should know better at 41 and she should too. They are both lost. Poor kid!

C2: Michelle has custody

MJ: No dancing. Leave him alone . . . . Talk is cheap!!!

COJ: 40 and 41????? U got to be kiddin me!!!!! They grown actin like that???? Damn shame. Nothing can be done. Two ding dongs old enough to know better.

HL: If a person can't hit the target at 6 paces, then why given them a shot at 4 paces?

Issue: Mark was relentless in his effort to get Michelle back or get into her panties by asking her out on a date without mentioning anything about his daughter. Michelle desperately replied "When you start spending time with your child, I might consider." Should this even be up for discussion.

Perspectives: When you know the nature of someone, you learn to accept them for who they are. Focus on your child and her best interest, and not any romantic encounters with Mark. Her conversation should be strictly about Mark spending time with Brazil. Conversations need to be about Mark giving up his parental rights. How many opportunities are you going to give someone to show their ass for you to kiss.

Knowledge: It seems to me that every so often Mark likes to test Michelle to see where he stands with her, more on a "I can still be with her tip," hoping she caves in; he has no intentions on being with Brazil on any level. He has other children and feels like Michelle was a slip up or something to have on the side to keep his whistle wet and fresh with something new.

Action: Again Michelle needs to carry on and love her daughter unconditionally, maybe one day Mark may come around, but for now, it is what it is and Michelle would be better served to just shut his request down because the request are only made to get a rise out of her and to stroke his ego.

Consequences: Brazil and Michelle are the ones suffering now because of Mark's selfish ways; under the circumstances, I don't know how Michelle felt for Mark and he does not have any emotional attachment to Brazil; but as she gets older, the need to have a male presence will be imperative. Mark needs to understand that due to his lack of involvement, Brazil will eventually seek out attention for nonworthy males eventually. Hey, Mark, are you going to sit it out or dance your way into Brazil's life?

Scenario 61 No Child No Future

Twelve yearrs ago, Rhonda was told that she would not be able to have children; she is now a thirty-eight-year-old and single. She met Don who is twenty-eight years old and single with no kids. Despite their age difference, they are very much connected to each other. They have been dating for eighteen months and unlike Rhonda, Don wants to be married, and have children on his own; considering Don was the only child, he would like to have several children. Rhonda understands this and told Don he should explore other options. Don was very upset regarding this comment and told Rhonda he cares for her deeply, and also is struggling with on how he would break the news to his parents who are looking forward to having grandchildren one day in the near future. Don's parents were very influential in the city of Charlotte and carrying on their legacy means everything to them. Rhonda continues to pull away because she does not want Don to feel cheated but he refuses to leave. Neither will commit because of this issue but they refuse to move on. Where do Rhonda and Don go from here? What is your take regarding the influence of Don's parents in his life?

WC: Try artificial insemination or just adopt if they truly care for each other they will make it work. Don needs to put his parents in their place.

C2: Don wants his own kids with the same blood line from his dad

DP: In this situation I can understand both sides. I think the need to carry on the name (seed) is very important to men, specifically black males. I think given the scenario Rhonda might understand that and hesitates to commit because that is something she cannot give. There is so many spiritual and historical precedence to this matter I think that is why so many couples and relationships struggle with fertility issues . . .

HL: Don is putting unnecessary pressure on Rhonda. His family's legacy isn't her problem, but his. She is justified in not trying to bare the burden of his family's expectations of grandchildren. At some point in time, they both must deal with this situation before it destroys them.

LN: Don should move on, he wants children and a wife, and he's dating a Woman that cannot bare children, it's been only 18 months, he only cares deeply for her not Love her. Don may have regrets and resentment if he settles with her. Due to death and incarceration, the rapid decline of many bloodlines of blacks I can understand the parents point too, um sure they'll love any child adopted or otherwise, but Don is possibly the last of his family's legacy

HL: Adoption may not be to his liking if he is looking for bloodline ties. Invitro maybe the best option, but other than that, you are right.

C2: Plus he is only 28, chill bruh you got some time

DP: I don't think they expected to develop feelings for one another and once the issue of children came into play then it became an issue. Seems like Rhonda has accepted her fate but Don either has to accept it or move on.

LN: That young man better run, Rhonda will be 40 in 2 years, her starting a new young family opportunities are closing fast, he is not even 30 yet, Don needs an intervention

RC: Don is still young and his feelings may change because of the fact that Rhonda can't give him children, But if he doesn't change because of the love he has for her then maybe adoption may become an option in the future.

C2: The old saying blood is thicker than water, that is what Don wants and wants to give to his parents

RC: Yes but blood doesn't always make you family . . . . ..there are many families that adopt and you'd never know!!!

DP: I have a question: Could any of us have made that sound of a decision at 28 if we had no kids and it certain we would not because of our partner . . . just a thought. Would it be easy . . . .To say adoption

TA: #1 - It is "his" life so his parents do not really get a vote in what he does with "his" life? We all should be guided by our parents but to be influenced to the point that you are allowing their decisions to become your decisions is how people end up living unhappy lives.

#2 - Decide what you want and do it. It's not that hard. If he wants his own biological kids then he needs to break off the relationship and go do that. She can't have kids. Where is the issue? Wait . . . I know, the issue is that no one wants to be an adult and have this conversation at the beginning of the 18 month relationship. He has to man up and make a decision to either not have kids and stay OR to move on and have kids with someone else.

MJ: If Don really wants a family then Rhonda needs to leave the relationship so that Don can find the person he can build a family with. She also needs to free herself for the man that will want the same things as her and not feel cheated. If they don't they will end up resenting each other in the end.

LN: I would very disappointed if my son came home with a Woman almost 40, while he's still ripe; she would be robbing the entire family of an heir.

Which brings me to this thought, Blacks should practice polygamy for race preservation. Rhonda would make a great sister wife, Lol, No really

C2: A 28 yr old man does not need to adopt when he is capable of having children, move on and they can be friends from a distance, Rhonda would make a great God mother.

TS: Some of these comments are unbelievable . . . . all of this "heir" shit. So many children that I work with don't have parents to love and guide them . . . not to mention that we live in a world of dwindling resources. Yet we still feel it is our "duty" to continue to procreate when we aren't taking care of the little ones already here left behind . . . .

C2: TS, how does your statement relate to the comments

TS:???

YWB: When u become an adult u got to live for u they lived their life

KM: It's 2014 and reproductive science may be an option. Don can still have a child and preserve his family's bloodline. It may not happen the traditional way but at the end of the day (or in this case, the end of 9mos) Don and his parents will have their heir, Don and Rhonda can continue their relationship, and some selfless woman will do a good deed and make some money by carrying Don's baby. And they live "happily ever after"!!

C2: The joy of bonding during the stages of pregnancy is lost with this method, no mental connection with the child.

MJ: I agree with David and then also some women might get a little jealous of the surrogate and then that would cause problems in the relationship.

KM: I totally agree David. But take for example soldiers who are deployed for the extent of their wife/girlfriend's pregnancy. They miss that bonding time but love the child no less and vice versa. I'm just saying it's an option and if Don and Rhonda agree that all parties involved would be satisfied, and then they should go for it!!

C2: But there is no better bonding than a mother carrying her own child

TS: okay now you're making me mad . . . I know plenty of families who have adopted their children I would like you to tell them to their face that they don't have a bond with their children . . .

KM: When something is so important to you and/or someone you love, you do what you can (within your comfort zone) to make it happen. Rhonda may WANT a family and this could be her chance to have one.

C2: They may have a bond but it's not the same and you and everyone else on here knows I. I am speaking about a mother carrying her own child I think it would be a difference but let's remember I can be wrong because I never carried a child, I love these discussion forums

KM: Rhonda would be raising the child from birth. That's different from forming a bond with a child who has already developed certain characteristics and phobias, likes and dislikes. She would be the only mother this child has ever known. She better has a ring first AND covers her ass legally. . . . Make sure she has maternal rights in the event something should happen.

LN: Its a beautiful necessity to adopt and give a home and love to children that are in need, but this about a 38 year old woman with fertility issues, with a 28 year old young man with no problems, they can adopt ten kids, and love them with no regrets, it's still not going to change the fact, if he stays with Rhonda he's sacrificing his birthright. Nobody denies adoption is needed.

DP: I think either way it is a sacrifice for both. I think Rhonda understands it a little more because she has been dealing with it for 12 years. Don not so much. If they decide to be together it will always be an issue. As I catch up on the comments even the dynamics of the group with the opinions presented here present the issues they will face. Don's parents may always be an issue as someone in the group said he has brought an "older woman" home and he is "ripe." Adoption is easy to suggest when we are outsiders looking in but no matter your race or creed birthing your own child has always been favorable over any other option. Even today same sex couples attempt to have their own "biological child" instead of adoption when possible.

Issue: Rhonda and Don have been dating for eighteen months; there is a ten-year age difference with Rhonda being the elder. Don wants to be married and have kids of his own one day. Rhonda can't have children and does not want to hold Don hostage from his dreams. Don's parents would like to have grandchildren to carry on their namesake; they are very influential in the city of Charlotte. What should Don do?

Perspectives: There is a thing as artificial insemination or adoption, but furthermore, who cares what the parents want. This situation creates a spiritual and historical precedence; I can understand both sides. Both Don and Rhonda need to handle the situation before it kills their relationship. Don needs to leave her; the two essential things he is looking for Rhonda can't produce. Man up, the choice is simple if Don wants his own biological children than he needs to seek it elsewhere.

Knowledge: Don does want his children badly, but it's important to continue the bloodline and Don values making his parents request come true, so essentially Don needs to have that important conversation with Rhonda. I am sure it's going to hurt like hell because they have a loving connection. I find it odd that if he knew Rhonda could not bear children from the beginning, why did he let this relationship go on this long of, unless Rhonda put something on his young wet behind the ear ass that he could not walk away.

Actions: This will be a very tough decision but at the end of the day, to follow his heart if that means remaining with Rhonda, then he needs to look into alternative methods to have children; but that's if Rhonda even wants to have children. If having his biological children means more to him then he needs to be out and prepare himself for the ups and downs before that comes into existence. Marriage and parenting are two of the most difficult things to do in this world. So Don better make sure he finds the right person but I am sure his parents will have the final say and which direction he goes.

Consequences: If he stays with Rhonda, he may have regrets about not having his own biological children; in addition, I am sure that he may be in a better for Rhonda although and these are Don's wants and the only thing she stated for sure is that he needs to explore his options, so I am not totally sure of her commitment level. If he opts out with Rhonda, although he is young, does it necessary mean he will find that special person who he falls in love with or is it all about having children because Mommy and Daddy want that to happen? Despite it all, I am sure who ever are chosen will have to meet high standards and then they'll probably take off before anything jumps off.

Scenario 62 Where Is My Daddy?

Scenario: Brazil will be turning five years old in a few weeks, she has seen her father a total of three times in her life, the sad thing is that he lives fifteen minutes away from her; he has never contributed any money toward her not even as much as buying her a blow pop. Brazil's mother has remained a good mother and has done everything on her own without missing a beat. Another issue is that Brazil's dad has told no one in his family about her. Brazil's mother has his contact info but has left him alone; what would you do in this case? Should she pay him a surprise visit one day or keep doing what she is doing?

C2: Mother doesn't know family, met him through match.com

LG: I think she should Keep doing what she is doing! I don't think it is her place to make him do anything for the child if he chose not to, not even introduce her to his family . . . She can one day tell her daughter who her people are but, the worse thing you can do IS TRY AND MAKE A PERSON BE APART OF SOMEONE ELSE'S LIFE, FAMILY OR NOT TRUST I SPEAK FROM EXPERIENCE!! It has been me and my son all of his life . . . I NEVER complained about his dad nor tired to make him or his family be apart of my son's life . . . He took it upon his self to get close with his other family when he got older. Anything that you may feel another person needs to do for you or your child is not up to you to make them do it . . . THAT IS BETWEEN THEM AND THEIR MAKER!!!! We as a people need to stop trying to play GOD, we all have our struggles . . . She should just keep being the best mother that she can be and don't worry about him nor what he is or is not doing...TRUST if he is not doing right, his life won't be right for him . . . But, there is always two side to a story . . .

YBW: Speaking from experience, mother and child are most likely better off without him.

PG: his an adult he knows that baby girl needs him! but baby girl doesn't know him so she has not missed anything. You can't miss what you never had so with that mom keep doing what your doing, Brazille will be just fine . . . fyi she has a father his name is JESUS the best dad one could ever have!

MS: I know this case and what was done. The mother left that man alone bcz it's his choice, he have 2 do what is right? Now the child will suffer bcz a little girl needs her dads guidance n a way that a Mom can not teach. Later on the girl may have issues on male/female relationship bcz her dad was not there 2 guide her process. The father will/may never try 2 meet his daughter unless family members intervene.

C2: MS we have all watched this movie before and it never ends with a fairy tale ending

MJ: Unfortunately this scenario is all too common and it's very sad. I agree with what PG said. Not one man has anything to say about this?

MS: No it does not but this tool is needed K.I.M. Keep It Movin this is a combination of forgiving and fulfilling ur potential meet.

Bcz u will NOT move forward until u forgive rather its a person, place, or thing!

TA: LG is 100% right. She has pretty much covered what I was going to say. The little girl is 5 so this does not mean that she will not ever have a father figure in her life. Right now it just looks like she will not have her "biological" father in her life. I know several people that have had relationships with step-parents that they call "mom/dad" because their "biological" parents were not about s***t. The only person that loses out in this is Brazil's dad because until a man does right by his child then he can't expect for life to be kind. It may look like it on the outside but many times those men are fighting demons that are tearing them apart on the inside. It is similar to the way people that are broke still walk around looking like a million bucks. Everything that glitters isn't gold.

MJ: Well said TM!!! My biological father was just a sperm donor. Today the man I call dad is my step dad and he raised me since I was five. The best father any girl could ask for.

C2: Well said TM

CA: He's a piece of shit. No I would not surprise visit him or his family. However, that lame as excuse of a father will be paying child support (if he even works). Asshole.

DD: As a father who has raised my daughter since she was 5 (she will be 13 soon) without much help from her mother. I think the mother should just keep doing what she doing. She dont need the dead beat.

C2: Thanks DD for stepping and speaking on behalf of the male gender

TF: She should keep doing what she's doing. You can't force this man to be a father to his child. If there is no love or attachment Brazil is better off without him. Once she's older her mom can give her the choice to know his family. Its sad that the father's family doesn't know she exists . . . they just might be a good family.

CA: Actually . . . I would call his mother and let her know, see how she responds, and then decide from that conversation how to proceed with regards to the family's involvement.

MM: I have a similar situation as MJ. Stepdad (Dad) has been my father since I was two and I'm thirty-eight. He legally adopted me when I was early teens . . . . . I've always known who my bio was. He'd pop n and out when it was convenient for him. My mom kept me n close contact with my grandparents until they passed. I still remember all this like it happened yesterday! Point being made is: my mom never demanded $ from him. She was blessed with a great job and took very good care of me. They never told me I couldn't c my bio and even encouraged a bond. My bio, jus would never step up. 2 this day, my 13yr old has seen him 2x (once when he was 6 days old and the other when he was 10). I told my bio all is 4given if u can jus b the grandfather 2 my son, since u weren't a father to me . . . . I got nothing! I teach my son that an absentee parent is not anything to strive 4 . . . . and those who purposely avoid responsibility r not the 1s to look up to or imitate. Do what's rt, b responsible and take care of ur children as I have dun 4 u, since I've known u were created. I do/did feel bitter 2wards my bio, but he taught me a lesson by being absent. I did end up having a child with a man similar to my bio, unfortunately but I teach my son to luv him unconditionally as he will evolve n2 his own feelings about the situation and draw his own conclusions. @ the end of the day, it should b the child's discussion and not a forced 1 . . . . . N my opinion CA It's not about the money. It's the principle of being accountable for your actions and taking responsibility, that's why I would file for child support.

C2: Thanks for sharing MM, very deep

CA: Wow! Who are these men, they suck! Makes me so thankful for the hard working men in my life. Wow. I am beyond blessed. Holy crap. Thank you God.1

MM @ CA, I said my mom didn't file (but help was also there if she needed it). I never said I didn't file. But, my reasons for doing so were very different from my mom situation. I can relate to both sides. But, on any given day I would have rather ha . . . See More

CA Yes. I agree . . . time trumps money all day every day.

C2: I thought the saying was time is money,

CA: The saying goes like this: "Time is priceless".

MJ: CA, David said that she doesn't know the family/mother to be able to call her. What does she do then?

CA: Why doesn't she know the family? She had a baby with a man without knowing his family? Why would anyone do that?

MJ: IDK people make mistakes . . . I guess that's irrelevant at this point. The child is here now so . . . oh well I guess huh?

CA: Not a mistake . . . impulsive . . . poor decision making skills. No it's very relevant at this point. Why would anyone do that?

CA: Choose your partners wisely ladies. Do your research.

C2: CA I guess that is mute point on why that person would do that, the child is here so how does that person move forward because in the grand scheme of things this child may never get to meet that side of the family

CA: I guess just make the best out of the situation at this point. I just cannot even imagine having a baby with some random guy from match.com. WTF! My son's Dad and I had a long relationship, loved each other, and lived together. I know his family and friends. I am annoyed by this scenario.

C2: Cheryl remember that is your story and ending but others may have a different story and outcomes with different characters

CA: Gotcha . . . .so I'll end with this . . . ladies, please don't have sex with other people's husbands and men you don't know. Problem solved . . . it's actually quite simple. There are consequences for all of our choices. Learn the ABC'S: Antecedent, Behavior, and Consequences.

C2: Only if it was that simple some men can charm the panties off a women while they are attending church

CA: Omg David! Be wiser than the charmers, ladies . . . I have faith in you! Focus on your goals and become self-actualized, strong women. Don't give away those precious cookies. You are WORTHY of respect.

EG: Now the serpent was more cunning than any beast of the field which the Lord God had made. And he said to the woman, "Has God indeed said, 'You shall not eat of every tree of the garden'?" Then the serpent said to the woman, "You will not surely die. (Genesis 3:1, 4 NKJV)

C2: Okay now translate that into your words because again not everyone on here is in turn with the Bible.

CA: Thank you EG. I was wondering when you'd chime in with your wise words of love. :)

CA: Pray for discernment . . . to be able to see the lies and deception of the charmers.

CA: Well more men would think twice about their behavior, if those were their consequences! :)

C2: Are the men at fault for all situations that end up with these results

CA: Long term is more than a few years . . . is doesn't sound like it from the details given here.

CA: Knowing someone and their family and friends well BEFORE you have a baby with them is going to increase the chances both parents being present in the child's upbringing. DO YOUR RESEARCH WOMEN!

CA: to look for: INTEGRITY, RESPECT, TRUSTWORTHINESS, LOYALTY, GENEROSITY, EMOTIONAL MATURITY, SELFLESSNESS, FINANCIAL STABILITY, AND HUMILITY.

Issue: Five-year-old Brazil lives fifteen minutes away from Dad but has seen him a total of three times, also he has made no contribution nor has he told any of his family members. Brazil's mom has his contact info but has carried on with her business being a mom. Should she remain this way or show up on Brazil's dad doorstep with Brazil?

Perspective: Continue doing what she has been doing, leave this situation in Gods hand; you can't force a man to do something he does not want to. She has a dad named Jesus and Brazil can't miss who she does not know. Sometimes stepdad's come into your life and fulfill that role and the child never misses a beat. Call the guy's mother to see what her take is on this situation regarding her son. People need to realize who they are lying down with and creating these children.

Knowledge: Brazil's mother felt like her biological clock was ticking and wanted to have a child by this other guy she was in love with, but he was not interested in having any more children. So to me it was more about having a child then the possible commitment from the guy. In cases like this, you may play with fire, your ass will get fried; so everyone, how about some cheese to go with that wine.

Action: Brazil suffers in this situation because of two adults who wanted to tango in the sheets instead of thinking about the consequences. As much as my heart aches for Brazil and we can put the blame on Brazil's dad, her mom is just as guilty. She made her pissy bed so now she needs to lie on it. Going to his doorstep can get that ass a beat down in front of Brazil. She needs to carry on with her life and pray that homie comes around for his baby.

Consequences: Hardship after hardship, a woman left with raising a young girl on her own and to face all of societal issues without her father's guidance. The ultimate goal is how we make this a winning situation for Brazil. I would warn Brazil's mom do not try to force Brazil on her dad, let his involvement with her feel genuine instead of a force obligation. When you make something mandatory without the other party's consent, you can end up making things far worse than they started off being. Women, don't believe the hype with online dating, you are playing a game of Russian Roulette with your life.

CHAPTER 9

Mistrust

Scenario 63 A Missed Opportunity

JANICE IS LIVING a life of regrets trying to find that silver bullet called love; but when she had it as a youngster, she let it get away. Evan was head over heels in love with her as they started their freshman year in college. Janice likes to drink in at times would get out of character, but it was okay when she was with Evan because he covered down for her, protected her like no other, he loved her hard, and thought their love would never end. Things changed once they got to college and she made new friends and suddenly Evan became an afterthought. Each attempt Evan made to see her, she declined him and it tore him into pieces. Finally she came home for the holidays; Evan just knew Janice would make him a priority, but that was not the case, she denied him for a couple of days. When she finally came around, it was not a joyous visit; she came to end it and she told Evan he was crowding her and he needs to get off her Bozak. Evan broke down and pleaded for her not to leave him. She denied him again, Evan was a hot mess for a while and never forget this experience and he has been afraid of commitment to this day. Janice has not had any luck be there in regards to relationships. Her heart aches because she has never found anyone that love her unconditionally as Evan did. Have you ever let a love one get away, and if so, how did you get over it? Just remember when that opportunity comes knocking at the door, be prepared to answer because you never know if that opportunity will come again. Missed opportunities are painful.

C2: It unfortunate for both parties that Janice decisions impacted both of their future relationships. But someway somehow they need to find a way of working through these issues. Maybe these 2 can give it another shot

HL: Selfish people behave selfishly

DP: Well Evan should value himself know his worth and know he is worth more than what Janice feels. Sounds like Janice is immature. Evan deserves better and as for Janice you never miss your water until your well runs dry. If Evan is willing to give Janice a 2nd chance than lucky for her, I would not blame him for moving on.

MJ: I agree with DP. People keep looking for greener grass until the lawn gets too overwhelming to mow. If he forgave her and gave her another chance she should take it. However, he shouldn't go backward. There will eventually be a good woman who will love him unconditionally. Neither of them should get back together just because they're lonely. They would just be settling if they did. Neither of them should make a permanent decision based on a temporary emotion.

MASJ: If it is meant for them to be together they will be.

JE: The only mention of love in this scenario is that he was head over heels in love with her. No mention of the vice versa. If Janice isn't head over heels in love with Evan then it really doesn't matter how much he loves her, sounds to me that the feeling isn't mutual. If so, it wouldn't be fair for her to string him along and ending their relationship was the best thing for them both, only thing she should have done is end it sooner instead of prolonging his pain.

C2: I never mention it in the scenario but before they started college, she claimed she loved him

MJ: Love is unconditional and it shouldn't be based on emotion. Love is a verb. She had lust not love because if they weren't so she would have worked it out.

JE: Doesn't matter what she claimed, her action showed otherwise.

KP: Going to college is a major change for individuals . . . it's a time for exploring and coming into your own . . . Almost a selfish state . . . Janice was wrong for treating Evan with such disrespect. The one person who truly loved her unconditionally . . . . Evan will hurt for a while but needs to move on and find someone who will respect him, love him unconditional like he deserves. Janice needs to feel the hurt that she had given to Evan. (I didn't miss an opportunity per say just put his wants and needs above my own and encouraged him to flourish and follow his dreams)

C2: Why would a woman play with a man's heart when a good man is hard to find? Despite their age

JE: The act of showing love is a verb, love itself is an energy, unexplainable and powerful. It should, at its root, be based on nothing but pure emotion, based on anything else it has ulterior motives. Love is the only true emotion that exists. There is only love and the absence of love, every other emotion stems from these. If she were in love with him it would show through her actions naturally. It didn't so it's time to let go.

MJ: Love endures long and is patient and kind; love never is envious nor boils over with jealousy, is not boastful or vainglorious, does not display itself haughtily. It is not conceited (arrogant and inflated with pride); it is not rude (unmannerly) and does not act unbecomingly. Love (God's love in us) does not insist on its own rights or its own way, for it is not self-seeking; it is not touchy or fretful or resentful; it takes no account of the evil done to it [it pays no attention to a suffered wrong]. It does not rejoice at injustice and unrighteousness, but rejoices when right and truth prevail. Love bears up under anything and everything that comes, is ever ready to believe the best of every person, its hopes are fadeless under all circumstances, and it endures everything [without weakening]. (1 Corinthians 13:4-7 AMP). He deserves that.

LH: Feel bad for Evan, he needs to jump back in the race. I'm not totally mad at her, she was young and immature. Why do I feel like the story is pointing in the direction of, should Janice try to get back at Evan?

C2: LH, I think the attempt was there but Evan gave her the cold shoulder other than having sex with her.

CA: You win some, you lose some. Plenty of fish in the sea!!!!!! ;) No regrets in

TA: Janice wasn't ready when Evan was and by the sound of it, probably thought the grass was greener on the other side. She was young and thought time was on her side. I am a believer in if it is meant to be then it will happen. They weren't meant to be together. Evan didn't need someone who didn't appreciate him. She was selfish. Also, opportunities don't come to anyone, from where I stand opportunities usually present themselves in the form of work. In other words, make your own opportunities. Its never that serious to the point of settling for someone just because you don't think you can do better.

Issue: Janice and Evan were together when they were younger and it truly felt like love for Evan, but Janice had other plans when they went off to college; she ended up breaking Evan's heart, and from this forward both of them struggled with future relationships.

Perspectives: Evan deserves better than the way Janice treated him, he needs to have more self-worth. Evan should not go backward, one day he will find a women that values his love, and loves him unconditionally. It's best they both go their separate ways, their feelings are not mutual. College is a time to explore and find yourself; Janice was too young and selfish to grasp that process. When it comes to opportunities, you have to go out and create your own.

Knowledge: Drinking was the root of self-destruction for Janice and her being gullible. She put herself in a terrible position at college with no one to watch her back; in return, she ruined the love of her life, many will say that karma came back very hard against her. In order for it to ever work for these two, Janice would have to eat a huge slice of humble pie and I am not sure that is her flavor of the month.

Action: Many people would think Evan is a damn fool for going back to Janice, but typically, those individuals are full of shit. I can say this if he decided to go back he better make sure he has the upper hand and becomes the future shot caller or else history will repeat itself. When you get older, what would you prefer, someone you already know but previously it did not work out or a random stranger? Those are the things you need to consider because this dating game is a biaaatch.

Consequences: If Evan truly loved Janice and he refused to give her another opportunity, he may end up regretting this decision. Life is about taking chances; either way, you just need to be conscious of the choices we make, but chances have to be taken to create opportunities no matter what you do in life. Become the best counterpuncher in life.

Scenario 64 Closet Lovers

Scenario time: you work at a nursing home with your best friend's fiancée Kevin; one night during the middle of your 11:00-7:00 a.m. shift, you walk into the linen closet and find Kevin and Nurse Jill having sex; you hurry up and close the door without them seeing you. What are you going to do with this information?

AB: haha you crazy

C2: AB that is not an answer

MMA: Im telling, point blank

C2: MMA without talking to Kevin

AB: it'll be hammer time

SL: I'm telling

C2: AB meaning what that Kevin was smashing the nurse
So SL you are going to ruin their potential

GCE: They won.t be getting married! No need to ask Kevin what was you doing!!!!

MM: What is it to talk about he got caught, point blank

C2: How are you going to deliver that hurtful info when they are scheduled to get married in 2 months

KJP: Go back and get my camera phone . . . hopefully I have it with me . . . then its click click . . . hey buddy I'm not saying a word... the pic I just sent to I cloud is talking not me . . . I swear . . . lol Then I will support her and let her decide . . . I've been in situations like that so I know not to judge and let her ride it out the way she wants to . . . cause she may wanna still get married and forgive him . . . who knows . . . she's gotta decide . . . I'm just her support system to fall back on.

MR: I think i would let kevin know I know . . . sometimes being in someone else business can back fire . . . Learned from experience . . . some people dont want to know anything about they men . . .

MM: He should have thought about it not done it...sorry once a hoe always a hoe

TA: I'm telling my best friend the same way I would expect her to tell me. Period.

SL: I'm not ruining anything him and his doggish ways ruined it. His bad

C2: You ladies don't believe in giving 2nd chance. What if he was trying to get out all the demons before he got married

SL: Bullshit. He should have gotten the demons out b4 he proposed

TA: SL is right, I call bullshit! He can get out his demons but thats his decision. Thats the beautifiul thing about freewill and freedom of choice. What he needs to realize is that every decision regardless if its good or bad has a consequence that may be intended or unintended. Therefore he made the decision so he needs to deal with the consequences.

KJP: David would you give your fiancee a 2nd chance? Or you can make thus a ? Are woman or men more forgiving when it comes to infidelity?...which is more likely to stay and make it last forever (in my keith sweat singing voice). lol I already know what my thoughts are . . . lol

C2: Absolutely if I loved her enough

HL: Letting my man know

CA: Well . . . was she with holding sex from her fiance?

Issue: You work with your best friend's fiancée Kevin, and one night while working, you walk into the linen room and you catch Kevin plowing the Charge Nurse Jill. What are you going to do with this surprise info?

Perspectives: Nothing to discuss, I am telling point blank; this marriage will not take place if it's up to me. I would get my camera phone and snap a picture. I would let her know but not judge the situation; this is a decision she has to make for herself. I would speak to Kevin and let him know I am aware of the situation; some females don't want to hear anything regarding their man. Could she be withholding sex from Kevin?

Knowledge: Just maybe Kevin fiancée may be okay with his act of discretion, get it out before you say those vows. I think it would be important to process this with Kevin before planning your trap and not knowing the entire situation. Far too many times, we overreact to situations instead of diagnosis before we prescribe (the great Steven Covey).

Action: I learned my lesson several times of showing my allegiance to friends in regards to looking out for friends and it backfired so now I keep my nose clean and you heard it; I will plead the fifth and I ain't seen shit especially if you are not going to do anything with the information I share. The less people you have in your business, the stronger the relationship may become.

Consequences: Again know your friend; are they going to go somewhere with the info you spare or will they let their partner sweet talk their panties off and you look like the nosey asshole who broke your neck to tell all for nothing. There have been controlling relationships where the guys have had the females turn on their friends for trying to destroy their love. So again, know who you are dealing with during these situations.

Scenario 65 Confirm My Schedule

Devin had been working two jobs for a while and his vacation had just started; Dena his girlfriend had made plans for them to spend the whole day together, but Devin had other plans. He did not want to let Dena down, but he had made plans to attend a summer beach party with Chuck and Antonio, his buddies. So off to the beach party he went, drinking and having a great time, a much needed great time; meanwhile Dena showed up and asked why did he break their plans and she wanted to stay at the party with him. Devin told her she needed to go home because he was with his boys and besides you don't bring sand to the beach. This instantly upset Dena who begin to cry and threaten to not be around when he returned from the party. Should Devin had let Dena stay or was he right for sending her away?

SS: He was wrong for telling her to leave but at the same time that was kind of Staulkerish for her to just show up like that. I'm conflicted and I don't really know what to say about that. That's why I'm single. Lol

COJ: R u kidding??? Men need time with the fellas just like women need time with the girls. Dena better go home and let that man be. She can see him later.

C2: Why is Dena mapping out his vacation without finalizing with Devin first? So damn intrusive

MIJ: He could have skipped the sand to the beach comment. She shouldn't have shown up uninvited.

C2: Welcome my friend MIJ, I look forward to your valued insight

SBC: I don't feel that he was wrong for telling her to leave; however, if he had perhaps approached it in a different way then Dena might not have gotten so upset. Couples need personal time away from each other.

TF: Devin deserved his vacation. . . Dena shouldn't have shown up . . . Devin's sand to the beach comment was wrong

C2: Welcome back Tee, you know I value your feedback

KP: Knowing he had vacation time coming up Devin should had communicated with Dena about his plans in advance . . . . . . They could have made plans after his boys night out . . . there would have not been any confusion if there was a conversation before hand . . . Communication . . . Communication . . . Communication . . . .

HL: There is two dynamics at work.

1. Her making plans without getting his input;

2. His insensitivity to her regarding the statement. It might be true, but IF he intended on making the relationship last, then he just put into her mind subtly that he might be untrust worthy.

HL: KP: Why is it necessary for him to advise her of his plans? He is a free man and should be able to have plans without having to advise her of his every move. Anytime anyone makes plans for two people without getting input from that person in advance, they have earned what they get. She was disappointed through all her own fault.

C2: When Dena threatened to not be around she was throwing out there suicidal thoughts to make him feel bad

KP: Well HL: if they are in a relationship then it's called respect . . . Not saying he should "ask" permission but communicate to her what his plans are . . .

HL: Well, I'm going to put it out like this . . . . I would have told her nice to know ya!!

HL: True KP, but where was that RESPECT when she didn't ask him?!

HL: I mean she made plans for THEM without his knowledge. Some how I see that as a double standard. Or is that just respect for women and not men? Hmmm . . .

HL: In trying to be dictatorial, she comes across as petulant. That does not fly in my book. Women like that are better off by themselves!! Or with children they can command.

KP: She shouldn't have to ask . . . Not saying anything in advance would assume he had no plans . . . . . Or was he trying to avoid a fight knowing she would be upset . . . . Either way . . . . Communication!!!!!!!!!!! I think it both ways . . . respect for each other

HL: Okay, then why did she not take it upon herself to ask seeing as she made plans for the both of them? IF he has done this and she had plans, would she have felt violated? When making plans, it is prudent to see if the other party(s) has plans. Must be me, but I usually do that.

C2: Communication is imperative, a simple Devin do you have any plans for your vacation if not can we do something on such and such date

HL: Just that simple. No muss, no fuss.

KP: No matter what . . . . No matter whom . . . . no matter why . . . If they had the open communication then it would have not come down to an unfortunate situation in which now has escalated into something much more volatile

CA: Enjoy your vacation Devin! This couple may want to consider improving their communication skills. Lol

C2: Should Devin consider her a basket case that does whatever necessary for attention

LN: Clearly his time with his boys was more important, and he's obviously looking for sand (women). It's a party, her plans may have included that same party, BUT, Devin is an asshole for his comment. She needs to move on. If a man is constantly working and when he's off, he didn't think to make plans to spend time with his Woman, leave him to hang with his boys. Make no threats, just move in silence. Silence speaks much louder than words.

C2: LN, maybe he made an asshole statement about bringing sand to the beach, but I will chalk it up as it was motivated by alcohol and besides, that particular day was not the end all be all she could have chilled with him another day

LN: Nah I'm thinking he's an asshole, drunken honesty is no excuse. He could have committed some time to her the next day, but instead he chose to make the sand statement. If it were the other way around, Men don't handle statements like that coming from their Woman well. No babe, you need to leave, I'm here with my girl's, who brings Hotdogs to a barbecue. Loll, Men would fly off the handle

C2: Would a man be that impulsive to show up I think that is the difference

LN: Definitely they would, especially if it's a public party and yes then. Would try to be all over you. Then only difference is, most Women wouldn't make that asshole statement to a man they care about I think she was good in trying to make plans, maybe she was going to surprise him by planning things he likes to do, clearly she found out, he's not interested in her plans, silly woman, should have communicated with him

C2: I am sure some guys may beg to differ

KM: Men and women are very different creatures. I think in general, men see "hanging wit da boys" as stress relief from the daily grind and unfortunately their significant other. Women like romance and quiet time with the man in their life. Since Devin was the one working two jobs, his day off should have been spent doing what he wanted to do. Dena shouldn't have assumed he wanted to spend it with her. So I agree, communication is key. But he was wrong for the comment he made and she needs to evaluate her place in his life.

KP: David Glover why does she need to be a basket case? Is she that so wrong that she wants to send some quality time with him? Maybe he made her into a basket case!!!! Loll.

C2: Because she pulled the I am going to kill myself role once she didn't get what she wanted

HL: Which is as I said are the markings of a petulant adult. Only a child will hold their breath until they get what they want. That is exactly what she did. I don't care who you are, to use that type of a threat should be met only one way . . . call the bluff

HL: LN: I can think many (_o_) statements that women have said to men. I'm sure you can too if you are being honest.

C2: We all know that most women executive and planning skills are better than men but this does not give them the right to fill up someone's calendar without approval.

KP: We all know that men only think with one side of their brain and can only see what is right in front of them without seeing the consequences that may arise . . . .need to remember that a relationship includes two people . . . . Sorry David just had to give a shout out to the females!!! Xoxo

LN: Definitely some inconsiderate Women make rude comments to Men. HL

CBH: One thing I feel is very valuable is your time and no one should plan it for you without consulting you first. She was wrong for going to the beach and looked rather desperate. I would hate for my man to to show up at girl's night out Uggh. He probably was showing off for his boys with the sand at the beach comment but that probably just opened a whole other issue because she won't forget that . . . .ever.

HL: KP: Judging by the scenario, I guess she was behaving as a man then?

HL: By the way CHB, I agree

ALM: He is an asshole. Obviously he's not concerned about her at all. She needs to move on and deal with someone who will leave the sand at the beach and cherish a good woman who actually cares about him.

HL: How did she come to be a good woman? Her making plans and not consulting him is not what I'd consider 'good', but rather selfish. That is not synonymous with good in my book. Might be me. *scratches head*

ALM: She may have been excited about spending time with her man who caused her to make plans. That's what women do we plan for the future while men live in the present. If he didn't want to spend his time with her he should have just said so. He is an ass . . . David Glover when did she say imma kill myself. It says that she won't be there when he gets back. That would usually mean that she's leaving him.

C2: ALM I know that comment to mean taking her life

ALM: Well if that's the case she's tripping. I thought she was threatening to leave him which would've been a completely logical reaction. He needs to head for the hills if she's going to off herself.

LN: ALM, LMao, Show her ass and bust it open for somebody else, Hahahahaha

C2: How does busting open your ass work?

LN: Twerk, tweak, it to the floor, Loll

C2: Oh okay the good ole freak dancing

ALM: Exactly loll

TA: Okay . . . I am trying to get caught up here but basically they are both wrong! These two people have zero communication skills. All of this extra drama could have been avoided with a simple conversation. She did not have a right to make plans for someone else's time without their input. She is his girlfriend and not his wife for goodness sake. Women need to know the difference. Then she just shows up where he is with his boys. I'm sorry but he is human so saying something insensitive when you are upset is not abnormal. At the end of the day, he is wrong for not communicating with her upfront and then she is wrong for pretty much the rest of the scenario. It should have ended at "I have plans with my boys". There was no need to show up and show out at the beach.

HL: ALM: I'll wait for you to retract that comment about men not knowing what a good women looks like, but I have a feeling that won't happen. The fact of the matter is that many men will try to appease women who are unworthy of their affections

ALM: I did generalize when saying that men don't know a good woman when they see one. I will not retract my statement but I will revise it and say that many men have trouble with that. Only because I do have good men in my life who have selected their woman well and treat them as such. What makes you think Dena was unworthy of his affection? All we see in this discussion is what happened in this situation. For all you know she could have played a major role in helping and supporting him in his time of need. Making plans is something that a woman who truly cares about her man would do. Given maybe she shouldn't have popped up at the party but maybe she planned to go there anyway and happened to see him there. His reaction was disrespectful and if he really cared about his girlfriend he would have at least been a gentleman about it. He could have even stopped at I'm with the boys.

People should treat each other accordingly but I don't see in this scenario where she deserved to be spoken to in that manner.

HL: I made no assumption on anything she did that was not posted. You show me where I said she was not worthy of his affections and I'll gladly retract that statement. I did make a statement about men giving their affections to undeserving women, but not this

ALM: Yes she should have asked first but she had no ill intent in making plans for them. She must have known that when making plans that he may not be interested in them. That's a risk she took that backfired. She could have been trying to surprise her man with something special there is no harm in that. I am not siding with her because she is a woman. I truly believe that sometimes good intentions get skewed.

LN: I thought it was a good thing to plan a spontaneous romantic evening with your man, especially if he's a hard working man with two jobs but it sounds like you guys are saying you should get permission first before planning a romantic evening with your man. The biggest complaint that I hear from men is that they don't feel appreciated and that their women behave like it's all about them and so many of them would love a woman to take charge and plan a romantic evening instead of waiting on him to take her on a date but I could be wrong

HL: Let me put it out; She did NOTHING wrong. She could have done it better. Here is how: Ask him if he has plans on said day/date. If not, then tell him/ask to not make any plans. When he ask why and he will, tell him that he'll find out in due time,

ALM: LN exactly. I get that men like to chill with the guys but sheesh. Are the boys that much of a priority that if your woman plans a romantic date that you would actually blow her off for a party wit the guys? This convo just makes me feel so blessed to have a man who puts me before his friends.

HL: If it is the Super Bowl, YES!!!

ALM: Loll o lord that's the next convo we need to have. A mans opinion on sports vs. women

HL: Why wait?! Lets do it now . . . .haha

ALM: Loll u go first HL

HL: I tell any perspective mate that on Sundays from September to February, don't expect to hear from me. I'm watching football. Unless she is dying, or someone is in the hospital or ER . . . don't not call!! I'll call you

ALM: Loll at least u added the dying part. Do men prefer to watch a game with the boys or their woman who is also into sports?

HL: Men will watch any sports with those who watch. Gender does not matter. If you doubt that, just go a Net's home game and see how many women come out of there. Rangers or Knicks . . .

ALM: Knicks!!!!

HL: Philadelphia Seventy sixers; See, we have a conflict already and when haven't even exchanged numbers LOL I'm also the type of guy that will teach a female about a sport I watch if she wants to learn and doesn't know

ALM: Boooo 76ers loll jk. Well that's a good thing. I can keep up with basketball. But I'm lost when it comes to football. I go to super bowl parties for the snacks loll is that bad?

HL: No. most Super Bowl parties are about that food, drink and such. Hardcore football fans will indulge in the food, but the game is the ultimate priority. I'm actually looking into putting a group together for women to learn about football. It's not hard to understand football, but it'll take some time, effort and willingness to put aside some time to learn. Let me know if you are interested

ALM: Loll a women's football support group. Yeah I'm sure that'll be a hit! U should also discuss fantasy football and what people get outta that. When folks start talking to me about their fantasy football team it sounds like the teacher from Charlie brown.

HL: Sure thing. I'll keep you posted on it. They go hand in hand actually. One can help you learn about the other.

Issues: Devin had been working really hard working two jobs and was going on vacation and planned some time with his boys attending a beach party; sounds like big fun, but Dena his girlfriend had made plans for them two to spend the day together. Was Dena wrong for planning his vacation time?

Perspectives: He was wrong for telling her to leave, but she demonstrated stalkerish behavior. Man need time to themselves as well, Dena take your ass home. The sand to the beach comment was a little bit too much. Don't show up anywhere uninvited. Devin should have communicated his plans to Dena in advance. Why does this grown man have to communicate his plans with her?

Knowledge: Devin and Dena had many relationship issues to begin with, so definitely, Devin was trying to hang with his boys to scope out some potential candidates; and as far as I know, he had some ladies there waiting to model their two-piece bathing suits. So we can see Devin had choices and besides he put in time at work to have a good time. Work hard play harder. Now he could have been more sensitive once she showed up, but it's never a good outcome to throw yourself on someone.

Action: Personally, unless I say "Babe plan something for us to do" and unless I confirm that, then it's a no go; I dictate my plans or vacation time. If we are having issues and then certainly my vacation time with you will be on a limited-time basis. It may be harsh, but its truthful; vacation is a time to relax and re-energize yourself to be prepared to get ready for a continuous grind at work or whatever you do. Obviously you want to be amongst good company, not someone you will be arguing back in forth bringing stress upon you. To Devin I salute, you deserve laughter, and sweet eye candy to begin your vacation.

Consequences: The downside of this attitude is you may hurt your significant other's feelings but again she forced her controlling ways on Devin. This was day one of his vacation so she could have simply let him be and fell back in line and waited her turn because day one belongs to that person who is taking that vacay. Sorry people, self-preservation comes first. Advice to you ladies, doesn't mark up my calendar without running it by me.

Scenario 66 Games People Play

Latanya was preparing for her weekend plans, it was Thursday evening and she was sitting around with her boyfriend Phil and she asked does he mind if she goes to happy hour tomorrow with a couple of her guy friends from work; originally Phil said yes; but after Latanya decided to go, Phil changed the script and said she should have known that it wasn't okay. Latanya really wanted him to say no to see where she stood with Phil. So when he said okay, Latanya was liked okay what the hell. Things hit the fan when Phil saw a text message to Mike, a friend of Latanya, which read that Latanya almost got plowed by Rick once Mike left because Rick was trying to get with her really hard; but she didn't mean it literally, and besides, she already told Phil about Rick. Everything got heated when Latanya found that Phil was sexting other women asking to taste their goodies considering he never tasted Latanya. After a major blow up, Phil thought both situations were equal, Latanya did not think so; she kicked Phil out of the house. In your opinion, was Latanya actions justified?

TS: Latanya may have been wrong for going out with the guys . . . but Phil's intent was much worse. Plus it seems like Latanya was open and honest about everything while Phil was doin dirt on the low . . .

TA: Who are these people? All of this is immature on both sides yet again we have a breakdown in communication. #1: She was playing a game. If she wanted to know where she stood with Phil then she should have asked him! #2: If he said yes, then he should have stuck to his yes. What is up with this changing your mind and then putting it on Latanya that "she should" have known better. Really? She obviously didn't IF she was ASKING him in the first place. #3: What is up with all of this checking each others text messages? It doesn't matter what the text say, the point is you shouldn't be reading someone elses text messages, period. If you are at the point of having to check text messages with the person you are in a relationship with then you don't have a relationship. Insecure people do not have happy long lasting relationships. She doesn't trust him and he doesn't trust her. Regardless of if she was justified or not the split was going to happen because there wasn't any trust. Relationships are simple. Its the people in them that make them complicated.

HL: LMBO . . . Okay first thing first, Phil should have his own place

GG: why does this sound like love jones? I hate games. put your cards on the table. If she wanted to know where she was in the relationship she should ask. If he didnt want her to go he should have said so. BUT if you are out sexting out here you get what your hand calls for and all the fall out. . . . . . . I happened to have male friends. If i thought it would make my signifiacant other uneasy I would invite him. I would let him get to know my friends. I would not be going out with anyone that would put my relationship in danger.

KP: Obviously this is not a relationship that has trust or communication . . . . For her to "test" him and for him to "yes" her was obviously a short coming in their relationship . . . .. For a woman to go to such lengths to see if a man truly cares is a cry out for the attention she needs from him . . . . And for a man to call her bluff is a just a way of him "showing her" . . . . As for the text . . . .Dumb asses!!! If they spent the time they did in the fabricating of the texting into building their relationship maybe they wouldnt have to worry about each others phones . . . for her to kick him out . . . Premature and just a power move she had on him . . . . But for him to call her bluff . . . probably the best thing he did to get rid of a women who wants to change him into what she wants him to be not be the part of his life that enhances him . . .

C2: No Love Jones here real life GG

LN: Latanya is childish, and when you play games you lose. She knew Damn well, that she shouldn't be hanging out with men from work. Unless she's not in a committed relationship, or they're Judy's, Lol

COJ: R these ppl over 30??? They need to break up and move on. Geee wiz

C2: Definitely over 30 COJ

KP: If after 30 they are acting as if they are 20 . . . . Both need to grow up and move on . . . .

C2: This behavior isnt based on age because we have people in their 50's that can act this way

KP: Maybe David . . . But as people age their behaviors and reactions should be at different levels of intensity

C2: It depends on environment, culture, values, professionalism. Its not cut and dry

KP: Absolutely David . . . but knowing nothing about this couples background . . . ie culture, values, environment and professionalism . . . . I only went with a general observation . . .

C2: KP, you are right that is why I only give you enough to base your perception on the info provided

ALM: Wooooow so much to address in this sitch . . . . Okay so first of all if they already live together she should not need to play silly games to figure out "where they stand". Phil probably said yes to see how far she would go since she is so eager to accompany her male friends. If she told Phil about Rick trying to come onto to her he could have been more understanding. But I do understand his anger because he did say he didn't want her to go when the time came. He was immersed in his emotions which caused him to do say something inappropriate and out of character (since he never "tasted" his girl). He was wrong for that because instead of approaching her about it and working it out he turned bad into worse. According to her a man made an advance at her and was turned down. According to his texts he made a sexual advance at another woman. Where did she come from? Obviously shes not a new fixture in his life. I dont think she was wrong for kicking him out because they dont trust each other nothing worse than sleeping next to someone who u dont trust. Seriously decreases quality of life. No bueno

C2: Just to give you an update after Latanya and Phil split up she has decided to attend the happy hour today with her male colleagues

ALM: Lol no strings for her anymore. Wonder if Rick has a chance.

C2: She is free as a bird right now

DP: This looks like both of them had commitment issues. Each one was testing the trust of the other. Phil sexting had him guilty that Latanya was stepping out on him and . . . .so on. This is the classic cat and mouse game. Tricks are for kids and if they want a solid relationships these sort of games need to cease. I fill like the scene from "The Five Heartbeats" - "I have to fight every night to prove my love." If they were in love and together then these things would not happen. Say what you mean and mean what you say. This is why so many relationships have problems to day. Keep you butts at home and clean your own house. *stepping down* This is not gender specific this goes for everyone.

Issue: Latanya was invited out by a couple of guy friends to a happy hour; Latanya asked Phil if was okay and he stated yes she can go. Phil really didn't want her to go and did not think she would go. This miscommunication led them to go through each other's phone and they had a big blow up from the content of the messages, which led to Latanya kicking Phil out of the house.

Perspectives: What's up with the lack of communication and the checking of each other's text messages; no trust, no relationship. This was bound to happen. Phil's intent was worse and he was doing dirt on the low, low. People should stop playing games and maybe Latanya should have invited Phil out to the happy hour. Kicking him out was a premature power move; they need to focus their relationship instead of playing games. Latanya is childish and she should not be hanging out with male coworkers in the first place.

Knowledge: Women like to use that bullshit that they like hanging out with guys because females are to catty; no, they like being the center of attention, and when they are with guys, there will be a lot of boob-and-ass watching from the guys. Throw alcohol in the equation and some inappropriateness will come out. Latanya is no less guilty than Phil. Stop trying to play chess when you are skilled at checkers.

Action: Phil should have shot this down from the beginning, no need to play "homie" unless you wanted to use this time to text the honeys you were trying to taste. Clearly like previously discussed, they had communication issues and were not mentally connected in their relationship, but yet they were shacking, go figure! What does love have to with it, relationships are more about the business side, hence them living together.

Consequences: When you play with fire, you will get burned; clearly these two could not overcome their relationship issues. It makes me wonder, was Latanya opening the back door for Rick to come in after sending Phil out the front door, something for you to marinate on, what a coincidence do you think this was premeditated? Well both are free agents; hopefully someone will sign Metta World Peace and Dennis Rodman. Totally cray, cray.

Scenario 67 I Can Make It Better

Scenario time: Gina and Bill have been struggling lately due to Bill recently losing his job for excessive absences; this has created a hardship for the family because Bill was denied unemployment. The bills are adding up and Gina does not know where to turn. She started staying late at work and started sharing her issues with Steven. Steven offered to let Gina borrow some money for one night of passion. What should Gina do?

FG: Gina should go rent the movie temptation!!!

C2: Renting that movie is not going to pay her bills

HL: It's not what Gina should do; it is what Bill should be doing. However, this is why I don't deal with women who put their personal business in the work place. NO GOOD for the relationship. It adds unnecessary pressure and puts people in bad positions.

HL: the simple answer is decline the offer.

FG: But it will remind her that one night of passion and. "Getting her bills paid" can end her life!

C2: This is true FG but most people respond out of emotion

TS: I think both Bill and Steven should kick rocks and Gina should find a real man that is responsible enough to care for her without strings.

C2: Gina opened up the flood gates by sharing her business

TS: That doesn't mean she was opening up other things . . . Steven was a douche to offer money for sex.

C2: Is he a douche or an opportunist?

HL: I'd say an opportunist. Everyone has decision to make. Gina is no different than Steve. Just in a financial situation.

TS: Lol . . . both. I just know that if I were Gina, any feelings that may have started would have flown out the window with that offer. If he had game he would have just offered the money and then he might have gotten some on the regular because she thought he was so generous. (Not saying that I would fall for that either . . . But some would unfortunately.)

PC: Bill, Gina and Steven must live in Niagara Falls. So many Gina's already paying her bills like this, and so many Bill's cannot keep a damn job and way too many damn Steven's ready to pay a Gina for some ass.

HL: TS, if what you are saying is true, then she was already contemplating leaving Bill. Emotional cheating is the first step for women into physical cheating.

PC: Steven is the smart one; he knows them bills gone be due again next month. Residual coochie! Smart man.

TS: I absolutely agree. But I still say that I would drop both men . . .

TC: Everyone is focused on Steven, I am focused on why Bill is missing so much work and can't find another job.

C2: Yes people, need to hold Billy Boy accountable for his mishaps

TC: OAN Gina should have put Steven in his place for disrespecting her. Also she should have never been talking about her marriage good or bad to him anyways.

C2: My issue with Steven is he that loose with his money.

TC: That's your issue? Not that he is a jerk for approaching a married woman like that

C2: There is nothing stating that they were married, she shared some info with Steven wanting him to go somewhere with it

EP: Yo David you know Steve and Gina has already had words before this and he knew that he would get a chance at her. She not shit any way, she and her man should have sat down an came up with a plan together but she (Gina) ran to a piece of shit nigga that she has already be kicking it with at work… No good chick . . .

C2: My man EP, I can always count on you to give it to us raw

EP: Raw but ole skool . . . And real . . .

C2: Yes Sir

TC: If they are not married, why are we even discussing this? Why is she taking care of a grown man who is not her husband?

C2: Just maybe when he was working they were splitting things 50/50 so it may not be that easily financially to walk.

HL: David: That is exactly why I said I don't deal with females like that.

C2: Talk to me brother HL, are you saying when things are going good it's good, but when it turns bad they bail out

HL: Not so much that. I was raised to keep home affairs in the home. You know how our mothers got down. There wasn't any of the running your mouth in the streets about what goes on in these four walls. That was an automatic (_._) whippin'. Now, before all of women kind jumps on me like Mr. Ed, don't misunderstand what I am saying. I am NOT saying he should hit her. I'm saying that she should have kept her home affairs HOME! Once a person opens up the door to what goes on in ANY relationship, no matter what it is, they subject that relationship to anyone who doesn't care and wishes to undermine it. Thus in this case, Steve, who has low to no scruples made his move like a shark does. He only does what she may have been secretly wanting and that is a man who can financially take care of her. If, and I stress IF, she was really into effective communication and the longevity of the relationship, then she would have sat Bill down long ago and made him aware of how his attendance problems at work is causing a major issue in their relationship and possibly preventing it from being a longer term. By him not being a responsible brother, he is undermining his position in the home as well is in her head. I believe that most of us will agree that when a thought such as that hits a woman's head, it's only a matter of time before she is going to seek greener pastures.

C2: Well said brother Herb

ALM: Being broke is no excuse to turn to prostitution.

HL: ALM: She didn't turn to it, it was offered. HUGE difference!

Issue: Gina and Bill were having financial problems because recently Bill lost his job and had no money coming in. Gina begin discussing her household issues with a male coworker who propositions her for one night of passion. What should Gina do?

Perspectives: It's not what Gina should be doing, it's Bill who is not doing, but she should not be putting their business out there. One night of passion can be disastrous. Steven is trash for offering money for sex. Why focus on Steven instead of Bill who lost his job. Gina has been having conversations with Steven for a while, which makes her not shit. She should have sat down with Bill and devised a plan. Why would someone be taking care of a man who she is not married to? When a women begins thinking about making a move, typically it's going to happen.

Knowledge: We all go through issues at home; the problem lies when you share your issues with others especially someone at work. When you let others know your weakness, they use it as an opportunity to exploit you. If you are committed to someone, then you entitled to at least have a sit down with them before you put others in your business. I can tell you this as the bills pick up, the better the offer looks for Gina to take; so at this point, Bill is a lame duck.

Action: Gina and Bill need to come up with a time frame to see how they can salvage their financially embarrassing situation; if things don't change, they may need to split up, there is no need to dog each other out in the streets. They also need to look at the core issue of why Bill lost his job in the first place; was it due to drinking, laziness, lack of motivation, this has to be addressed before any plans is put in place.

Consequences: Bill's lack of employment has put them in serious jeopardy financially as well as him losing his women to another man. As a man, this is a hard pill to swallow and the way I was raised and taught that a man is not a man without a job, but clearly you don't want a big mouth woman who goes running their mouth every time you have issues, so maybe Bill needs to walk away; the last thing as human being that you want to do is drag someone down because you are down. Maybe they can pick up the pieces once Bill gets his shit together.

Scenario 68 Income Tax Sniper

Food for thought: Attention ladies who will be expecting an income tax return, beware of the income tax snipers. Profile: Male, unemployed, underemployed, in between jobs, may state he has his own business, vehicle in the shop, looking for somewhere to stay until his closing on his house is completed, just lost his mother looking for a companion. If you hear any of those lines run fast, his plans is to move in, juice your pockets and bank account, and he will be gone soon as the weather breaks; don't get sucked in because you will end up ass out.

LBS: Word

C2: LBS I know I am a butt hole, I just have to put it out there

TD: Talk about it Mr. David Glover, YOU LEFT OUT THEY NEED SOME CHANGE TO get back on the feet :)

C2: TD we see it happen every year

TD: Your right, it happens so bad now, that even men are telling women to be on the look out, well at least real men like your self.

NM: People fall victim every year I'm sharing this

C2: Go ahead fam, please share

NM: I did

MJ: Sad but very true

HL: haha . . . funny

HL: Men have been saying to be aware of things for quite some time. It's just now that women are starting to listen.

Issue: Every year around February, you have men that play on vulnerable women who they perceived will be getting a nice income tax return, and once they wiggle their way in, they're there until they squeeze every cent out of them.

Perspectives: They use all kind of excuses to get in your home, and work their way into your pockets such as I need a little change to get on my feet. Women fall victim every year. It is happening on such a regular that good men are warning women. This is so sad but very true. Men have been warning women about this but women have just started listening.

Knowledge: Many guys lives for the season, they may leave the household but will return during tax season based upon what the female is getting back dollar wise. It's a means of stepping up their wardrobe, putting their piece of shit car back on the road, or re-upping in the dope game. Some women are so desperate that they fall for this every year, and soon as the bank account is depleted, the sniper is on to his summer fling. Pay attention to your guy's behavior during income tax time.

Action: Women need to step away and let this sniper go; who cares if you don't have a New Year's Eve date or someone for Valentine's Day, you need to maximize your money to the fullest so you can build on your savings and do something special for your children. Focus on the definition of a sniper, someone who is highly trained, a marksman who operates alone and they maintain close contact with you during income tax season. They aim to target your assets during that time and once the final W2s come in and you hit the local Jackson and Hewitt or H&R Block, they make sure they hit you dead center in the heart to get half of your refund.

Consequences: You know nothing last forever, and once the funds are depleted, the sniper will strike up an argument to purposely be thrown out the house and he moves on to his summer residence. This leaves you broke financially and heartbroken, but clearly you live for this treatment because you know as well as I know the sniper will be returning around Thanksgiving time. The definition of insanity is if you keep doing what you are doing and getting the same results; but hey, if you like it, I love it. (SOS) Stuck on Stupid.

Scenario 69 Snake in the Garden

Is Melvin a snake in the garden, Melvin and Tina became friends at one of the lowest points in Melvin's life. Melvin was totally broken emotionally and mentally. He was going through personal struggles. Tina did not know much of Melvin and he was brought into her life by a close friend. Tina and Melvin became very close during this time and began dating and eventually moved in together. She helped him to gain his strength back, help him with his finances as well as to help with other issues in areas in his life. Now that Melvin is back on his feet, he feels the need to move out on his own after living with Tina for two years. Tina felt used and betrayed and she felt that they have built a bond that he is now breaking as he says he needs to live on his own. Tina feels that they can no longer be friends. Is Tina being selfish or Melvin? Melvin is still asking for some help from Tina, should she be the bigger person and help someone who she thought was a friend who respected, appreciated, and care about her? Or should she just cut our losses now?

RC: Seems to me like he used her to get back to where he was, I couldn't/wouldn't talk to him. But if he was also helping her because her finances wasn't that great or she didn't have a job and also needed his help then that's different maybe they should just go their separate ways...She helped her and she helped him!!!!!No hard feelings.

DP: Now unless I missed something he didn't say he was breaking up with Tina just he wanted his own. He has been living "off" or with someone and never provided or had his own. Perhaps having his own lease for the first time or buying his own car. This could be the final step in his recovery is gaining a sense of self worth. Perhaps his home may be bigger and he invites Tina to move in with him. We always say we want a man to be a man well living with a woman a being taken care of is not always cool for all men. Now he is in a position to provide for himself and he is asking to do so. Tina may be overreacting

JE: Sounds like Tina is confused about Melvin's motivation for moving in with her. If Tina believes he moved in because he wanted to be in a long term relationship and be closer to her I can understand why she's hurt. If he failed to clarify the fact that it was just a temporary situation until he gets back on his feet then he did in fact manipulate and use her and it's time for her to move on.

EG: Stop playing house, she knew he came with issues and should have offered help from a distance or ways he could have gotten help and still been a friend. It's important to know a person before you share your world with them. The Spiritual way of human interaction should have been followed . . .

C2: It seems like he was nursed back to good health and buddy boy wants to play no help this way benefit card denied

YWB: He is a user period it is the man's job to take care of his woman. Many women make more than their mate but dude got to pull his weight. He got what he wanted now he gone typical

TA: I'm not sure if selfish is the word to describe either of them. Tina made a conscious decision to take in a broken man. She needs to put her big girl panties on and deal with it. She made several classic mistakes that women have a tendency to do because we are nurturers by nature. She became his mother, counselor and probably nurse and required him to do what? At the end of the day she is giving and he is taking because she didn't ask for anything in return (based on the scenario). She is pissed and says she was used but she volunteered to be used so I am not mad a Melvin. Personally, I would want him to move out. Why would she want a future with a man that hasn't proven himself able to manage a household by himself? Now the time has come for him to do that, she wants to be mad about it. The way I see it is if he moves out and still wants to be with her then he really wants to be with her. If he stays then she will never know if he is there because he needs her or wants her. I want to be wanted, not needed. Once the need is gone then you have nothing. It also sounds like she has a little codependency going on too.

NG: They were in a relationship, she thought she was helping her man get back on his feet, so they can have a better relationship, but all he did was use her . . . . so she needs to cut her losses and move on.

C2: person x, stated if they really didn't know each other, for someone to come into someone else's life and be a supporters mentally and emotionally and they treat someone like that (wow) what is he looking for, that is sad that she did all of this and now he repays her by leaving. She seems to be the idea women. If he was living off her and wanted to go be a man I can agree with DP but if they were playing house working and paying bills together than what is the point of getting his own. If he needs to feel like it is his place, why not get his own, and bring her? Crazy to have someone in your life helping you with everything, and now you want your own, still be with her, go from two places to one to two again. Sounds like a game. I don't understand how some people can live with themselves. Doesn't sound like he was even ever her real friend, sounds like he is just a user, how else cans a person do that to someone else? He obviously doesn't know true love is, he will find out his major lost

TA: I don't understand why it is so wrong for him to leave if he doesn't want to be there. I'm sorry but I don't know anyone that wants to be in a relationship with someone who is only there out of obligation. That's what it would be if Melvin stayed. She will be better off in the long run letting him walk away and cutting all ties.

C2: I guess the time invested hurts Tina so bad, Melvin would have been better off with just telling her he wants to be roommates with benefits when they both are feeling lonely. Again most people are in love with the concept of being in love.

HL: Sounds like a situation from which only he benefits and when it's convenient for him.

C2: What is your recommendation for Tina (HL the Great)

HL: She really has no option in my opinion. As the saying goes, 'the die has been cast' and he is making his choice to move on and attempt to be an adult. She does have the option of supporting him in that endeavor, but anything else she allows him to do, would not be prudent IMO. She has spent enough time assisting someone who hasn't valued a great deal what she did and meant to him. If this scenario needs any clarity, just refer back to yesterday's about the break up of the friendship of two former colleagues. I see some people are putting the onus on Tina for making the decisions to assist another human getting back to stability. I wonder how many would still blame the 'woman' in the relationship if this had been a homosexual relationship. Just curious. I'm a proponent of helping someone and that means putting oneself at risk sometimes. That is what Tina did and she is to be commended for it, but that is the downside of helping someone who only wants the help and they don't wish to see anything else beyond what has been provided.

HL: DP: You make great points, but I would ask if he is really interested in making things between them work, then why not move into a place where they both can plan to live long term? That is one sure way to show how much he valued her allowing him to regain his self worth. To build together is the best way to gauge what they could become. She has shown that she isn't a fair weather person which I believe every man wants. The true test of character or least one of them is to see how a person treats you when you have nothing to give. Clearly she has shown her's is no one of selfishness.

TA: HL, for the record I wouldn't care if they are straight or gay

HL: Ha-ha . . . .it was just a thought . . . .

KM: It depends on if Melvin led Tina to believe their relationship was headed toward something long term. If he didn't, Tina should just take that loss, learn from it and keep it moving. If he did, he was wrong for that and should keep in mind that Karma is a bitch. Situations like this one is what makes a woman not want to get involved with men who don't have more than or at least equivalent to what she brings to the table. Financially, sexually, emotionally, etc . . . . . . Then if things don't work, neither leaves feeling robbed or used.

KP: Tina needs to cut her losses at this point . . . She has helped him enough . . . .It seems as if he wants to keep her close enough to help him get out of trouble when needed but not close enough to reap any rewards . . .

KJP: Sounds like Tina had expectations of Melvin that he didn't know . . . She also has the right to do whatever is in her best interest when it comes to continuing to help him . . . . to me Tina is in control and she can't blame Melvin for something she allowed and if she didn't know she does now and had control again to do what is right for her . . . Hopefully she has learned a lesson.

C2: When Melvin ass moved in with her while they were dating he should have known there would be expectations

KJP: Nah . . . It's up to the expectee to let that be known . . . That's a problem for me . . . Take accountability and so assuming.

C2: Unless his ass is incompetent no one has to spell that out but certainly Tina could have given him due process by letting him know what the deal is

KJP: Loll . . . not everyone is as competent as you . . . Lol. You can not do anything to anyone if they know with out them letting you . . . The blame game is why most of us don't enjoy life. David Glover

Issue: Tina and Melvin became friends; they begin hanging out and spending a great deal of time together, he was down on his luck and she took him in and really gave him the support so that he could get back on his feet. Meanwhile he was planning to place his feet elsewhere once he begin to get it together. After two years, he felt like it was time to go find himself and start over. Is Melvin wrong for wanting to leave?

Perspectives: Maybe both parties helped each other out, go your separate ways with no hard feelings. Doesn't sound like he is breaking up with her, he just wants his own. Chill out, Tina, stop playing house with someone with issues, help from a distance. Melvin is a user; it's a man's job to take care of his women, but the role has reversed, men get your weight up. Tina made a decision to take in a broken man and became his nurturer, counselor, and nurse, and gave, gave, and gave while he took, took, and took more. She chose this life for herself. How can someone be with someone for two years, and instead of working to build something together, they want to go their separate ways to do everything on their own; does not make sense to me.

Knowledge: Tina was searching for love in all the wrong places; sometimes women put too much emphasis on time instead of doing things the right way. They rushed into situations because someone is paying them attention for the time being. They need to check individual vital signs, and if something is going on with the heart or mind, you may need to refer them elsewhere because you may not be equipped to handle their issues.

Actions: If I were Tina, I will let him go and cut my ties with Melvin. I just don't see how they can remain friends, but she needs to learn a valuable lesson for the future that it's not worth nursing someone back whose vital signs clearly indicated he was in need of critical care. Tina could take advice from Iesha (Poetic Justice) that she is not in the line of business of keeping ninjas that don't want to be kept. You need to find your way and never make someone else's problems your problems.

Consequences: It sucks to spend time getting close and trying to build an empire with them; but meanwhile, they are looking at real estate elsewhere. Of course, the pain of being alone hurts like hell, but it's part of separation. Tina, you still have your health and beauty to go out and find something greater than Melvin. Don't beat yourself up pondering about what went wrong; Melvin had no intentions of staying, he was looking for a room and board with some ass on the side.

CHAPTER 10

Dating Game

Scenario 70 Don't Settle

DON'T SETTLE; CAROL has been really hard up for companionship, she has been spending time talking to a guy who spent some time in jail; this person had had some drug issues, but overall, he's really nice. They are supposed to meet for lunch on Friday; meanwhile Carol has never met him. She requested that her friend Janice do a Facebook background check because she was more tech savvy. After further review, Janice find out some not so good news. Should Janice pass this info along? Will let Carol find out for herself? Will the news was that he was in jail for stabbing his father in a drug-induced rage and now he keeps falling off the wagon for his crack and cocaine habit. When he is clean, which he happens to be right now, forty-five days clean, he is really a great guy. Would you give someone like him a chance? Well Carol decided to give him a chance; after lunch, she slept with him three times that afternoon and evening. He got up and left and promises he will return back the following day. I guess Carol got her groove back, what are your thoughts?

TS: What the hell?

TS: Janice would be the worst friend ever not to share the information . . . .

TS: And "hard up for companionship" is an understatement . . . .

C2: TS, everyone needs a little love, no one should die lonely. Get it while the getting is good.

KJP: She's grown and can make and hopefully handle whatever she has done . . . If she asked her friend for help then, if her friend is a friend it shouldn't matter the news . . . She should tell her.

I personally don't think it is so much about her giving him a chance . . . I think it's more about him giving himself a chance . . . 45 days clean is great and all . . . But he will need to decide if that is enough time for him to stay on the right path and not get caught back up.

C2: Do you think she is letting her state of loneliness impact her common sense; he has a lot of risk factors working against him.

KJP: Of course I'm sure that plays a big part in her decision making . . . However she is grown and it's not like she didn't know what she was working with. Once you know . . . You now have to take full responsibility for whatever you do with what you know if you are competent

HL: Her life, I'm not a believer at taking risk to stave off a lack of companionship . . . .

C2: In this day in age many women and men are putting them self in harms way just for some Instant gratification.

C2: Are women guilty of sometimes taking the little good in some men and making that supersede the enormous wrong that they have done.

LN: This Woman has deeper issues then loneliness, Janice should tell Carol all information she's gathered as asked, Janice should have chosen the latter. Women and Men are both guilty of trying to build on potential, instead of accepting that you chose for who they are.

C2: Is it safe to say terrific women are not having terrific relationships with terrific men.

LH: Drugs? Only 45 days clean? No. Run, lady. Come back when you've been sober a bit longer. Surely there are more fish in the sea.

Issue: Carol has been desperate for companionship and hooks up with a recovering addict, who has spent time in jail. Her friend finds out more disturbing news about homeboy, should she tell Carol what's going on?

Perspectives: She would not make a good friend if she does not tell. If Janice was a friend she would share the info regardless; whatever her friend does with the info is on her. Being lonely should not cause you to take major risks for companionship, she is a grown ass women who knows what she is getting into.

Knowledge: Simply put, Carol was looking for someone to screw her brains out and that is all she saw, she had her blinders on. These are the situations I talked about making poor choices for some sex; if she wanted to get screwed that bad, I am sure some high character guy would top her off every so often.

Action: The reason why Janice is obligated to tell is because of his past history of stabbing his dad; this damn dude can snap at any given moment, don't leave your friends life hanging in the balance with this lunatic. There is no such thing as confidentiality when someone is endanger of hurting themselves or others, be a friend sharing is caring.

Consequences: I can easily see this romantic fling, or let me correct myself, this freak fest going bad as soon as homeboy uses up Carol and he doesn't get his way and throws a temper tantrum; Carol will be at risk for getting hurt. Okay, you got your groove back, but now shake your ass out of his life, he is not worth it, let him find a rehab romance that is more his speed.

Scenario 71 Free Spirit Doing Me

Sammy was living the life as a young twenty-nine-year-old man, handsome, charismatic, fun filled, and free spirited. Sammy worked as a custodian bringing home about nine hundred biweekly, his rent is three hundred, and he has a low-level cell phone so his expenses were at a minimum. When he got paid, his daily routine would involve heading to the bank to withdraw $875.00 of his paycheck, next stop to the liquor store to purchase the $50.00 bottle of Peach Ciroc, and then off to the mall to pick up those fresh Nike Ones, Polo Shirts, and crisp Levi jeans, and let's not forget the nice fitted cap. Finally, he would stop to pick up his Friday fish dinner from the local fish market. Sammy did not have a vehicle so he would slide his boy $20.00 for gas. Reading up on Sammy's lifestyle, you would think he was single man, but in fact he was dating a forty-three-year old who had seven children ranging seven to twenty years old. Sammy had it definitely going on, but what are some of the presenting issues that Sammy has going on?

PC: None, them ain't his kids and he works to support his own habits. Outside of his poor spending habits there's little for him to work on.

DP: Beside his poor spending habits and lack of developing a sound foundation for a strong financial future. Sammy only is really concerned about himself. He should really consider investing in some solid investments that might secure in long term such as a home or 401k. Financial education counseling would be beneficial for Sammy. Although the kids are not his he is not setting a great example to his girlfriend kids about financial responsibility but he shows the benefits of having a job and your own money. Their mom needs some relationship advice in that she has 7 kids and no stable relationship for them. Unless one of the children belong to Sammy, he as no obligation to his girlfriend except just provide companionship.

C2: I know he has no responsibility to his woman's kids but out of all the women in the world why in the hell would he hook up with her, 7 kid's wow

DP: I often ask that question myself. Single man no children and they fool around with a woman who has 7 kids and vise versa

TS: Maybe she could just get it I find it actually more remarkable that she would be with him . . . does she want an 8th child

DCJ: Being that his expenses are at a minimum, he should be saving a huge portion of his pay check. He should be investing in his future. He has a decent job, for an individual without responsibility. One should not assume that people with a lot of kids are looking for someone to take care of them. However, of he's eating over there, spending the night etc, he needs to help her. Hell, he's eating up their food, using their water etc . . . ..

C2: I can imagine what her mailbox looks like, Jones, Davis, Williams, Simmons, Baker and Thomas and weekend daddy pickup probably looks like dismissal time at a school

HL: Believe it or not, none.

HL: Anything else, he can learn. His money habits are those of a person who isn't living for tomorrow. That can always be changed with a few adjustments and understanding that his earning potential will change. Other than that, he is fine living his life as he is.

C2: When will he learn? When he is 40

HL: As long as he is only impacting himself, it doesn't matter. If he is content with living in an apartment eating as he does, not owning a vehicle, then that is well within his rights to do so. Hopefully, someone a long the way will show him the errors.

TS: Which was why I was wondering why she would want to be with him . . . simply because they are at very different stages of life with different priorities . . . ?

HL: Maybe he sees her as just his toy. Or both see each other as that

HL: KP: You would be shocked by how many people have their priorities in reverse order.

HL: He has his own place, so he comes and goes as such. No roommate situation here

MJ: What the what??? She has no business dating this man. Although he is not responsible for those children, they are part of her. She needs to not be in a relationship with such a selfish person who doesn't seem to have any future goals. I'm not saying he doesn't have a right to be selfish, because he does. I'm saying this is not a good match!!! Like TS said . . . . that's another child waiting to happen.

C2: Maybe she has lost all her self worth because of previous relationships and Sammy is nothing more than her maintenance man

CM: Sammy has issues period. Why is he dating a woman with 7 kids?

MJ: David that's exactly why she needs to NOT be with him. I agree with CM as well.

C2: KP you said she should be with someone is setting example, why don't you think Sammy is a good example, the young lad is holding down a job while she is holding down her mattress

TA: I agree with HL on this one. Sammy doesn't need to do anything other than what he is doing. It's his life and he can live it however he wants to do it. He isn't hurting anyone. He has job and taking care of himself, which is all you can ask anyone to do that is an adult with no kids. We need to give people the right to be who they are. If Sammy wants to do this till the day he dies that is fine. He is "dating" the woman who has 7 kids. She isn't his girlfriend or wife so what's the big deal with that since people date all the time. ALSO, why is everyone tripping on the woman with 7 kids? The scenario didn't say she had multiple "baby daddies". She is 43, so she could have been married and widowed or divorced or adopted some kids that were less fortunate or that adopted some foster kids or . . . ALSO, she could be financially secure. Once you remove money and kids (which is what everyone is focused on) from the scenario all you have is a 29 year old man dating a 43 year old woman. She just may be a cougar . . . lol! What if she is just using him for sex? It has been known to happen

HL: BINGO TA!!!!

ALM: This scenario presents allot of potential issues. He is living young and care free. She has many kids some of them almost his age. His income may present a problem for her. He pays all his bills and stays fresh but doesn't seem like he has much spending room for much else. He should be saving money or investing. She has several kids so she cannot be as spontaneous as he can be. She is at a place in life where she is more settled. He might want to have kids of his own and that may not be an option for her or even something she wants. Not to mention if the kids (especially the younger ones) don't like him, or get too attached to him and he leaves that would be no Buenos for the stability in her home.

COJ: What 43 yr old woman wants anything to do with a 29 yr old guy who has no car????? Boooooo

C2: When the 29 year old works it right and shows her how to drive a stick everything is all good

ALM: Lol

HL: COJ, One that has 7 children and no husband

HL: Besides, why does he need a car? He seems to do well without one.

Issues: Twenty-nine-year-old Sammy living life very free spirited, sticking to his typical routine of spending his money loosely and living life, single minded; wrong, he has a forty-three-year woman with seven children. What's wrong with this picture?

Perspectives: Those are not Sammy's kid's; no issues there, but needs to work on bad spending habits. Sammy needs a financial advisor and be more of a role model to the children. Why does this woman want to be with Sammy, they are at two different stages in their life? Why is this fool dating someone with seven kids? Sammy is not doing anything wrong but living his life, he is entitled to that; he is not married to her. Many issues in this scenario; Sammy stays fresh, but everything that looks gold doesn't always glitter.

Knowledge: Sammy really does not have any standards when it comes to choosing women, this may be more about sex than anything. Also Sammy did not have rocket scientist as parents so in certain areas he may be challenged. Some of our habits we pick up from our parents and it becomes a generational curse, and of course someone needs to break the curse. Personally, I don't see Sammy being the one.

Action: Seven kids really, Sammy, I just don't see it, and if it was a sex thing then it would be from a distance as a last resort thing. I am Jacked, Ciroced, and Henny'd out of there. How do you deal with all the babby-daddy drama? Sammy may be living his routine life; around holiday season, he will wake up and realize he has gotten over his head with this situation.

Consequences: One of the consequences to this scenario is what if she is too experience sexually for Sammy and she seeks pleasure elsewhere to make up for Sammy's deficits, this can be heartbreaking for the young lad. What if Sammy slips up and gets her pregnant then she will be four kids away from a starting lineup for a football team. Sammy, advice to you, stick and keep it moving on this one bruh, take the *L*, it's all good.

Scenario 72 I Don't Do Dutch

Gerald has been asking Melinda out for months but each time to no avail, he seem to be a nice guy with no serious baggage, she has been through the ringer in her past relationships and was very guarded. After consulting with several close family members, she decided to go out with Gerald for breakfast; during breakfast, Melinda ordered the Grand Slam French toast meal, and because Gerald was not big on breakfast, he ordered one pancake, which was two dollars. When the bill came out, Melinda offered to pay with her card, Gerald declined to let her pay and they ended up going Dutch. What are your thoughts after reading this scenario?

SS: This happened to me b4. A guy continuously asked me out and I finally agreed but when the check came he asked if we could split it. I agreed and never had the need to deal with him again. Because asking me out gives me the impression that he's paying for the outing. If we were going Dutch it should have been stated before hand

SG: He should have let her pay if her offer was sincere. It's not 1950, after all. If she suggested going dutch instead (because her meal was so much bigger/more expensive) after he refused to let her pay for the whole thing, i.e. it was a mutual decision, and then I see nothing wrong with going dutch.

SS: Gerald asked her out therefore he should pay however maybe at the time he couldn't afford to do so and that's why he only ordered one pancake. If you can't handle your own business then don't try to invest in a new one.

SG: But it says he only ordered a pancake because he's not big on breakfast, not that he couldn't afford something more.

SS: If he wasn't big on breakfast then he shouldn't have taken her to Denny's okay, LOL

C2: It sounds like he was happy to be in her presence no matter where they were

SS: Good point David.

C2: Thanks SS

SS: Your welcome David :)

ALM: What's the point of asking her out all those times if he was going to make her pay for her own food? That's not a date it was literally just breakfast. She probably won't see him again.

SS: Exactly ALM. She could have stayed home and made her own if that's the case! Wasted her time.

ALM: Exactly. I would have felt bamboozled. He tricked her into going out. He should've let her pay so he could have gotten something out of the deal because she's def not seeing him again

SS: I know that's right ALM lol

C2: Should as women we come with preconceived notions that guys will always pay, come prepared you never know, don't be left at the table with the bill on your lap

KM: I would make her my wife . . . ..where the hell did that one come from

HL: I'd have to question why they went to Denny's. Other than that, I have no thoughts.

C2: Real life this stuff can't be made up Champ

C2: HL, should women always have expectations, should Gerald be cut off after one date?

HL: David: It's my weekend so you know I'm going to ream some (_._) s!! Gerald shouldn't have been persistent in his desire to date this woman. She made it clear that she wasn't into him for whatever her reasons are whether they're valid or not. Usually when a female behaves like this, it is for a reason. He should not want to go on another outing with her PERIOD. She didn't even show any regard to his dislike of eating breakfast. At the very least, she could've gone out with him for lunch. What I find disconcerting is the use of the terms 'bamboozled' and 'tricked' as if the man didn't make it know about his desire to eat breakfast and she did have the opportunity to say no as she had previous. Those are the worst things I've ever heard from a female and I've heard plenty. No expectation of a dining experience being paid for should be levied against anyone! For any female to expect to have her meal paid for, no matter who is asking one out on a date is only 'dating' because there is a free meal. That mess kills me. That is the equivalent of men only dating a female if she is going to have sex after the date. None of you would even agree to something so absurd! I would say that dutch was wise. Hell, I wouldn't have asked her out more than once!! Men need to start holding these females to a standard they hold us to!! To hell with all of you ask, you pay. How about every time a date is made, that dutch is the way to go. I'm sure all of the BS would be cut out and we'd find out who is into whom and not what they can get.

LFJ: The name Gerald says it all. This Gerald I know is too tight with his money that he can stop his blood circulation with that GRIP, can we say TIGHT! AND too cheap to pay attention! I say it's nothing wrong with going Dutch HOWEVER, DON'T ask me out of if you're having financial strain beat you down.

HL: And I have NO PROBLEM with asking a female to go dutch and I'll make it know before we even get to a venue.

SS: David you asking a women out to dinner is no different then me telling my daughter that I'm going to take her out to lunch (she knows my treat) and further more if I'm going to get all dolled up in my dress and high heels and you try to take me to Denny's for dinner you best believe that will be the last time ok

LFJ: Ditto

HL: SS: The difference is telling someone and someone agreeing. If Gerald had told her that he was going to take her out, that means he pick the place. I'm sure he wouldn't have picked Denny's to eat at and if he did, then he is a damm fool!!!

HL: And the option to pay is ALWAYS reserved no matter who ask. Stop with he asked he pays

BS. Women want it all without having to give up a thing!!

LFJ: Well now he is a damn fool without Melinda and still hungry!

SS: Lol

MJ: But Denny's though??? OMG run girl run!!! He's been pursuing her and he takes her to Denny's??? Then . . . doesn't pay for her meal??? NOT ACCEPTABLE!!!

TC: Why would Gerald take her for breakfast if he is not into that and then allow her to pay for her own meal, its a date. I think she declined before because her gut was telling her not to waste her time and her gut was right. I wouldn't go out with him again, he wasn't man enough to say he doesn't like breakfast or man enough to insist on paying for the date.

SS: Exactly!!

HL: I'm going to go out on a very BIG limb and say that in the O/P, it said he was not very big into breakfast meaning he doesn't like that meal. I might be wrong so I'll go re-read it . . . ..

Nope, it says that. Now, back to this date. He did not or it is not specified that he said when he was going to pay. Women, you all need to STOP thinking that just because you are asked out, that your meal will be free. In many cases, that is the reason why some women end up with broke men fathering children they don't take care of. DAMN expectations as opposed to having it stated. Pathetic I tell you!!

MJ: I'm so disagreeing with you HL. It is specified that the person who asks pays unless he states from the beginning that it's dutch or whatever. He did not specify that so he pays!!! How does he know if she had money or not? Furthermore, he was chasing her not the other way around. HE PAYS! Your argument does not stand in this case.

CBH: HL you don't invite someone out and not pay. What is she doesn't have the money???? Should she continuously turn him down? I was asked out before and I drove. When we got there he asked were we going Dutch? I said you should have asked me that before I decided if I wanted to go. I excused myself from the table and drove off and left him there.

TC: HL, I don't want you think I am speaking for all women but generally, if a man takes a woman out on a date (even if I ask you out) the man should pay. Also if a man is not big on breakfast, don't take me to breakfast. And I don't understand how baby daddies even came into the conversation.

HL: Where is that rule written at? When you show me, I'll relent all I have posted. It is ASSUMED because of the past practices that we due to societal issues with women not having the financial means to pay. Today, that no longer is true. Women nowadays earn just as much and in some cases more then men. So why is it taboo to go dutch?

LFJ: In my opinion all arrangements should've been specified PRIOR to the date. Simple clarification could've handled this tug -of -pay situation. Personally I rather go Dutch because these days people believes dinner and sex is a combo pack and I don't have those combos on my shelf. It's all about speaking up. Learn to agree/disagree without SO much emotion.

CHB: I disagree TC. If I asked him out I wouldn't expect him to pay . . . . He was courting her . . . ..

HL: TC: Your statement is why I don't date often. Even if women ask a man out he should still pay. I can't believe the mess I'm reading today!! Women have lost their damned minds!!

RO: Well HL has some great points. I always pay, but I'm open minded to the comments being made. Let's say the guy was not broke, and matter of fact he is wealthy. Also let's say they agreed to breakfast. Then what????

CHB: HL if a woman asks a man out she should pay.

MM: He ordered a $2! Obviously he had intentions on paying since he had been pursuing her. He should have stated b4 the date that he doesn't prefer breakfast. Or go to a place that serves both lunch/breakfast, so both can enjoy their meals. That's crazy a damn $2 pancake . . . .. He could jus ate 1 of her damn pancakes and saved his $2 lol

TC: RO if a man is broke he needs to be working on getting himself together not trying to be dating.

MM: If I ask sum1 to go out to eat with me, I have no problem paying for them. But don't insult me when you're the 1 pursuing me and I finally agree and u turn out to b a cheap date. But order a decent meal (unless you're not that hungry) so we can have a conversation.

HL: I can tell you how the father of children comes into this conversation . . . it has to do with holding men to certain criteria that they haven't not held others to. She has had bad experiences . . . I'm willing to bet that those experiences aren't due to men who were honest and stepped up to handle what they said they would do. It goes to a man not having to say what he will do. He will do it, no questions asked. This man did not say he will pay. He asked her out and she agreed to it. Therefore there he didn't not say he would pay. When engaging in dating, a man should be able to choose if he wants to pay and not forced into it when there was a mutual agreement to go out.

HL: Three Time's Dope . . . "Funky Dividens" . . . .that is my motto!!!

MM: Okay I'm lost . . . .. When did we start talking about broke men fathering children?

TC: Okay if you want to go into broke baby daddies, there are broke baby daddies because women allow them to be. It starts with a woman allowing a man to think that he doesn't have to pay for date.

CHB: HL you failed dating 101. And my son's father who is now my husband was held to that expectation. I never ever had that issue with him he just did it.

HL: MM: I was making the comparison of what is expected by women and how that reflects that choice. So of the choices those women make about men and why they do. I just happen to use dead beat fathers. That is how

MM: Okay, just read HL response . . . . Thx 4 clearing that up!

HL: CHB: No such thing in my book. I don't subscribe to old world notions. I break all of those rules when I date. If I want to do dutch, I'm going dutch. That is the problem with many women today. They want it all. They want to be taken care of while having to do nothing at all to earn that care. No on my watch!! Homie don't play that!!

CHB: Well my husband doesn't take care of me . . . . We are a team but before I joined that team he did what was needed to be done to peek my interest.

RO: Okay I agree a man should pay if he ask a woman on a date, but do the women agree she should give it up if she accepts the date??? A lot of women like to mislead or get free meals. Not all, just saying.

MM: your entitled 2 your opinion and so r we! I choose to pay when I go out if I asked that person . . . .. Male or female . . . Peps don't have $ all the time. I expect the same n return from whomever. I take care of my kids because I want 2, have 2, and need 2 because they're my responsibility. The same way a man should. That's an expectation that should be made across the board. But back to the pancake, maybe she returned his call and agreed to meet him for breakfast and that's why she was going to pay.

CHB: RO are you implying a woman prostitute herself for a meal???? Of course not especially if you are just getting to know someone . . . . Who sleeps with someone for a meal?????

HL: I'm going to run down a few things for some of the women who read this post or will read it and not post on it as to why men should not pay for first dates unless she has proven worthy of such treatment 1. It sets up a precedent that he has to live up every time they go out no matter how inexpensive it is. 2. Don't do it one time and all of a sudden, the man is branded one of one hundred names no matter if they marry or not. You see if the woman is truly into being a team player. If she has no issues with it, then she has earned the right to have the next outing paid for. 3. Men will find out if she values money and how she handles her finances as well as how she spend their money if their become married. 4. In order to find out if a woman is a keeper, men have to start from a position of what he will not do. Then, he can relent when it is shown that she is worth it. Not before. 5. When men allow societal expectations to run them, they have effectively given up being a man that can make decisions without fear of being branded by women, feminist or other men who have already given up being their own man.

TC: RO No she will not agree to give it up. Dating for a man should be seen as an investment. You put time, energy and money into it and sometimes it pays off and sometimes you lose. :)

HL: An investment into what? How he can spend and she has the power to say thanks, but no thanks?!

HL: The biggest trap in dating today. I'll pass. I'll invest in penny stocks!!

TC: I hope those penny stocks give you companionship and keep you warm at night.

HL: I'm CTHU . . . sometimes you lose . . . .and the women never lose . . . comical!!

HL: MM: That is true. All of what I said is my opinion and are not to be taken as gospel, but most women will not think about paying for their meal on a date even if she asked. So how is that truly the way to build?

TC: Maybe you don't appreciate what goes into dating for a woman - we could be at home in sweats watching the Golden Girls eating ice cream. But instead, we get dolled up, we hold in our burps and farts until we are ready to explode, we wear uncomfortable shoes and etc. We lose when it doesn't work out too; we lose our time, energy and money too.

CHB: HL it's funny that most of what you say my father taught me the opposite when dealing with men.

MJ: LMBOOOOOOOO

RT: Denny's are we serious he should have paid; men should always pay for dinner unless prediscussed.

HL: TC: Why would you make such an assumption? Could it be that you think I'm too harsh in my stance when it comes to dating? I just don't settle. Getting dolled when it comes to dating is the reason women give so they are deemed worthy of having a man pay for them as if men are just there to pay. I just don't care to pay for good looking person who has invested nothing other than a few hours of prepping and getting dolled up. If a woman wants to impress me, then put on sneakers, jeans and woo me with talk about Descartes, politics or how she volunteers her time helping others better themselves. Then I'll know she isn't just in it for what she can get. Pretty faces area dime a dozen women who value my money and have something to offer besides her looks, not so much.

MJ: Wait . . . how did we get into all of that? It was a first date! The point we are trying to drive home is that he pursued her and asked her out. He should have paid unless he stated otherwise BEFORE they went out on the date. It's during the first date that they could have discussed all of that stuff. They could decide after that if they wanted to see each other again. HL why should she assume she has to pay when he didn't say anything about it and he is one who asked her out? That's just cheap

TC: HL: Obviously I have invested more than just being pretty, my family has invested in my upbringing and I have invested my time, money and effort in educating myself and making myself visually presentable. So dating is serious for me, I don't like to waste my investments.

HL: TC: I don't recall saying you didn't. My statement was generic. Not meant for you or anyone on this post.

HL: MJ: There was no assumption of her having to pay. I'm not sure where that came from. Go back to the O/P and see how it came about that the discussion of how the bill was going to be paid originated. She said she would pay, he said no. They went dutch. Where is there an expectation of her paying? The onest is being put on the man to pay and the sole reason is because he asked her out? That is exactly why I posted those reason men should not pay on the first date 1 stand by them.

HL: The word 'should' . . . .just kills me!!!

MJ: You're entitled to believe that but I believe the man should unless stated from the beginning that he wouldn't. She opened the door for this nonsense when she asked if he wanted her to pay. It's her fault for that. I don't have a problem paying for something if it was discussed before hand but definitely NOT on the first date. That's just me though

HL: No, that is every woman who thinks that their gender allows for such treatment. Not that it is wrong to think like that, but it puts men in a no win situation. A situation that I won't be in.

MJ: See this whole burning bras and women's lib just messed it up for us women. What happened to chivalry? It can't be dead!!!

HL: No it isn't, but you have to ask yourself . . . when did women stop doing things that women used to do? When you have answer for that, you'll discover chivalry. ;)

HL: Ladies will ALWAYS be shown chivalry by true men. But it is the out spoken Women's Rights Movement who say 'I don't need a man to do X, Y or Z' that kills it. So don't blame men who have taken a stand. In stead, blame women who have force men to take that stand by abusing men who would otherwise be glad to pull out your chair, change your oil, change your flat tire, fight for you, etc. All for a simple "thank you" as opposed to expecting it.

MM: Oh please . . . . . It's a damn $2 pancake 4 crying out CHEAP . . . . . Who really cares who pays for it . . . . ..? Nice 2 hear a guy's opinion. I guess I'm a bit different. If I went out on a 1st date and he paid, I wouldn't think or assume he should and will cont to pay for every date there after. Lol @ least not in this day and age. I'm not going to assume that he has $ just because he paid for my $ 2 pancake. Lol! All it said was that she finally agreed to go out to breakfast with him. We don't know who called who in the end, but who really cares, it's not like they went to the Buffalo Chop House.

MJ: MM!!! Bahahahaha okay every situation and every one is different. In this specific situation I believe the man should have paid because he didn't mention it in the first place and he seems cheap. So having said that, every person must hold themselves for their actions and inactions. I will not lower my standards either. For me personally, the man should pay for the first date. If he the pursuer. Being cautious is good, but being overly cautious of the baggage the last person left is not good. You can't blame all women for what previous women did.

RO: TC I believe it's an investment both ways. I'm not knocking the women who don't have selfish ulterior motives when wanting to get free movies and dinner with no intentions of getting with the man in the future. It's a lot of women that take advantage of a man kindness to take a woman out and pay for it. So the men who think going dutch is reasonable until they see the value of her. I myself has always paid and don't have a problem with it, but I do see the point both ways and from both sides.

C2: If you start paying all the time, next you will be expected to move furniture for free, when does it end

MJ: LOL at David you men have a valid point in that there are SOME women who just use men. However, that's not all women and just because some of us expect you to pay on the first date doesn't mean we wouldn't pay on future dates.

C2: Do you fault men if they are booty motivated?

MJ: Fault? No not if they're provoked. It would be her own fault if she was provocative. For me personally, yes I would because I don't like that.

HL: Here is the question to ALL WOMEN . . . .how often do ANY of you chastise women who knowingly take advantage of men because they ALREADY know, there isn't going to be a second date? If you do

NOT, then guess what? You are part of the problem. What to know why? Because men will check another man on some BS move. He will let him know that he is grimy and that he needs to stop using women. Very few women will do that to other women. Their response is get em girl; take him for what you can get or bounce or some other nonsense.

KM If a man asks me out on a (1st) date, I EXPECT him to pay. Once/if the dates are more frequent, I would offer to pay occasionally by saying something like "please allow me to show how much I have enjoyed you and our time together by paying for dinner tonight". He won't feel offended nor should he expect me to pick up the tab ALL the time.

MM: Not true for all women fellas! No 1 is saying men should pay 4 everything all the time. All women r not seeking 2 cash n. Geez . . . .. and most men, who have a grimy friend, aren't going to tell him he's grimy. They're going to lol and congratulate him. There r plenty of men who use women 2 guys 4 all kinds of stuff . . . . Like credit, meals, car/gas . . . . Hell and try to use their friends behind they backs lol . . . . . .

MJ: I just checked another female today so yes HL I do. You reap what you sow and I surely don't want to reap a bad harvest.

HL: As men, we do understand and realize that there are those of our kind that will abuse/use women for their benefit. Most of them travel in packs and are selfish. Won't debate that. I'm speaking mainly of those men who have friends that actually work and earn. Stand up men, will not allow those men in their circles.

HL: There is that ugly word again . . . 'expects' LOL . . . . .*runs* CTHU

HL: I wonder when more often becomes half of the time. Before or after the wedding? LMBO . . . .brothers are going to go broke trying to date in this world . . . ..LMBO . . . ..can't win so I don't even bother . . . the whole dating world has been hijacked!!!

MM Lol @ HL. Dating isn't the only thing that's been hijacked.

HL: LMBO...true that. That is just the topic of conversation. What other things in your opinion have been?

RHS: I think it's cool, nothing wrong with dutch! Now days the game has changed in dating but ladies it's about how you play it. When asked on the next date is upfront about who is paying and if you're not in a position to pay decline the date and if he really wishes to go out, he will gladly pay. Why? Because you were honest and upfront a trait that allows you to stand out from the rest

C2: Ladies let's be real who sits around and have prearranged conversations about who is paying the bill, the notion is expectations and that is why when the bill comes the waitress or waiter hands the bill to the guy.

MM: The dating scene, relationships period have been hijacked by a bunch of bs, lies, domestic violence, phonies, etc . . . .. The list goes on and on. A lot if situations just aren't authentic anymore. It's crazy!

HL: It's not the situations MM, it is the people involved in those situations. The situations are timeless. Trust me. There is a reason why many authentic men don't date often. It is because they aren't deem to have enough 'swag' or don't stand for the . . .

MM: Agreed, yes it's the peps involved . . . . Some not all.

RHS: Sorry David Glover I do, because now days so many sisters have no expectations . . . ..

C2: RHS, that is great and women need to follow this quote from the Great Michael Jordan, "You have to expect things from yourself before you can do them" so in other words don't have expectations of others.

Issues: Gerald had been asking Melinda out for the past months and when she finally agreed to it, Melinda offered to pay the bill; Gerald sounded like such the gentleman that he could not let Melinda pay the bill, so he ended up paying his portion of the bill which was around

$ 2.00 and Melinda paid for her French toast meal. What are your thoughts?

Perspectives: Since it's not 1950 and she offered to pay, there is nothing wrong with a female paying. It appears that Gerald had some financial issues going on; he should have handled his business before trying to go out on a date. Why ask someone out if you are going to make them pay. Cut if off, he is a waste of time. If I were him, I would not have gone out with her; she didn't have the consideration to go to lunch since he was not big on breakfast food. Men need to start holding women to the standards they hold us men to. If a man invites a woman out, he should always be expected to pay unless you made arrangements prior to going.

Knowledge: Do women do a poor job of holding firm to their original stance. If you are not interested in someone, then don't go out with them no matter how many times he asks. It's a form of using someone for a damn meal. Why waste your time, his time, and his money. I know they say people can grow on you, but when you go into something with a negative frame of mind, you are going to get negative results.

Actions: Now under the circumstances, I am trying to figure out why would someone go on a date with short money. First impression is your last impression so I can easily see Melinda being done with Gerald. He basically wrote checks his ass could not cash. Don't step to someone unless you are ready. Gerald wooed Melinda for a while and finally got her interest but could not cash in on the check literally because he was broke.

Consequences: Gerald flat out blew it and I don't know if he is able to turn it around from the $ 2.00 pancake episode. Is it better to lie or front to a women because no matter what, the whole U.S. and China will know about it before the sun sets. More than likely if he is giving a second chance, you are lame sitting duck and nothing you say or do matters. Fellas never try to come back after a date has gone bad to make up for something you have done wrong. You will be the laughing stock of that crew; just bow gracefully unless you are in the business of giving people personal entertainment.

Scenario 73 Let's Try It Again After Going Dutch

Gerald and Melinda part two. Remember the popular scenario about two-dollar pancake? Well Gerald has offered to take Melinda to the Outback Steakhouse and stated that everything will be on him as far as the expenses, he also apologized for the other day and stated he was in a bad spot; he really enjoyed Melinda's company and stated he had a surprise for her, Melinda feels that he seems sincere. In your opinion, should she give Gerald another chance?

ALM: He has already been put in the friend zone; he might as well let it go.

TS: I would . . . because I would appreciate his honesty.

MJ: If she feels he is sincere I don't see a problem with giving him a 2nd chance. I would make sure she has money on her just in case there's an issue.

CHB: I would give him a second chance. The fact that he apologized and was able to acknowledge that he was in a bad place is worth seeing where it will take them. I hope she updates us on on the outcome

C2: I will provide you with an update; I am wondering what the surprise will be myself

ALM: Since he acknowledged that he was not able to pay last time and apologized she should give him another chance if she enjoyed his company last time. I think it's admirable that he confirmed that he would normally pay if he asked a woman out on a date. That must have been bothering him for him to admit that.

KM: I would give him another chance just based on the fact that he was "man enough" to apologize and be honest about his situation. We don't know the details of the first date. She may have enjoyed his company as well. Dismissing people so quickly is not only unfair to that person but possibly to you too. Could miss out on a "good thang"

SG: I'd probably accept in her shoes, though would be a bit thrown off by the mention of a surprise. I might be up front and say it's not necessary, but it's the thought that counts.

HL: Her call. There is no right or wrong.

C2: Everybody deserves a second chance, just hope he steps his game up, when you have the opportunity to be in the presence of a wonderful woman, step your game up and get your weight up

HL: I would go so far as to say that if he intended to pay for their first date, then he put himself in a bad light. He should have dictated when that date was going to be putting himself in much better situation to be successful. Poor planning leads bad results and I think that is what we saw.

C2: Yeah put its still was viewed as negative experience no matter how you slice and dice the pie

HL: LOL . . . no question . . . .

HL: I knew that. That is one reason why I always call the shots on when I go out. Where is up for convo, but when has to be for me to shine. Only fools and half steppers don't.

TC: I can't wait to hear about the surprise, hope it is better than the surprise she got on the first date.

C2: That was more powerful than a surprise it was damn electrical shock

MM: It's entirely up 2 her! I think if they had good convo and they hit it off during the 1st date, then he deserves a 2nd 1. Who no's the 1st date may b something they lol about later . . . . . . If they go on a few more

HL: David: Either the rest of the male populace run from here or am I the only male on your friends list . . . haha

C2: HL you are comfortable conversing no matter what the topic is, number 1 screening tool for women engage a man in a random conversation and see how he responds, and he may run and hide in the bathroom stall before he has anything to do with the conversation

HL: Haha . . . I chalk it up to politics and working with the public for as long as I have.

COJ: Where in the hell do u get these stories from? Are you writing a book? I love it. LOL. Keep 'em coming

Issue: Gerald wanted a second chance to redeem himself after the first date with Melinda; he had a nice dinner planned at Outback Steakhouse along with a surprise. Should Melinda give Gerald another chance?

Perspectives: I respect his honesty so I would. Since he was genuine, I would; but I would ask about his money situation before I agree to it. Never dismiss anyone too soon because you can be missing out on something. No right or wrong answer, poor planning did him in on the first date. If she enjoyed his company as well, maybe they should laugh at the previous situation down the road.

Knowledge: Despite what the consensus of people said, Melinda decided that experience was too much and she declined the second date. Clearly it was a struggle to accept the first date so to think he was going to get a second chance was far-fetched to believe. Sorry, Gerald, you did not answer the bell after getting the shot at the title.

Action: There had to be a gut feeling on why she declined the second date, there is no need to star in that movie again. When you work so hard to get a shot at the title and you fold under pressure, that opportunity may never happen again. Seize the moment or else ponder in what if land. Keep it moving, Melinda, he had his chance to dance and he chose to be a wallflower.

Consequences: I guess at times curiosity gets the best of us and you may think in the back of your head, I wonder what the surprise is going to be, or maybe I am missing out on something good, well let me give you a hint on the surprise, and are you ready. This time you may get stuck with the whole bill surprise! Move on and never look back.

Scenario 74 Life or Death

Life or Death

Susanna met Jason, got her job, and really started liking him because he was the complete opposite of Fernando, the commander in chief of the gang the Siberian Knights. Fernando was sentenced to ten years for drug distribution; he left Susanna to raise their two sons ages ten and eight alone. She wanted so desperately to get out of that lifestyle because she feared for her family's life. After spending time with Jason who showed her the finer things, such as Broadway shows, day trips to wineries, Elton John concert, and weekend ski resort trips, Susanna was all in. She had met the man of her dreams and has some good news to share with Jason that she would be having his baby girl. Jason was elated because this would be his first child. Somehow, this news got to Fernando that his woman has moved on and we'll be having another man's baby. Fernando had a note delivered to Susanna ordering her to terminate the pregnancy or he would see that her and her new friend would die and Susanna knew he was not joking. What should Susanna do? Someone will be hurt in this scenario. How would you handle this life or death situation?

MJ: Pray and seek help from the authorities

C2: What can the authorities do? When they may work in conjunction with these gang bangers

MJ: That's why I said pray first. Not all of law enforcement is evil. Is this a real-life event David? If it is I will pray for these people.

MJ: To answer the questions . . . . .. 1. NO terminating the pregnancy. She should not murder her own child. 2. She should tell Jason so he knows what he's getting into and PRAY PRAY PRAY . . . . God can put a hedge of protection around them. He did it for Daniel, the 3 Hebrew children, etc.

TA: I'm not running scared for anyone, period! What I would do is relocate my behind somewhere far away and pray that God will make it a smooth transition. The death threat would be reported with hopes of making sure Fernando doesn't see the light of day again either or at least get more time so she can raise all of her kids with him around bars. A mother's job is to protect her kids by any means necessary so I would probably go and get me a couple of carry permits and be at the gun range too (that is the country girl in me . . . lol!)

C2: This is risky business a lot to consider

KP: This very serious situation!!!! Susanna and Jason need to have a very intense conversation about what they need to do. Going to the authorities and making it known about the note is the first step . . . For the sake of her unborn child and the other children she needs to seek out a shelter and get away fast!!!! Fernando is not someone to play or stand up to. This is an unfortunate situation that happens all too much when these controlling men think that their woman should wait around for them to get out!

C2: KP I could not agree with you more, Fernando and his associates do acts like this for a living and they have no remorse and no regards for human life.

Issue: Susanna has moved on with the perfect guy who is showing her a different side other than the Gang Bang Life that she was living before. Susanna ended up getting pregnant by Jason, and once Fernando found, out he sent her a death threat note. Knowing Fernando's history, what should Susanna do about this situation?

Perspectives: Pray and seek help, call the authorities. Don't murder your child, God will protect you. Relocate and make sure you go get a pistol permit. Hopefully Jason is the man he says he is and can live up to the lifestyle he is portraying. Susanna needs to talk with Jason to see how serious he is about their relationship. This is a very serious situation, seek out shelter, consult with authorities; it's very unfortunate when you have controlling men who are locked up and don't expect women to move on with their lives.

Knowledge: Many people can say get the authorities involved but these damn gangs are so big and you never know who is in a gang and when they will be coming after you; this is a major situation that will lead you to live a life of fear, one of the main reasons I am against posting too much info on social media along with your children because if you dealt with someone in the game, you and your family can always be at risk. Please make good choices.

Actions: Susanna really need to sit down and talk with Jason; I am pretty sure she never shared anything about Fernando, and because of this letter, she got it's only fair to give Jason a chance to opt in or opt out of the relationship. If he chooses to stay, you need to develop a safety plan on how to make each of your lives as you work toward having a future together. This certainly will not be an easy task; but if it's not worth working hard for it, it's not worth having it. Especially if you believe in love will conquer all.

Consequences: This situation can go many ways, of course the obvious is that someone getting seriously hurt or potential death, and that would be the worst scenario. Susanna can share the info with Jason and he can bale out on her, because trust me, that young man better load up on the Excedrin's because he will have daily headaches if he stays. No matter what happens, Susanna will have to live with her choices of poor quality of a man she chose and she will forever be connected to Fernando. Remember, some choices you make will be life or death decisions.

Scenario 75 May Day

Discussion scenario: it's your best friend's fortieth birthday party, and you don't have a babysitter for your six-year-old daughter. This guy you have been dating the last two months is sitting around getting ready to watch the Mayweather fight and volunteers to watch your daughter for you. Do you go to the party that night?

EB: HELLLL MF NO!

MJ: ABSOLUTELY NOT!!! You just don't give the devil any room PERIOD!!!

C2: Okay let's change it to 8 months

MR: He a stranger he not even getting no booty so why in the hell will he be able to keep my baby

MJ: EXACTLY MR . . . . it's inappropriate for one and for two your babies are way more important than some party. It doesn't matter how long we're dating . . . . I don't trust anyone!

CA: NO FUCKING WAY!!!!! ANYONE WHO SAYS YES TO THIS QUESTION IS INSANE.

C2: That same man has spent many nights over so your daughter wakes up to seeing his bum ass on a regular basis

YWB: Two months isn't enough time to leave your child with a new "interest"

LFJ: absolutely out the door and out of wack. No! I don't trust people I met a guy that offered to watch my son and I was like no thank you you don't have children of your own and your self centered so no and carry on. It's sad to say but this world is sick. I don't even trust some family members because others will NOT treat your children the way you do. Children are helpless to the attention and discipline from others. No a man I been dating can't watch my kids not even a few of my friends. No no and no . . . That's my final answer.

C2: That's the purpose of this to get you amped up and thinking bright and early

MJ: You're right David some women do it and some of those situations have ended up on the 6 o'clock News

C2: Also in the scenario bum ass is sitting around eating your food and convinced you to order a 70 dollar PPV fight (wow)

MJ: lmbo at David. Why does it necessarily have to be a bum? Couldn't it be a guy like you?

C2: Why wouldn't he watched the fight at home, why would he commit to watching a six yr old on fight night, suspect that's why he couldn't be me

C2: On top of that he will be smashing when you get in, this guy must be the man and some ladies eyes

MJ: No I meant that he could have a job and not just being a vacuum. I didn't say you. I was referring to someone who appears to have the similar qualities as yourself. Just putting a little twist into it.

C2: I know and I like that you are thinking outside the box

TD: Ummm NO!!!

C2: Tee come on now you have to give me some explanation.

JP: A real BF would help you find a babysitter and pay for it so that he can accompany you to the party. Hahahahaha. My bad, you said Mayweather was fighting right?

C2: Lol@ Jerry Perez

IM: I would NEVER, however, I know some women that have met men in a club, took them home with them that night and they never left, smh . . . it happens . . . sad

CA: This scenario is precisely how children get mistreated and abused. The people who would actually do this to their child/children disgust me. This makes me SO ANGRY!

TF: Okay here goes . . . if we are just dating for 2 months my child doesn't know him yet. I don't know him well enough yet. If he's watching a fight . . . he can't possibly watch a 6 year old at the same time. Plus if we are dating he should be attending the party with me . . . right???

IM: I value the safety of my child more than partying. No reliable sitter, I'm staying my tail home

TF: I just don't believe in putting my precious jewels in awkward situations . . . no party is worth that

C2: Tee not when Money May Is fighting your friend is out of line for planning that party that night

C2: IM so they moved in off the muscle now that is pathetic on both parts

TA: I'm with MR! HELL TO THA NAW!!!! That is my child. If I don't have a babysitter then I don't need to go. Kids come before everything and everyone

MS: No

C2: Unfortunately MS I can't let you off the hook with just a simple no, please explain

Eg: I'm with MS, no, marriage creates a better bond. Invite the friend over to your home for a special birthday dinner and celebration and explain your position. Don't put your children in harms way for self gratification!

LR: Hell no!!!!!

CM . . . . any old ways, to answer Dave question to be a good sport . . . .. dude should have been in Vegas watching the fight instead of being in the house asking his new chick to watch her child.

MS: Too many bad things can happen when u r a child.

There's a movie called "Minority Report" and n it there r special people who have the ability to predict if an awful crime is going to happen, well I don't have that ability so I rather not put my child at risk. As my daughter says "safety first"!!!!!

C2: CM good answer but maybe his pockets are low

C2: Hey TR I am about to call you to the carpet, please explain your answer no

CA: Maybe he stayed back because he had sinister intentions . . . .EW! I would kill that MFR. He would suffer.

CM: In that case, he needs to evaluate his career and make a change? Get a second job and grind a harder

CM: Vegas may not be his cup of tea so he may decided to watch it at his lady friends house

CM . . . . . . so he can take advantage of the 6 year old . . . sick . . . . . . lol

CA: Why wouldn't he watch it at his own house or with his buddies somewhere or at a sportsbar?

C2: CM and CA those are concerns and I would think what's his agenda, Mayweather fight night and babysitting don't go together at all

C2: This scenario shows You how many of our perceptions are formed, and we live in a nontrusting society where a potential innocent man is already marked as a pedophile because he offered to help his girlfriend. Everyone agreed that our children are vulnerable and we wouldn't want or do anything to harm them.

CA: Wiser to be cautious than trust and put an innocent child in harm's way. I hear way too many stories of abuse that were very preventable.

EG: But Dave, I disagree with the trust aspect of your argument. When the process is outside of His will for our lives Marriage, children, forgoing gratification of selfish desires, we will always experience worldly behavior. The approach to have is a Kingdom mentality, where you say to your mate, my friend's birthday is coming up and I would like to do something special for her. The couple coordinates hated word from pervious post, their calendars and pick which day works best for all involved.

C2: What do you disagree with involving the trust aspect, most people stated no they wouldn't allow Tyrone to keep their child due to not knowing him well and not trusting the situation

CA: EG . . . please clarify your response. I don't understand any of it.

AA: It's your best friend and you don't have child care to go wig out with the girls? Where are the girl's parents? What happened to the daddy? Damn, homeboy is watching the fight alone? You said you'd pay for the fight right home girl, that's half a hundred? Hold up, this is from the girl's perspective right? I can't understand woman, let alone a procrastinating one. It's your home girl's birthday dammit. And wait; who's watching your home girl's kid, she's 40. Somebody had to make the birthday woman's womb grow by now. Lots holes in this scenario.

EG: Marriage-family, Dave has given a worldly example that currently exists in the world that can only be reconciled by God's plan therefore allow trust to exist in our fallen world.

C2: AA now you are thinking outside the box I only wanted to create a basic scenario and let people thoughts expand on the basics, you are funny as hell

CA: Your response sounds analogous to not taking your child to a doctor when sick b/c God will heal him or her. I call that child neglect.

RH: I think NOT, in fact . . . NOT AT ALL!!!!!

C2: RH I am going to ask you like everyone else why not considering he is already posted up at your house

RH: 1st of all, did you call me LR (lol). Because, he's posted up in my presence, not alone with my precious cargo . . . the child!!!

CA: RH . . . are u responding to David's original question or my response to EG?

RH: David's question. But I see your response.

CA: Thank you for clarifying. :)

EG: Loll Dave, that's my point, he shouldn't be. Call me old school but he shouldn't be posted up at the house-Pr 22:28: Remove not the ancient landmark, which thy fathers have set.

CA: So what exactly are u saying EG? First u say trust, then u say something contradicting that . . .

C2: Okay RH, I got you so is there ever a time frame that you ladies will feel comfortable with Tyrone being left alone with your children

EG: CA, there are no contradictions in my statement, His plan for our lives should be walked out. My pervious scripture concerning land marks, our parents lay the foundation for our lives and if we witness a successful marriage then we are going to want to emulate that example.

EG: Dave you have started up again-Ro 7:15:

For that which I do I allow not: for what I would, that do I not; but what I hate, that do I.

C2: EG how have I started up this Is good grown folk discussion don't you agree

CA: Okay . . . well in the real world David's scenario is happening . . . many people do not witness Leave It to Beaver home lives . . . so sacrifices in one's social life may be required when presented with a situation as David is describing.

EG: CA now you're talking, I have been saying the same thing but in a different tongue (Kingdom is mine). Dave said we are grown folks, having grown folk discussions so as grown folk I think language should be Kingdom minded lacking any worldly influence.

CA: I still don't understand your opinion on this given scenario . . . what is your response to David's original question?

EG: No, was my answer, why put your child in that situation. Then I went on further to say, why is Tyrone posting up in your home in the first place?

CA: Okay, great! Thank you for clarifying your response. :)

C2: EG some women may respond that they are grown and can have whoever they want over, Tyrone has been helping with bills the last couple of months

EG: Now this young lady in the scenario needs Steve Harvey's book-she needs to stop giving up the cookie! Lol, does that make it right?

C2: Not at all my friend

TM: No . . . haven't known him long enough . . . and he wouldn't be staying at my house while I'm out . . .

C2: Question to all so Is there a timeframe that this is acceptable for Tyrone

EG: The only moral way to look at it is once Tyrone commits himself to that family by way of marriage.

C2: Don't you have to build trust before you get married?

EG: Dave, you're correct but shouldn't trust be built outside of the home before he is introduced to the child and also what foundation should that trust be built?

EG: Excellent scripture for today's topic-A good man deals graciously and lends; He will guide his affairs with discretion. (Psalms 112:5 NKJV)

C2: EG that's the truth

BM: You don't goo! You never truly know someone in a year . . . let alone two months . . . and how comfortable does your daughter feel is the question

CA: A 6 year old child does not have the capacity to make a decision about what is in her best interest. She is a CHILD NOT THE PARENT.

BM: Cheryl you are more than right!

AL: What if you were the new man of two or eight months would you be exempt?

C2: Are you asking me this personally?

PG: hell no stay yo ass at home your bay should be to have mommy daughter time, you don't know that man women are to quick to leave their babbies with men they don't even know! Your time is up rise your children you had them babysit them for as long as it takes that's what real women do! Good one Dave the man might just be the peddie waiting for your baby

C2: PG You haven't change one bit, school those young ladies or old ones that are reading this

RHS: Stay my tale @ home! Kids come first over here, all day!

MMA: Okay I read all postman have a 7 yr old and my ass can't do shit, i don't trust her with any body, and if u got a live in man and u have trust issues with him then he is not the one.

C2: So MMA you will be staying in that night

MMA: Yes I will, mommy say it will be days like this . . .

C2: I guess each of you who stayed home will be boo loving with Tyrone

MMA: I never talk about this, my daughter was 3 yrs old and I caught the cable guy rubbing her stomach she had a dress on I was in so much shock when I went for my bat he was gone, when I called her dad we went looking for him, so I don't trust men around her.

C2: What the hell, That is crazy freak ass cable dude

MMA: I know aint that some shit . . . and they up hold him for it it was my word against his . . . so my point is some times u have to take a rain check on life my kids come first . . .

C2: Understandable for sure

MM: Naw, I'm staying @ home . . . .. As a matter of fact, more than likely he hasn't even met my kid(s) n the 2 months I've known him.

C2: So MM when do you decide it's okay for Tyrone to meet the little ones

MMA: When the woman feel right, and if he pass the interview . . .

MM: Only time will tell! But, I have to get to know u 1st b4 I introduce u to my kid(s). 2 months isn't enough time for me . . . . Also, if I don't c it going anywhere serious, there's no point n introducing u to the FAM or my kids. Unless, your n the familiar friend zone. I'm jus extremely cautious when kid's r involved.

C2 Agreeable I wonder how many women take heed to that or there is a sense of urgency to get Tyrone acclimated to the family so he can step in and pay next months bills

MM: Personally, I'd rather have my OWN, than sum1 else's !

C2: With the economy being the way it is sometimes it leave women with no option to bring Tyrone a long for the ride

MMA Every woman wht help and need help, but why have some one u don't care for their, i know we have some tht don't care, at

C2 Bills with shut off notices are real, along with refrigerators where you see straight to the back so sometimes it's not a matter of how long you known Tyrone it's a matter of how much he can give you.

Issue: It was your friend's fortieth birthday party and you have no babysitter so you may not be able to attend. Your new acquaintance, Tyrone, offered to keep your six-year-old because he was going to just hang out at your place and order the Mayweather fight. Should she attend the party or not?

Perspectives: A real boyfriend would have paid for a babysitter for her. This is the first step on how children are mistreated and abused. No party is worth risking my precious jewels for a night of dancing. Invite your friend over for your own personal celebration on another day and explain the position you are in. Tyrone should be in Vegas watching the fight instead of asking his new chick to watch her child (freak). Safety first, view the movie Minority Report. He may have sinister intentions and I would kill the m-frrrrrr if that's the case. Shouldn't he be watching the fight with his boys or at least at a sports bar? Where is the girl's dad? What about the mother's parents? Who is watching her friend's children because I am sure she has children at the age of forty. Two months is not long enough to have any man in the presence of your child.

Knowledge: This scenario seems to be a no brainer, but every day people make bad choices out of loneliness or just can't stop running the streets and they put their precious babies at risk for rump shaker contest.

We have to make better choices for one that was mentioned why was Tyrone chilling at her house so hard; did she already know this man? Most men who got something on their mind is not too quick to meet the woman they are dating children too early because when a women is quick to introduce you to her children, she is basically saying I need a daddy for my child.

Action: She needs to chalk this party as an "L" and please stop bringing men around your little girl, and I don't care if you do know him, he does not need to be posted up at your house. Your friend should have done better planning, because she really can't expect guys to show up at her party during the time Money May is fighting. That is a party in itself I mean an event. Always think safety first when it comes to your children.

Consequences: Well we know how things could play out if she does not attend the party in most people's eyes. It's a shame how our thought process is so negative and we have condemn Tyrone of child molestation before Mom has committed to the party. We all know that in most cases, molestation typically happens with someone a child has a relationship with, point for Tyrone. But all jokes aside, we can't take these situations lightly, and as parents, you have to protect your children from harm; trust me I know, tore and broken children become torn and broken adults. Mom, sit this one out and tell Tyrone you will get with him at a later time and pop in a Disney movie, and all will ends well with you and your daughter.

Scenario 76 No Texting Rule

Evening scenario: get your cocktails ready, Jennie and Doug hooked up after twenty-one-years since graduating from high school. Doug was in town for business and Jennie stopped by his hotel room to have dinner and drinks. One of Doug's favorite forms of relaxation is unwinding watching sports; this evening, March Madness was on so during the time Jennie was there. Doug was texting one of his boys talking about the great games; Jennie thought Doug was being rude because she was ready to get it in but Doug never wanted to give her the impression that her visit was all about the sex. Do you think Doug was rude for texting?

DP: Miscommunication. Jennie pick up your face and self respect. Not everything is about sex. Did she even stop to think if Doug was married or involved? Seriously, we get mad when they ask us to give it up and we get mad when they won't take it. After 21 years things have changed, maybe Jennie is not as attractive as she was then. Jennie should just go home and thank him for the night.

MJ; There was a lack of communication. All cards should have been put on the table instead of getting attitudes. That's childish. No Doug wasn't rude because he didn't treat her like she was a ho

HL: LOL . . . Doug should have never allowed her to come by. Problem solved!

RC: I would think he'd want to catch up being that it's been 21 years even if he wasn't trying to do anything!!!

C2: Sometimes people have needs to be met and why do all that talking if the goal is too accomplished your needs being met

HL: LOL . . . .

HL: That freight train is starting to get going!!

RC; Well if one of the parties wasn't feeling it then talking is very necessary!!!

C2: Meaning that if they talked he could lay the foundation for next time, I think the issue in hand was Jennie wanted his undivided attention and was upset because he was texting

SG: Mixed feelings. It was rude of her to drop by without calling ahead, but if they've recently gotten back together, he should have set basketball aside to spend time with her. (Unless I am misunderstanding what you mean by 'hooked up'...)

TS: I'm guilty of being a crack addict when it comes to my phone but I know that the general rule should be no texting when you're with someone.

C2; Who made up that rule, never heard such a rule?

TS: Well my men apparently have felt slighted when I haven't given them my full attention . . . so I've learned to play the game.

C2: It sounds like they were insecure and needed your attention like a child.

HL: No texting/phone use on dates unless you are checking in on a child/baby sitter. Just my personal rule. If that is done to me, you're going to pick up the tab because I'm out.

HL: TS: I've found good and insightful conversation will kill much of the desire to use cell phones.

TS: I think I like you HL . . .

HL: LOL . . . careful . . . .I'm like that Bavarian Chocolate . . . .the more you try, the more you want . . . ..LOL . . .

MJ: So HL if you don't get attention then you throw a fit and walk out?

HL; Never had that happen. But, I also give attention.

MJ: Okay just checking because that didn't sound right.

HL: Haha . . . .I was jus speaking from the standpoint of bad manners . . .

Issue: Jennie and Doug hooked up after twenty-one years since graduating from high school, she stop by his hotel room and had dinner and drinks; while relaxing watching March Madness, he was texting one of his buddies talking about the game. She thought Doug was rude because she wanted to sex him but Doug did not want to give her that impression it was about sex. What do you think about Doug's behavior?

Perspectives: Jennie, slow down, pick your head up, and go home, you have not seen him in twenty-one years, it's not about sex. Doug was not wrong; he did not mistreat her at all. Maybe she should have never stopped by. Whatever happens to small talk about the past twenty-one years, getting reacquainted? General rule of no texting, when you have company. Doug could have pushed basketball to the side and spent quality time with her.

Knowledge: Okay people the sex had already went down the day before when Doug arrived and she left that afternoon with an attitude. So when she came back the following evening, Doug was not pressed to sleep with her he did dat, she was already to dive in to bed five minutes after arriving, but Doug was watching March Madness and texting about the games.

Actions: Doug eventually ended up breaking her off something that night, but his mind was distracted; she felt Doug was rude and they had a verbal exchange and eventually she left to go, back to her husband feeling angry and buzzed. Doug felt like no skin off his back because he was not going to be arguing with a controlling woman who had other issues.

Consequences: Jennie would get too attached and get sloppy at home if Doug puts it on her good enough. Texting, phone calls, to Doug can be a red flag to her husband. Just by her getting upset with Doug over texting shows she has some stability issues. These two may need to let the past be the past and keep it moving.

Scenario 77 Nothing to Offer

Good morning, requested topic, scenario. A guy who is doing well for himself meets a young lady who he is very attracted to mentally as well as physically; they enjoy spending time with each and their relationship seems to be growing. The young lady although is having a tough time financially as a single mother of one daughter; she has to ask him for some money to help her get through the week. He is totally turned off from this and drastically pulls away from her and stops spending time with her as well as contacting her. Is he wrong or should stay around to help?

NB: Good morning love these . . . we all go through ups and downs but if the only problem is cash I say wait and c what happens. Think on this what if that child were me the woman my mom and his man's help became encouragement support the struggles stopped and that child is miss a successful citizen that Ugghhhhhh I wasn't finished hit the wrong button o well I am now lol

CHB: How long have they been together? He probably should not stay because if you see someone struggling I don't think they should have to ask for help on either side. If this is his character I don't think this will work.

TCR: She better off without him, if she was woman enough to ask he should've stepped up as a man. Her blessings are going to be even better being he acted like that. I could see if she weren't trying

VS: I think he should stay . . . one hand washes the other and both hands wash the face, so with that being said . . . if he is attracted to her mentally already than he knows of her current situation and I'm sure of their talks on what she plans to do to get out of it. I think it's selfish for anybody to walk away from somebody in time of need. What if he one GOD forbidden day looses his job? He too may need a bit of help to get himself back together. And like above mentioned if he saw her struggling and didn't offer he's the bigger turn off than her needing to ask, she obviously felt comfortable enough with their dealings to ask . . . my opinion!!

LN: I say run as fast as he can, first off, If they're only dating, she should have done whatever she would have done, if she weren't dating him, No begging on dates for your one child, her time would be better spent, not on a date, but looking for how she can earn money she needs, He needs to look deep before he leaps, if he was so into her, He would know she's broke. BUT, If he's having a problem finding a woman he may want to lower his standards just a bit, it's much more difficult I think to land a independent woman, then one who needs the help at that point in life. Tell me if I'm being harsh, in my opinion

MMA: She should leave, because she shouldn't have to ask for anything she should be getting it already, and if he knows what she is going through he should have her back that's what a real man should be doing helping her in a time of need

TCR: LN, that was harsh, I hope u don't ever have to ask for help DAM!

RO: This is a good one. Interested to hear responses lol. Because if the man ask for sex it's the end of the world. Now she asks for some money it's all good. I'm not stating my response yet, just want to read first

MMA: Yes u are being harsh, why should he run he pick her if he wanted ass then he should have put that on the plate first . . . no woman should not lack when her man or her friend has money . . . yes see need to better herself.

TCR: I am a single mother of two and I give my kids the world on a silver platter, and I always let a man know in the first round of the draft, if u not into me n my two it wont be me n you!

RO: I changed my mind I will respond. I would give her the money if I see potential in the relationship, just how I was raised.

TCR: To RO:IS it wrong for a man to want ass and has only spent one day with the woman, no dinner, movies, concert, drinks at the bar or anything?

TCR: That's what u better had said!!!Ron, lmao

LN: My only issue with her, they're (dating) spending time together, this is how a smart woman would do it,
Guy; Want to hang out?
Gal; Sorry can't right now, having a major issue?
Guy; Can I help?

Gal; I'm working on it, but I really must get this handled, then maybe we can hang
Guy; Maybe I can help, what is it?
Gal; I'm a Lil short this month, you know how it is.
Guy; I got you,
Gal; Thank you boo, let's go

MMA: Thanks LN for putting it a little better, what if she ask him all of that and he told her no not this week.

C2: Lisa is it really that easy, what if this guy views her as an extra bill, CHB they have been dating for 4 months

MMA: Well David, if he view her as an ex bill should not got an ex bill . . . .

LN: Then tell him she's busy and cant go out, if he doesn't offer to help, that says much more about him, It is absolutely that easy, easier not to ask, HOWEVER, 4 months indicate he getting the cookies, In that case she's the one that should run, with her dumb ass. MMA said it best; he already supposed to be sharing the cash

LN: David Glover he should view her as a bill, like a bill, he will be responsible for spending with or on her every month, Dinner, Dates . . . .the way it's supposed to be

KJP: See this is where I have an issue with us ladies . . . why???? Because we have these expectations of me that are not fair to them or ourselves . . . they don't owe us anything and until me stop compromising our box and self esteem for some money or gift . . . we will never arrive and be who we are destines to be.

Before you start dating u should be 100 with who you are and not depend on anyone to complete you . . . only enhance what u already have . . . if your not there yet then put that relationship on hold.

This is why so many women are abused!

C2: Okay KJP that's adding a different perspective

CHB: KJP I would help anyone out that I see struggling. I would always help a friend so why not someone I'm dating or vice versa. Are the rules different if you're dating?????

MMA: Thank u, thank u CHB cause I was raise to get it in a lady way.

TF: If he cared about her and knew she was struggling he could have helped her without her even asking. If he was hungry . . . wouldn't he expect dinner? Relationships work both ways . . . .So he can move on to the next . . .

KJP: I was also raised to be a giver and help anyone on a struggle for me . . . because of what is going on for us as woman . . . it's all going to depend on her motivation in asking. What if he wasn't in her life . . . who would she have gone to . . . that's where she should have started then explained her situation to him without asking and that would have told her what caliber of man she was dealing with and if its worth investing in.

JC: It's all about the potential of the possible relationship . . . if there is no potential in it then he should let that be somebody else problem. All that he should be sharing his money 4 months in like its automatic is BS ladies. That's what's wrong with society everybody feel entitled to shit they haven't earned based on no true foundation . . . Help is one thing if by our recent dating you have earned that . . . It's also not always known that she may be struggling because people live fake lives and hide things very well nowadays. So all in all it depends on the person, relationship established and situation. Because if the shoe was on the other foot, a lot of these responses would be he can't do nothing for me if he can't handle his own and/or broke n***@ quotes!!!! Smh. Always look before u leap in any fashion . . . mistakes has taught me that . . . everybody isn't deserving, many just scheming! Lol.

KJP: I don't think anyone on this is saying they wouldn't help out someone in need . . . but things are much bigger than that when it's between woman and man . . . this isn't a relative we r talking about.

RO: Very well put JC

CHB: JC if there was no potential he should have left it alone before the question even came up. I guess I have been lucky to not to never have had to ask for help. The few times I needed help it was offered to me without me having to ask. I would do the same for them.

MM: This is sum good convo peps! I'm going to chime in and say . . . . It would really depend on a few factors: how long they've been dating, how comfortable they r, the trust level. Now sum peps mite actually need the $$$, while others will test u 2 c if u would actually help out. I think that if they haven't known each other that long, then she should try fam 1st or not go on the date (as it mite b an extra expense, she can't afford right now) and explain that she doesn't have it right now. If they both feel comfortable n asking that of 1 another, then it's solely on the individual asked 2 either give or not. I don't think sex or $$ should b asked 4 2 soon! N my opinion! Vise versa . . . . If he'd ask, it would depend on the same circumstances . . . . . @ Least u no if u give $$$$ and they don't pay u bac, then don't give anymore! If she paid for a few meals, etc., then y not help her out!

TF: If there was no potential of a relationship . . . he shouldn't be 4 months in. If there is a relationship . . . it works both ways.

TA: The problem in relationships is that people jump in them before they are ready. The top 2 reasons relationships fail are 1. Cheating and 2. Finances. The guy in this scenario is wrong for being turned off immediately by her asking for money because he needs to know the "why" she is asking first. People that struggle financially usually do so from one or two main reasons: Income or Spending. If she is struggling financially because she works 40 hours a week and her income still isn't enough to make ends meet then that is something that can be fixed and shouldn't walk away from her. If she is struggling because she is financially irresponsible (buying a new outfit instead of paying the phone bill) then he has a decision to make and if he chooses to walk away you can't blame him because that has RED FLAG written all over it. You always throw single parent in the mix. Who cares? That is irrelevant. I'm a single female of two and know other single female that makes this point moot. Being a single parent (male or female) should make a person more financially responsible not less. Whether you are a single parent or not if you are stupid without money you will be stupid with money therefore the key is making sure you get in to a relationship with a fiscally responsible adult and it doesn't take long to figure that out. If not, then how will you ever be able to build wealth?

JC: I have been fortunate to never have to make this decision because usually the people I have been around. I would do this for in a heartbeat but everybody isn't worth it, just like every man that women date isn't worth everything they have to offer. Hence the trial n error of dating to me. Everybody I have dated hasn't actually become my girlfriend and likewise with u ladies I'm sure.

RO @ TS I don't believe in no Steve Harvey 90 day rule or any time limit on when to have sex for first time between two people. If the two r Grown whenever the two feel comfortable.

JC: TA said it all

RO: Hold up. The reason should not matter. If I'm going to loan u money, I'm going to loan it to u regardless of the reason. Bottom line is a person can't get mad about mine. If I ask a woman for sex and she say no, it hers and I can't be mad. Same thing goes if she asks me for some money

JC: Thanks RO! OAN I loved how the announcer use to say your name after u made a basket. My bad yall. Lol

JC: 4months in could be a short time to busy people as well, especially if your the type to try to have an understanding of the person your interested in.

TA@ RO - the reason always matter. Money has a tendency to ruin all kinds of relationships (not just male/female). If someone asks me for money then I need to know why. Is it an isolated one time only type of deal or is this person putting a band aid on a gun shot wound? If it's a one time only, cool. I'm in and no big deal; but if it isn't, then my answer will be yes BUT do not ask again unless you have done X, Y and Z to show me that you are serious about getting your financial life in order. I'm responsible with my money so at minimum the person that I'm going to be in a relationship with needs to be responsible with theirs too. I'm not asking for anything more than I'm willing to give.

TS: RO u r something else lmbo

PC: This guy is not only selfish but he is an idiot. Anyone who puts money over and above the woman in his life is a walking, living and breathing contradiction of a man. As a man we must be great providers and protectors of the woman in our lives. A woman is a man's heaven! As a man he should never look at the short comings of this woman . . . it take heart and courage to ask someone for a favor, especially if the person asking has never been in that position before. He was not that great of a boyfriend to begin with if he sees her struggles as a single parent, let alone as a person and his significant other; and sits back and watch the woman that he supposedly have these strong feelings for struggle. If it was me as her man her struggles are my struggles and we will work through them together . . . . .I would never put my woman in a position of having to ask me for something that I can obviously see with my own eyes. There are are no safety nets in life, when we leap we take a leap of faith together knowing that everything will be alright.

C2: It all boils down to the screening and interviewing process of getting to know the next person, KYP know your personnel, if you know the young lady and her heart is in the right place you can work with her if it seems like she has sketchy dealings you made need to fall back or examine further.

TF: Wow PC well said!!

PC: TF TF now if it was a white girl . . . .lmbo

RO: We talking about helping a woman that's not his woman. It's a big difference. Money is not everything, but let's see how many women put up with your ass if you're broke. I'm not saying not to help her, but a man is not wrong if he don't. It's his money, and his choice. Don't start anything u can't finish, because the hand is going to be out again lol

TF: LOL PC . . . don't start!

JC: Reading these responses are enlightening but damn some of y'all jump into relationship status a little too quickly for me. Smdh. Some of y'all men got dudes in ya crew that y'all don't show this much instant love too! Lmao. I'm joking but damn. I'm personally a helpful and giving person but wow on some these!!!! Lol.

PC: JC lol when it comes to men . . . ..sink or swim . . . .two male lions cannot occupy the same territory no matter how cool they are . . . .goes against the laws of nature. Same goes for dudes . . . .friends or not . . . .if your a grown man I am not giving you shit . . . cause its going to be a problem one way or another collecting that loan . . . . . . KM is my best friend we rarely loan money to one another but we lookout for one another . . . .money is never an issue amongst great friends male or female.

TF: Wait . . . .are they in relationship or not! David Glover . . . .

JC: @ PC y'all should choose better friends then because that sound likes some bullshit! Maybe because my friends are family and I subtract who can't build! I'm too damn old for fair weather friends so they don't exist in my cipher. But I respect it and to each his own

PC: JC not sure what you mean by "choose better friends" and I will never have to play the victim role . . . you know the one side of the story you seem to be holding on too . . . life is continuous...You win some and lose some . . . .even in relationship. That's the problem with men these days they are either way to feminine acting or afraid to give love or receive love.

JC: A sucka the same thing my dude in my eyes because as a parent we have to repair that when that happens to our sons. So reaching is the key not always trial and error. So idk where you're going with that. The scenario stated dating for 4 months not giving up house deeds and shit for something that may never be . . . .we don't bat .500 this way my dude!

JC: Teaching

JC: Now if we are in a committed relationship that's entirely different . . . as the youngins say there is levels to this shit my dude!

PC: Oh . . . so you believe that you can build a great big house on sand . . . .I am not living life through my son's l teach them and they have to experience it for themselves...just as a momma bird pushes the baby bird out the nest, not for its own amusement but to give that bird one choice fly little fucker or splat . . . . ..lol

JC: That's some bullshit but u have sons and I have daughters. Lol. But we both have kids and I respect it because your kids are older than mine so u have been doing this a little longer. But that's some bullshit because teaching is a life long process just like learning!!!! I'm out . . . u and I can build on this another time! Mr. Protector. Lmao.

TCR: Who said BORROW????That would have to be established also, but he can't borrow that. Loving he gets

PC: JC . . . ..Levels. . . . lol yeah your right like candy crush . . . . . . I don't live my life like a game . . . ..preparation and opportunity is how I live . . . .no need for levels that shit is for the lame . . . ..life is in abundance...There is nothing greater in life then sharing it with your loved ones . . . ..you used to live by this cree as well or you wouldn't have kids . . . .what happened? Get back to the basics.

TF: LOl TCR

PC: JC I also have a 13 year old daughter.

TCR: I'm saying tho! I don't have to worry about issues like that. Ladies just keep it right with your exes and u don't have to worry about SHIT!

JC: It's a Hierarchy in every walk of life my dude PC . . . Are u sure you're older than me???? Matter facts are u serious? Candy Crush, really? U say a lot of sly shit to impress people who are easily impressed. Lol. That's not for the lame it's for the living

C2: TF he has been seeing her on a regular basis for 4 months

PC: Lol . . . .no need for me to be slick or sly with my words . . . .we are grown men having a discussion neither of our positions are right or wrong . . . ..relationships are what they are . . . .and I didn't mention anything about levels you did . . . ..in the realm of relationships there is only one ultimate level . . . .marriage! Outside of marriage the relationship is on level 0.

PC: Yes there is a hierarchy in every form of life and if the hunter cannot maintain his ground he becomes the hunted . . . ..no lion stays on top forever.

C2: Shit many marriages are on 0 as well because many people are in love with the concept of being married

CA: Is she working?

C2: In between jobs when she asked him for the money

CA: Receiving child support?

C2: Limited 200 a month

CA: Car payment?

C2: Not sure but let's say no for the sake of it

PC: Many marriages maybe functioning like level 0 but they are married to say the least.

CA: Let me just be honest here . . . I would have been annoyed too . . . just like the guy in this scenario. My freeloader 'red flag' would be popping up.

Issue: A couple had been dating for four months and was starting to get a nice connection all until she asks for $50.00 to get through the rest of the week. His phone calls and texting came to a major halt. He was totally turned off. Do you think he was wrong for turning his back on her during a time of need?

Perspectives: If a person sees another person struggling that they are involved with, you should offer help instead of having them ask. He needs to run as fast as he can and find someone that meets his standards. If the roles were reversed and men ask for sex, what would women do? If I am that guy and I see that she has potential, I can work with her. Women should stop depending on men for help; if you need their help then maybe you should put dating on a hold. He owes her nothing after four months of dating, which is the problem expectation of others. Relationships work both ways, you help each other out in a time of need. No one would be upset if the tables were turned, women would dog out a man if he came at her broke.

Knowledge: The whole issue in today's society is the expectations we have for our partners but don't have for ourselves. Now certainly he could have extended his hand out; but if he decided to leave, that is his choice as well. So we can debate all day long that a man should help a woman financially and men may feel if I am helping you, you need to be sexing me straight like that, so this has to be established from day one; what is the intent of your relationship going to be, put it all on the table, all fifty-two cards, and stop hiding some of the cards.

Actions: Again the key is where they are going in this relationship; if the guy doesn't feel comfortable, let her know what the deal is; if you got burned before, let her know, give her due process and maybe she can explain her disposition on her game plan and why she needs the money. Remember, cut the bull about; he should know because that may not be the case and plus a closed mouth will not get fed. This is just a start on how to proceed with this matter.

Consequences: She will be left hanging and may need to seek this money elsewhere; and if it's desperate measures may cause her to get with a dough boy to help her out, which a prerequisite may be sex. So now you turned someone you cared about back out to the wolves and who knows how that story will end, I have an idea, let me tell you. Next time you are out and about, the word in the streets will be that "She is pregnant by Fat Cat." So think long and hard if you want to let her go because she may not have anything to offer at the time, but if she has a good heart and cares for you, then maybe you can build off that; if it's a reoccurring thing and she is setting you back, than its understandable if you bow out gracefully.

CLOSING STATEMENTS FROM THIS FIFTEEN-MONTH JOURNEY

MY BOOK *COCKTAIL Conversations* will be a major catalyst in helping the world around me for several reasons, and whoever reads it will improve in many areas of their life involving problem-solving and critical thinking. *Cocktail Conversations* will provide opportunities for a meaningful self-reflection of personal values and the perceived values of others. It is always helpful to consider different perspectives when navigating through the difficult terrains of life. My book will provide perspectives in reliable real-life situations and allow people to better understand the reasoning behind other's decisions and the point of view of others in their lives. Understanding others can open up doors for more effective relationships and communication.

Cocktail Conversations gives a sounding board to people who may need advice in their everyday lives. We are all in need of advice once in a while; and through the diversity of the readers and participants, we can learn something from each other to open our minds and hearts as human beings, to grow and love one another. As I traveled through this process, this book has enlightened me to a learning experience, and I have taken some of the advices given. I have learned that no matter what our options are, we need to respect others for what they believe in, embrace the passion that people have, and that each day has so much hope and promise. Thank you for allowing me to share these dialogues with you. Hopefully, they have touched you in a positive way.

Free Preview: *Something Just Ain't Right*

Kenny and Dolly dated when they were in college fifteen years ago. Kenny was physically and emotionally attached to Dolly but they ended up going their separate ways. Dolly ended up getting married but has been divorced the past two years. Recently after finding her on Facebook, Kenny has been trying to hook back up. Dolly decided that that would be a good thing since Kenny was such the gentleman before. Kenny invited her over for dinner where he prepared baked salmon, roasted potatoes, corn, string beans, Caesar's salad, and a light and fluffy lemon pound cake. Kenny also made sure he had Dolly's favorite wine, Red Moscato. When Dolly arrived, Kenny was trembling with excitement, but it all went sour when they went to kiss and Kenny realized that she was missing all of her front teeth. Should Kenny terminate this date? And what would you do if this was you?

Edwards Brothers Malloy
Thorofare, NJ USA
March 2, 2015